D1610779

Rational Action

Rational Action

Studies in Philosophy and Social Science

Edited by

Ross Harrison

Lecturer in Philosophy, University of Cambridge

Cambridge University Press

Cambridge
London   New York   New Rochelle
Melbourne   Sydney

Published by the Press Syndicate of the University of Cambridge
The Pitt Building, Trumpington Street, Cambridge CB2 1RP
32 East 57th Street, New York, NY 10022, USA
296 Beaconsfield Parade, Middle Park, Melbourne 3206, Australia

First published 1979

Printed in Great Britain at the
University Press, Cambridge

Library of Congress Cataloguing in Publication Data
Main entry under title
Rational action.
Includes index.
1. Act (Philosophy) – Addresses, essays, lectures.
2. Social sciences – Addresses, essays, lectures.
I. Harrison, Ross.
B105.A35R37   128   79-10280
ISBN 0 521 22714 3

Contents

Contributors

MARTIN HOLLIS is Senior Lecturer in Philosophy at the University of East Anglia.

BERNARD WILLIAMS is Knightbridge Professor of Philosophy in the University of Cambridge and Provost of King's College, Cambridge.

ROSS HARRISON is a Lecturer in Philosophy at the University of Cambridge.

RICHARD WOLLHEIM is Professor of Philosophy at University College, London.

CHRISTOPHER PEACOCKE is a Fellow of New College, Oxford.

JAMES COLEMAN is Professor of Sociology at the University of Chicago.

ALBERT WEALE is a Lecturer in Politics at the University of York.

AMARTYA SEN is Professor of Economics at the University of Oxford.

J. E. J. ALTHAM is a Lecturer in Philosophy at the University of Cambridge.

RICHARD TUCK is a Lecturer in History at the University of Cambridge.

JOHN MAGUIRE is Professor of Social Theory at University College, Cork.

Introduction

Understanding human action is understanding the product of people's beliefs and desires. Once the appropriate beliefs and desires have been attributed to the agent, the action is then explained and may also be justified. The concept of rationality has an important, but disputed, role in such explanations and justifications. According to the different relations which it is thought must, or should, obtain between beliefs, reasons, desires, and behaviour, so we have different views about the possibility of understanding or criticising the actions of both individuals and groups. Rationality may, for example, be thought to be primarily an evaluative notion in which particular actions are selected as being rational by contrast with others. These evaluations, in turn, may be thought to depend either on the interrelations between particular beliefs, desires, and behaviour; or, alternatively, on the independent assessment of particular beliefs or desires as being rational. In the former case, it is held that someone's beliefs and desires cannot by themselves be criticised as being irrational, but that, given that an individual has these beliefs and desires, then he is rational if he acts to get what he desires given that the world is as he believes it is. In the latter case, it is thought by contrast that someone's desires (for example, the desire to treat people in the same situation in different ways) can be independently criticised as being irrational, no matter how they relate to his beliefs or behaviour.

Alternatively, rationality may be thought to be primarily a descriptive notion so that, rather than selecting among human actions, all human action is considered to be rational. Rationality on this view is stipulative of humanity; it is the essential medium through which all human behaviour is viewed, and it is only because we assume it that we can attribute beliefs and desires to people at all. One form of this view is the doctrine of the 'holism' of the mental, associated with the American philosopher Donald Davidson. The thesis is that we attribute beliefs and desires to others as a whole: given a certain belief, we can attribute a certain desire; given a certain desire, we can attribute a certain belief; but what we are attributing are complete sets of beliefs and desires on the unavoidable presupposition that these beliefs and desires fit together in a rational way. Rationality is the inevitable glue which holds the pairs of beliefs and desires together.

Whether evaluative or descriptive, these differing views of the nature or importance of rationality all relate to the explanation and justification of individual behaviour. They explain and control the place of desire in the moral economy of one individual human being. There is also the problem, or further area of dispute, about how the desires of individuals relate to the actions of groups, the structures of groups, or to the beliefs of groups. Can the actions and the beliefs (ideology) of the group be explained as the net product of the actions and beliefs of individuals? Or should we start with the language and moral beliefs as a whole in order to explain the beliefs and actions of an individual? Rationality can on the one hand be regarded as an evaluative notion in the language or ideology of the group which helps (or enforces) the selection of behaviour by individuals. On the other hand it can be a notion which describes the actions of individuals, as self-interested maximisers of their individual satisfactions, on the basis of which the behaviour of groups of individuals can be constructed and so explained.

The following collection of articles is concerned with the problems involved in the concept of rational explanation, that is with the interrelated set of problems with which I started. Taken from the standpoint of desire, we could put them in terms of the three questions, what is the nature of desire? What is the relation of desire to reason? And what is the relation of individual desire to social behaviour? I start the collection with Martin Hollis's paper not only because he opens up all of these three questions but also because he argues powerfully a thesis about the correct relationship between reason and desire. Used as a descriptive notion, Hollis does not think that rationality has much explanatory force; however he does not think that the concept can be used only descriptively, or even used evaluatively just in gauging the instrumental effectiveness with which someone links together particular antecedently given beliefs, desires, and behaviour. Reason for Hollis is a fully fledged evaluative notion in the light of which the particular desires themselves may be criticised. It is exactly this thesis which Bernard Williams attacks in the following paper. He distinguishes between what he calls 'internal' and 'external' reasons for action, according to whether the reasons are or are not based on desires which the agent already possesses. Williams concludes that statements about external reasons are either false or incoherent, or really statements about internal reasons. He holds, that is, that reasons which are unrelated to desires which an agent already possesses could not give rise to a new motivation for action, and so criticises any external, evaluative, use of reason of the kind which Hollis recommends.

Williams's contribution to this collection is a natural consequence of earlier articles in which he wished to assimilate moral judgements to desires rather than beliefs, holding that this could be seen from the different way in which the notion of consistency applied to them. In terms of the present dispute, this fits in with thinking that reasons are not antecedent to desire (and so may not be used to criticise desire) in the way that they are antecedent to belief (and so may be used to criticise belief). Holding beliefs that are inconsistent is one thing, holding desires or moral judgements that are is quite another thing. In my piece which follows, I criticise this position of Williams. I attempt to show that the role of consistency is much more analogous in the two cases of moral judgements and of purely theoretical beliefs than he allows. If this criticism is correct, it means that at least moral beliefs, and so some mental states which result in action in the way that desires do, are capable of independent rational criticism, and so that all reasons used in evaluating desires do not need to depend upon some desires being already given.

These conflicting treatments of the interrelation between desire and reason may well be thought to be over-simple in two quite different ways. On the one hand it might be thought that it ignores the much deeper understanding of the nature of desire that we have gained since the writing of Freud and Marx. On the other hand, in treating desires as separable mental states, it might be thought that it ignores the problem of the holism of the mental which I referred to at the beginning. These objections are met by the following papers together with one printed later in the collection. The first objection is met by Richard Wollheim, with respect to Freud, and by John Maguire, with respect to Marx. The holism of the mental is the topic of Christopher Peacocke's paper.

Richard Wollheim draws upon Freud in order to give a full and careful analysis of desire, and the way in which desire relates to normal and aberrant types of satisfaction. The paper which follows, by Christopher Peacocke, can be used to provide an argument showing that even if our description of an area is holistic in nature, this does not have the consequence that we are not able to handle and understand the separate parts that are so linked together. Peacocke adopts and defends an even more extreme form of the holism of the mental than Davidson, holding (against Davidson) that it does not admit even of the kind of surrogate for reduction which Davidson allows and which Peacocke calls 'quasi-reduction'. He establishes this, and other points about this kind of holistic explanation, by considering the explanation of someone's experience in terms of his spatial location and of the states of the world at those locations. Peacocke shows that there is a structural similarity between this case and the case of explanation of action in terms of beliefs and desires. I take it that part of the point of doing this, as well as the more specific conclusions he derives, is that it provides the basis of a powerful *ad hominem* argument against anyone who thinks that the holism of the mental means that we cannot attribute individual beliefs and desires to people. The argument would be that since we can obviously handle independently spatial position and content in a structurally similar case, so here we should feel equally confident in our attribution of beliefs and desires. If this is right, it means that the holism of the mental is no block to the kind of explanation or justification described in the other papers in the collection.

If we suppose, therefore, that we have available an account of desire, and of its interrelation to beliefs and reasons, the next question is how we should use description of rational desires in the explanation of individual and social behaviour. There is a model of explanation, popular in economics and in sociology inspired by economics, in which it is assumed that individuals are utility-maximisers, and in which group behaviour is explained as the net product of the interactions of such 'rational' actors. I have already remarked how Martin Hollis attacks the truth and the explanatory force of this type of explanation in his contribution to this collection (and in his earlier books, *Rational Economic Man* and *Models of Man*). Lest it should be thought that Hollis in this work is tilting at unoccupied windmills, I have selected the piece by James Coleman. Coleman does exactly what Hollis attacks. He shows by means of several examples how rational behaviour models at the level of individual persons can prove fruitful in the explanation of social behaviour. Albert Weale, in his contribution which follows, also wishes to defend the use of this kind of explanation. He argues that the economic theory of rational choice is a coherent and successful way of explaining the actions of organised groups, in particular their political decisions. He wishes to show that use of this theory is also a practically efficient method of distinguishing what the correct choices of a group should be, given that they start with particular, potentially conflicting, political principles. For this it is important that he can demonstrate that the method is itself value-neutral, that is that it does not by itself bias the selection of public objectives, and this is the central point which Weale aims to establish in his paper.

At the end of his paper Weale notes that he has not considered cases of lack of information, or uncertainty. This is normal, so that when choices of action are compared, it is supposed that the evaluations are independent of the amount of information we possess. In the standard model, we independently affix utilities and probabilities to various outcomes and then choose (or ought to choose) that course of action which leads to the greatest product of the two. Amartya Sen's paper suggests a wholly new way of looking at the question. He examines the interrelations between the information we possess and the way that we evaluate outcomes. He shows how the relationship works in both directions, so that, on the one hand, moral principles can usefully be considered as limitations on the amount of information we are allowed to consider, and, on the other hand, that different amounts of information may lead to different choice of moral principles. Moral principles which might diverge if we possessed total information need not necessarily do so given the information that we actually possess; viewed like this much of the present conflict between moral principles might seem to be pointless.

The following two papers are, like Coleman and Weale, concerned with the emergence of social behaviour from independently given individual interests and desires. They are both concerned with justification, and with two famous and fundamental problems of how participation in social behaviour can be justified from the point of view of the individual. J. E. J. Altham is concerned with the legitimacy of the state, Richard Tuck with the free-rider problem (that is, why an individual should co-operate with society in the production of some benefit which would still be a benefit to him if he opted out). Altham criticises the recent arguments of the American political philosopher Robert Nozick, which have been held to provide conclusive justification of how a certain limited form of the state is both preferable to anarchy and does not require violation of individual rights. He argues that the possibility of a rational anarchism is still open, and that Nozick's project of explaining the political realm in terms of prepolitical rights alone is doomed to failure. He suggests that the only promising political theory that starts from a state of nature is one that makes direct appeal to the needs and interests that government might serve. For Altham, therefore, the long-running problem of the social contract is still a problem. By contrast, Richard Tuck thinks that the free-rider problem is not really a problem. After explaining why it has been taken as a problem by those concerned with justifying group behaviour in terms of the satisfaction of individual interest, Tuck draws upon co-operative games theory in order to show that it is soluble from this point of view. The real problem about the free-rider, Tuck holds, is quite different, in being a form of the Sorites paradox, the paradox that repeated application of a process which makes an imperceptible difference (removing a hair from a man's head) in the end makes a perceptible difference (makes him bald).

The objection urged by Hollis against the model of rational explanation which explained or justified group behaviour in terms of individual self-interest is that such explanation or justification was vacuous. An alternative objection is that it started at the wrong end. Rather than explaining group behaviour or interests in terms of antecedently given individual interests, what individuals desire (what they take to be their interests) should be explained by the group to which they belong and their position in it. This is what happens in Marxist styles of explanation in which desires are expressed in terms of ideology, ideology reflects social structure, and social structure is determined by economic relations. In his final contribution, John Maguire gives an account of Marxist explanation which brings out this importance of the concept of ideology. However, Maguire is concerned to make comparisons as well as oppositions between Marxism and the prevailing individualistic styles of explanation represented by the majority of papers in this collection. He talks of the relations between classes in Marxist theory in terms of the kind of exchange, or bargaining, theory which is used by Coleman and Weale in their contributions. Furthermore, Maguire gives a subtle account of the causal relations between social structure and economic base in Marxist theory, holding that Marxism is not committed to the automatic temporal priority of changes in the economic base. He gives a similarly untraditional account of the room that is left for individual free choice and undetermined desire in Marxist theory.

This collection is a selection from papers orginally given to a series of meetings of philosophers and social scientists organised by the Thyssen Philosophy Group and financed through the generosity of the Fritz Thyssen Stiftung. They have all been specially rewritten for this volume, and have not appeared elsewhere. I would like, on behalf of the Thyssen Group, to express our thanks to the Fritz Thyssen Stiftung, and in particular to its Director Dr Gerd Brand, for the financial support, encouragement, and advice which made possible an enjoyable and instructive series of discussions.

Rational man and social science

MARTIN HOLLIS

Water was short in the torrid summer of 1976 and there were soon calls for restraint. Where I live, the Anglian Water Authority quickly threatened to ban garden hoses, if the calls went unheeded. The sun blazed down in emphasis and the Authority made an ostentatious purchase of standpipes for the streets, in case households had to be cut off. Philosophising amid my limp lettuces, I wondered how much notice it was rational for me to take. It was plainly in the general interest that water be saved and this premise will not be challenged. But was it rational for me to save water? This is the common or garden problem I wish to put to you.[1]

The question is one about collective goods, meaning goods which can be provided only by collective or central action. They benefit all yet it seems that, if contributions are voluntary and if everyone acts rationally, they will never be provided. Examples are parks, schools, trade unions, national defence and democracy but I pick my own to save getting embrangled in a cluttered landscape. I shall remind you of the two standard ways with collective goods, usually dubbed the economic and the sociological, and shall complain about both. This is the middleground of the paper. There is also a background in the nature of rational action and its bearing on method in the social sciences and we shall have to touch some hard puzzles in epistemology and ethics. But let us start in the foreground with a lazy gardener growing his own lettuces during a drought. He is asked to save water. Is he to respond?

The Water Authority opened on a gentlemanly note of logic and ethics, with only an offhand gesture to my self-interest. All (good) citizens should save water, I was told; you are a (good) citizen; so you should save water. I granted the minor premise with smug alacrity. Undoubtedly I was a (good) citizen. But I disputed the major. Why should all (good) citizens save water? The aim was for enough water to be saved in sum now to see us through later. That is the collective good whose value to all citizens, including me, will not be challenged. But it did not depend on whether *all*

[1] My warm thanks go to Amartya Sen, to Quentin Skinner and to those at the 4th Thyssen meeting for their criticisms of an earlier draft.

I

citizens save water. Enough is enough; why should I help? Well, came the soft answer, very little is being asked of you. It would not hurt you to put half a brick in your cistern, for instance, and, if a million households do the same, the region will be a million gallons a day to the good. Nor would you really miss the odd bath and, if you showered with a friend, you might even enjoy it. At worst any marginal unpleasantness will be outweighed by your marginal self-satisfaction. Every little helps postpone the crisis and so benefits you too. Virtue brings its own reward, you see.

As a philosopher with lettuces at risk, I was unmoved. The question being initially not what was right but what was rational, it was too soon to appeal to virtue. My beautiful friendships might survive the odd bath skipped but my lettuces would die. Bluntly, my costs would outweigh my benefits and so, by an 'economic' definition of rationality, it was irrational to incur them. The reason was not that a dead lettuce now would outweigh my present joy in contemplating an uncertain future gallon of water. It was that the Authority's case involved a flaw akin to a fallacy of distribution. I stood to gain, only if a million others saved water too. Unless they did, my efforts would be vain. But, if they did, my efforts would be unnecessary. Hence my efforts would be either vain or unnecessary. Since they cost me something, however little, it was not rational for me to make them. It was fallacious for the Authority to argue that what all would rationally want to have provided each would rationally help to provide.

Meanwhile a lady wrote in sorrow to the local paper to lament 'the odd person who thinks that washing his car or watering his garden cannot make all that difference.' Yes, but was he so odd? Taking the question numerically, the Authority found that he was not and so doubled its exhortations and put a formal ban on hoses. The letter columns of the paper began to glow with the Dunkirk spirit, as citizens pooled tips on bathing in a bucket and boiling eggs in the tea pot. One man reported that his dahlias were blooming on dishwater as never before and was printed under the heading 'Virtue Rewarded'. But the figures told another story. Surveys showed that, while 10% were saving like mad, 40% were making only token economies and 50% none at all. Let us invent a random citizen from each group, called Lock, Stock and Barrel. Lock is one of the 10% all but keeping their taps locked. Stock is one of the 40% making a few stock gestures but no more. Barrel is one of the 50% using water by the barrel. Let us suppose that all grow flowers and lettuces but none earns his living from his garden or has any other special claim to water. Also none is a magistrate, councillor or local bigwig, with a special need to set an example (or not to be caught out). Lock loses both flowers and lettuces, Stock loses his flowers but waters his lettuces by hand. Barrel hoses both impartially. Which is the rational man?

Insofar as three men have resolved the same problem in different ways, logic suggests that at most one is rational. Nonetheless it can be argued that all are, since each had objectively good reasons for his response. Lock and his 10% had the reasons considerately supplied by the Water Authority. Stock and his 40% had the legal ban on hoses as a reason for abandoning the flowers and economic reasons for saving the lettuces. Barrel and his 50% kept rather quiet (except for a man who announced that he had paid his rates for unlimited water and meant to have what he had paid for) but there were reasons to hand. For instance the City Council was still visibly watering lawns, flowerbeds and even hard tennis courts. Besides, domestic water consumption is trivial compared with what industry uses. Also the argument about the fallacy of distribution could itself be cited by Barrel as a reason.

But, I reply, even though all had good reasons, it does not follow that all were rational. We cannot decide that, without asking who had the best reasons. It can turn out that all had equally inconclusive reasons but not that all had sufficient reasons, since a sufficient reason for doing x is also sufficient for not doing y. Admittedly Buridan's ass, placed midway between two bushels of hay, has a sufficient reason for eating either. But he does not have one for preferring a named bushel; and, in any case, Lock, Stock and Barrel are not in the same fix. If they all face the same problem set by the drought, we need a way of arbitrating between them and that is why logic will accept no more than one winner.

The reply depends on the problem's being the same for each and this too can be doubted. Each man had his own projects, desires and beliefs. Each did what appeared best to him and could report, like the legendary fellow who leapt naked into a bed of nettles, that it seemed a good idea at the time. Each had apparently scored 100% in a private examination which he alone sat. Economists often give this answer and it taps one common interpretation of utility theory. Here each man faces a situation defined by the utilities for him of various combinations of services of goods and is blessed with a complete, reflexive, and transitive scheme of preferences. In trading off the utility of plants saved against that of freedom from sanctions, Lock, Stock and Barrel all act differently and all consistently. Or so it may be said.

In simple form, this approach sounds vapid but I am not trying to poke fun. Even if the universal fact of ordered preferences in each man is the merest of tautologies, it cannot be known *a priori* how much of what a particular man would prefer to what at what prices and empirical work is still needed. Also, like drones in a beehive, tautologies are nowadays seen to be useful on their own account as categorial axioms or statements introducing paradigmatic concepts and it need not be trite or vapid to say that explanation should be concerned with preference and individual satisfaction. Nonetheless the circularity should not pass unnoticed. Indifference maps are drawn by taking a man's actions as signs of pair-wise

3

comparisons and then projecting the comparisons on the assumption that the man has a consistent scheme of transitive preferences which result in his maximising his utility. Any apparent discrepancies between the assumption and his revealed choice are removed by drawing distinctions among apparently similar occasions of choice. The distinctions are regulated by a principle of producing the simplest map consistent with the assumption. Yet, even if the process recalls a traditional culture preserving its belief in witchcraft, oracles and magic, that need not be to condemn it.

Nevertheless any purported explanation of action becomes a redescription, premised on making all men not just equally rational but necessarily so. With more space I would argue that such redescriptions are not explanatory. As it is I must be content to note that they cannot answer the original question. How much notice was it rational for me to take of the drought? I refuse to accept the answer that, however much or little notice I take, I shall always have acted rationally. Fortunately there is another way to read utility theory, which supports this refusal. Many economists, still subscribing to Edgeworth's dictum that 'the first principle of economics is that every agent is actuated only by self-interest',[2] would urge that Lock, Stock and Barrel could not all have succeeded in maximising their self-interest. They put a hard-headed gloss on 'self-interest' and the question is who gained the highest benefit at lowest cost. The hard-headed reply is clear. Since each individual saving of water is either vain or unnecessary and since it involves some cost, however small, Barrel is the outright winner, until hoses are banned. Thereafter the judges must decide whether there has been a change in the price of water. If penalties and risks of detection are low, then the price is still effectively zero and Barrel retains his title. If they are high, Stock moves into first place. A change of price does not affect the principle, however, which is that it is more rational to gain a fixed benefit at lower cost.

The moral for government is equally clear. The water campaign used the terse slogan 'Save It', borrowed from the campaign to save energy when oil prices doubled. In both cases each consumer could reason rightly that his saving would be either vain or unnecessary as a contribution to the total. In both cases the total benefit is shared among all, whether they have contributed or not. Yet the energy campaign had far more success. Why? Unlike water, energy is usually metered and each man pays for what he uses. So there is a selective incentive, even if not one of quite the sort which confines a subscription concert to those who have paid the subscription. It could only weaken the energy campaign to extend the 'Save It' slogan to water or, for that matter, chastity. There has to be an effective spur, like a real risk of a huge fine or an outbreak of VD among teenagers. Without

[2] *Mathematical Psychics*, Kegan Paul, London, 1881, p. 16.

4

one, it is merely irrational to work for charity, pay bills, vote in elections, take litter home from picnics or volunteer in a national emergency. In all such matters Reason stands like a proverbial sergeant major, inviting those who can play the violin to step forward and marching them off to scrub the latrines.

In fact, of course, people do vote in safe seats on wet nights without Australian-style fines. They do demonstrate amid hostile crowds, collect money for spastics, speak out against tyrants and bath in five inches of water. But they are being stupid, given the hard-headed economic argument. While they are stupid, the moral does not apply and there is no need for selective incentives. Yet the moral is still there, only waiting for the spread of education and enlightened self-interest. Theories of the social contract sometimes fancy that men need law because they are irrational. On the contrary, by the economic account men need law because they are too often rational.

The implications for social life go deep but time is short and I propose next to pick out the assumptions of this economic account. (It is, I confess, a very crude account and there may be subtler notions of rational choice in economics which threaten my argument. But at least it is the account which is carried over into exchange theory and, however crude, it bears at least a basic resemblance to common assumptions in economics.)[3] There are three assumptions to note especially. First rationality is taken as *Zweckrationalität*, a matter strictly of the means to a given end. The rationality of ends does not arise, except insofar as ends can be means to further ends. The criterion for what is a better means needs not be in crude cash. For instance the value of a lovingly tended lettuce may be much more than the few pence the greengrocer would charge for an apparent substitute. But even with a loose notion of opportunity cost it remains irrational for each man to do as the Water Authority wants. Such is the result of an economic means-only analysis of what it is to be rational.

Secondly an egoism has been assumed. There is no fallacy in arguing, 'The public will need water later; there will be none later, unless the public saves it now; so it is rational for the public to save water now.' The same holds, although with diminishing force, as we substitute smaller units, like industries, still large enough to affect their own future supply. The flaw emerges, when we argue, 'Each man will need water later; so it is rational for each man to save it now.' Egoism exposes the flaw by pointing out that it is irrational for a man to do for himself what others will do for him. This is not to say that he has no interest in the interest of others, since he often has goals which he can attain only by co-operation. Also the fact that he

---

[3] I am encouraged to find it also the account which Amartya Sen makes his target in 'Rational Fools', his Herbert Spencer lecture, 1976.

loves his mother, for instance, may both condition his goals and act as a selective incentive. But the puzzle set is the classic egoist puzzle of finding terms under which the interests of each will coincide with the interests of all including himself. Since its solution lies in selective incentives, it follows that men are by nature much the sort of creatures Hobbes took them for.

There is also, thirdly, a social atomism. Lock, Stock and Barrel have featured throughout as abstract atoms or individuals. They could be picked at random from their groups, because it made no difference *who* they were. Each was simply a member of the set comprising all like him and the sets differed merely in the skill with which they tackled the same problem. This is not the only way to conceive human beings. For instance had Lock been made a social atom but not an egoist or an egoist but not a social atom, other solutions might have emerged. We get the 'economic' solution only if he is both an atom and an egoist and therefore stupid. But with these three assumptions it truly follows, I submit. It is irrational to contribute to a collective good at positive cost, even though the good benefits each and will not be provided for anyone if all act rationally. The secret of harnessing the General Will is to find the selective incentives which force men to be free.

Those who dislike the solution must challenge the assumptions. Let us start with the third by making more of the thought that Lock, Stock and Barrel are citizens. Could it be that Lock is not a stupid atom but a rational citizen? Certainly the fact that he is a citizen helps explain why he saves water. There are norms of citizenship, exploited in the original appeal to all (good) citizens to economise and evidenced by the indignant tone of letters to the paper. So far a citizen has been merely a member of the set of individuals attached to the national water supply but, if the idea of norms is introduced into the argument, a fresh inference emerges:

1. A citizen is required to do his 'duty'.
2. His 'duty' at present is to save water.
3. So he 'should' save water.

Previously there was no valid step from, 'It is in the interest of all that water be saved' to 'It is in the interest of each to save it.' Now it looks as if we might pass validly from 'It is the duty of all' to 'It is the duty of each.'

There is, admittedly, a doubt about the meaning and truth of the premises. 'Duty' in the first two and 'should' in the conclusion bear a special sense deriving from the concept of a norm. Whether this is a proper sense is too long a story to unravel here. To set the sociologist off, I shall simply assume that there is a social position of citizen with normative expectations attached, which every citizen has a 'duty' in quotes to discharge. I shall also assert that citizens did truly have a 'duty' to save water. Someone may protest that this is preposterous, when half the population was taking no notice and another 40% very little. But in that case why should the Locks

6

be so smug and the Barrels so silent? At any rate, assuming that talk of 'duties' in quotes is licit, we can see the difference between economist and sociologist by citing the fate of Lord Finchley as immortalised by Hilaire Belloc:

> Lord Finchley tried to mend the electric light
> Himself. It struck him dead and serve him right.
> It is the business of the wealthy man
> To give employment to the artisan.

To the economist Lord Finchley's fault was that of a wealthy man who forgets in a situation of choice under risk and uncertainty that the hire of an electrician would be worth the opportunity cost. To the sociologist his Lordship erred in transgressing the bounds of his station and found that *noblesse oblige* was reinforced by lethal electric sanctions.

At first sight there is nothing here to embarrass the economist. He can grant that each citizen has a 'duty' to save water and simply ask why that makes it rational to do so. The prize still goes to Barrel, who has calculated that the costs of doing his 'duty' outweigh the benefits and has therefore rationally shirked the 'duty'. But the sociologist has a fresh answer. It is that each citizen has the goal of doing his 'duty' and saving water is the only means to this end. Rationality being taken as *Zweckrationalität*, of course it is rational for a citizen to save water. Similarly, a citizen may or may not have a duty to vote but, if he does, then it is rational for him to trundle to the poll, whatever the weather.

The economist is now awkwardly placed. Insofar as he has disclaimed all interest in the source and rationality of goals, it seems that he is bound to concur. To do so does not put him out of a job, since it not always so plain what 'duty' demands of citizens. The Chancellor of the Exchequer, for instance, has a duty to combine a high level of GNP with high employment and will need the best economists in the Treasury to tell him how to manage it. Equally, with a looser test for what counts as an economic problem, most social policy offers scope for cost–benefit analysis in implementing it. More loosely still, there is huge scope for thrusting the ambitious claims of exchange theory on an already confused world. But, on the other hand, he has now forfeited his claim to judge between Lock, Stock and Barrel. Instead of ruling clearly in favour of Barrel, he must suspend judgement until told what goal is being sought and what sociological constraints there are on the rational economic choice of means. Indeed, for the particular case of a typical householder in a drought, he no longer has any standing at all, since it does not take a degree in economics to decide what to do about a few buckets of water.

This raises a hard question about rationality assumptions in neo-Classical economics. They are usually claimed to be neutral, in that they serve to isolate the mathematical aspects of problems in allocating resources, without prejudging what competing ends are in themselves worth pursuing. But in fact they go much further. For instance in the theory of supply and demand, the rational supplier produces to the point where marginal cost = marginal revenue. But it is not self-evident that this is a rational way for a supplier to behave. Whether it is depends partly on whether the supplier's goal is to maximise profits or, as champions of satisficing models suggest, merely to make enough profit to keep going. It depends also, however, on whether it is rational to maximise profits – not surprisingly since to equate MC with MR is necessarily to maximise profits. Satisficing models, although dethroning profit, still take it to be rational to maximise something, for instance the satisfaction gained from a style of life, which needs at least minimal profits. Either way, a life devoted to maximum return at minimum cost is assumed to be rational. Otherwise sound neo-Classical theory gives solely bad advice. It was only by making assumptions about the rationality of ends that the economist could give a clear ruling in favour of Barrel.

These assumptions did not obtrude earlier because they were dressed as assumptions about human nature. Rational economic man is an egoistic social atom who answers an appeal to save water only if it is in his own interest. The judges cannot award the prize to Barrel without knowing the real interests of egoistic social atoms. Lock, saving every spoonful, is utterly efficient in pursuing the goal set by the Water Authority and his mistake can only be that it is the wrong goal. But we are not quite ready to exploit this finding. So let us leave the economist in his awkward position and attend to the sociologist.

In place of an abstract, individual, yet universal, homunculus, we are now asked to assume a social being, essentially located in a scheme of positions and roles. It is important to see how very strong the postulate must be. At first sight positions are merely abodes and roles merely trappings. If a man dislikes being a fireman he can change his job or not work at it so hard, just as he can move house or wear old clothes. But in that case he will always be wondering whether it is rational for him to answer the 999 call. The sociological solution depends on an inference from 'It is his "duty" to answer the call' to 'It is rational for him to answer it.' The inference is invalid if the goal served by answering the call could be better achieved by some other means and so validity is secured by making the goal that of doing his 'duty'. This is a flimsy device unless 'him' and 'his' refer not to a pre-social atom but to an essential role-bearer. Otherwise the economist springs back with minimax calculations about when it is rational to do one's 'duty'. Ultimately, failure to perform must be failure to be himself.

I stress the word 'ultimately'. The point is not that a fireman cannot rationally change his job but that he cannot escape all positions and roles and remain human. A rational fireman need not be a totally dedicated

8

fireman. Being also a husband, father, footballer and second trombone, he may rationally wonder how best to combine his roles. A sociological scheme has room for doubt within it and, witness the Chancellor of the Exchequer, scope for economists to resolve the doubt. But, ultimately, there can be no extra-social goals to judge the return on role-playing against. For the solution to work, *homo sociologicus* must be a very strong assumption indeed.[4]

Nor can *homo sociologicus* be an egoist. The economic solution assumed *Zweckrationalität*, egoism and atomism. It is not enough for the sociologist merely to switch goals by rejecting the atomism. Egoism has turned out to be a thesis about real interests and so about goals. In disputing that these are a man's real interests, the sociologist also disputes that egoism contains the best analysis of how to achieve them. The problem is no longer set because the self-interest of each does not coincide with the self-interest of all including himself. Instead, there is a new problem set when roles are so assigned that the discharge of each frustrates the discharge of all. Thus, on Marx's account, the rational and dutiful capitalist finds himself behaving in ways which destroy the capitalist system. Similarly rational and dutiful democrats would take so much part in government that it could not function. Moreover, men socialised into egoism are conditioned to want more than they can possibly have. The solution accordingly no longer lies in finding the selective incentives which let egoists wax fat. It now lies in finding a scheme of positions and roles which can all function at the same time and in socialising men into accepting them. Rational action is no longer action which yields an individual more for less but action which lets a man be himself.

We now have two answers to the hose-pipe problem. One makes it rational for Barrel to use as much water as he can get away with. The other makes it rational for Lock to use as little as an obedient citizen needs. I myself like Lock no better than Barrel and, even as he receives his embossed scroll from the Lord Mayor, I shall try to strike him down. One way would be to challenge this version of *homo sociologicus* directly, as a true model of man for whom all questions of rationality arise within a role and are settled by calculated obedience. But that would lead to a ham-fisted bout of assertion and counterassertion and there is more virtue in a fresh look at the idea of rationality itself.

Both answers started by assuming that rationality is an instrumental notion, relating means to ends but neutral among ends. Both turn out to commit themselves about the rationality of ends. The reason is that both make (implicit and perhaps inadvertent) assumptions about human nature,

---

[4] I do not, of course, mean to suggest that all sociologists make this assumption. But it is a frequent strand in orthodox sociology and one which has been taken over into politics and exchange theory. Also it does at least have the merit of giving a firm answer to questions about the identity of the individual.

which, in stating what men essentially are, imply a thesis about where their real interests lie. I shall contend that this is neither an oversight nor a peculiarity but arises because *Zweckrationalität* is not the sole nor even the primary notion of rationality.

What, then, are the conditions for an action to be *zweckrational*? They are often said to be that the agent must believe, after deliberation among alternatives, that he is doing what is most likely to achieve whatever he happens to want. Let us start by spelling these conditions out too weakly and then tighten them, until we reach a defensible answer. Too weakly, then, *S* acts rationally in doing *a*, if and only if:

   (1) *S* wants to achieve *g*

   (2) *S* has a choice among alternative ways of achieving *g*

   (3) *S* believes that *a* is the best way to achieve *g*.

Such an account say too much and too little. It includes too much by specifying a conscious choice among alternatives. The minor objection is that there need not be alternatives. Whether drinking water is the rational way to stay alive in the desert does not depend on whether there is an inferior way to stay alive, nor on whether there is anything else to drink. The major objection is that to insist on conscious deliberation is to miss the place of habit in rational action. The rational way to drive a car is precisely not to deliberate each change of gear but to master the skill so well that no deliberation is needed. There are rational habits and, were there not, we could not talk, plan, associate, build, reason or perform many other tasks which make social life possible. Rational action is a skill requiring habit and, if the point is missed, large areas of social action are wrongly classed as non-rational, with great harm to the social sciences.

The conditions include too little by resting content with the agent's wants and beliefs. The lesser objection is that mere belief that *a* is the best way is not enough to make the doing of *a* rational. Since knowledge would be too strong a condition, what is required to distinguish subjectively from objectively rational action is rational belief. Much hangs on the definition. When the Tameside council tried to unscramble the scheme for comprehensive education in Tameside, the Minister tried to stop them on the grounds that they were interfering unreasonably with children's education, not because selective schooling is unreasonable (although he thought it was) but because it was too late to organise it before the school year started. On appeal the Law Lords overruled him, not because the council did have a viable scheme and time enough but because, they said, the law recognises that a man may be reasonable, although wrong. The only limit to reasonable error, in the eyes of the law, is that a man cannot be 'so wrong that no reasonable person could sensibly take that view.' Blatant circularity aside, the judgement is surely mistaken. It holds a man to act reasonably, provided that he has *some* warrant for his view, even though he has ignored or not bothered to discover that there is better warrant against. The Tameside council indisputably had the weight of expert evidence against them and so resembled a man who shuts one ear and protests that he is doing his best with the other. Objectively rational belief is belief justified by the balance not of evidence actually taken into account but of evidence which should be taken into account. Otherwise irrational actions are wrongly classed as rational, with harm to, for example, the study of mental illness.

The larger objection is to treating what the agent wants as given *desideranda*. It is tempting to do so, since it seems to explain why what is sauce for the goose is not automatically sauce for the gander – why, for instance, one man will rationally spend his holiday in Spain while another climbs Mount Everest. Indeed, if rationality were a purely instrumental notion, it should be possible to infer straight from '*S* wants to achieve *g*' and '*a* is the most effective means' to '*S* would act rationally in doing *a*'. The temptation may also make us doubt whether Lock, Stock and Barrel are in competition. Nonetheless the inference is to be resisted. The most effective way to get rapturously high, let us suppose, is to take large doses of heroin. Is it also the rational way? Well, the agent must first realise that he is likely to become addicted and perhaps shortly dead. But, provided he wants this result or at least accepts the risk as a tolerable price for the intervening experience, is he not rational to go ahead?

The answer is certainly No, at least insofar as it is irrational for a man to act on a desire which he should realise that he will regret having acted on or which will prevent his achieving other goals which he would desire more. This much is uncontentious and, as noted, economists and sociologists do distinguish what is merely desired from what is rationally desired. Indeed the sociologist often complains that the economist's egoistic individuals have inherently irrational goals, whose pursuit can only leave them chronically alienated from themselves and their fellows. But 'rationally desired' here is usually said to be solely a matter of what is attainable. Thus the goals of a dedicated consumer are irrational, if they are to be sought in a social system which depends on seeing to it that everyone always wants more than he gets. The implication, however, is that any attainable set of goals is a rational set, implying in turn that the most efficient way to close the gap between expectation and reward is always the most rational way. There is usually a presumption here that we are to take men as they are and rewards as they might be. But nothing said so far justifies the presumption and it may well be more efficient to take rewards as they are and men as they might be or, less cryptically, to adjust the men to the system. It is not always rational, I shall argue, to lower the ceiling instead of raising the floor.

This possibility is not allowed in the previous answers. The economist who gave Barrel the prize must say, I think, that action which brings about a lasting match between desire and reward is *eo ipso* rational. He is squarely committed to a thesis about real human interests, one which, because no question of the essential identity of social atoms arises, cannot object to turning a discontented man into a pig satisfied. What is rational for a man cannot depend in principle on who he is, while his identity is in principle a variable open to social or psychic engineering. The sociologist, however, seems at first more resistant, since he takes identity as something closer to a constant. If a man is defined in terms of positions and roles, then to dislocate him is to destroy him. (Admittedly identity is not quite a constant since the fireman could rationally change position; yet neither is it quite a variable, since the fireman survives only if his new position is somehow congruous with the old.) But, although the sociologist thus has a fresh view of human nature and, with it, of human interests, it is still more rational to be a happy slave than a frustrated citizen. The transition is still advantageous, even if it can only be made gradually. No sense yet attaches to the idea that the rational man needs an identity in which he can be fully *himself*.

The contentious issue is thus whether there can be desires which a man could act on without regretting the result and yet be irrational to act on. You may know the science fiction story where human civilisation comes finally to rest with what seem to be bunches of shimmering grapes. When the time traveller looks closer, he sees that each grape is a cosy, irridescent envelope and inside it there lies a happy, slug-like human forever stroked by a mechanical arm. These creatures would never regret their terminal state, if only because they had programmed themselves not to regret it. Yet it is not obvious that a human being would act rationally in choosing this irreversible happiness. That depends on where our real interests lie and real interests, I submit, are bound up not with what we want but with what we are.

This line is appealing enough but ambigous. Does it claim that each man has his own identity and destroys it at his peril? Or does it claim more grandly that every man, in virtue of being human, has the same real interests? Fortunately we need not establish the latter in order to show that *Zweckrationalität* is not the primary kind of rationality. We need only show that it might be in a man's interests to change his desires, his projects, his character or whatever it is that tempts us to say there is no one answer for Lock, Stock and Barrel. Nonetheless the weaker claim is too weak, since it makes men into monads, all essentially different and each entitled to rejoice in his uniqueness. When Barrel is found with his hand on the tap, we have already refused to let him settle the argument by saying 'I would not be me if I did not turn it on.' Yet we cannot just give Lock's reason that orders are orders, since an analogous argument would make it rational for a member of the gestapo to torture obediently and with enthusiasm, provided that he is happy in his work, has a proper career structure, and enjoys the esteem of his peers. Rationality has to consist in identifying with some set of principles neither merely because one wants to nor merely because they are the going norms of one's station but because, whatever it may mean to say so, thay are in one's real interest.

We are not far from the idea that action is rational when it is expressive. Is it rational for a man to climb Mount Everest? Instrumentally it is, provided he wants to get to the top and has no more efficient way up. But that answer sees action as a way of achieving. An expressive view sees it as a way of being and becoming, of expressing and developing the self. Cost-effectiveness is no longer crucial and men can act rationally from, for instance, honour, respect or gratitude without having to be found a goal rationally achieved. The idea is attractive enough to have invaded political sociology, where it is sometimes used to deal with the puzzle of the determined voter. This is the stubborn citizen, who turns out to vote regardless of discomfort or prospect of affecting the result. Since he makes up most of the electorate, he is an embarrassment to a science premised on the postulate that men are rational. But that, it is often said, is solely because voting is often not an instrumental act; hence all is resolved when we see that the determined voter is acting rationally by acting expressively.

Yet mere labelling explains nothing and we may still ask what is rational about the voter's gesture. If the answer is either that he merely felt moved by a desire to record his true preference or that he was a mere creature of the electoral norms, we are still just where we were. There has to be a reason to explain why it is rational to act on the desire or accept the norm. I do not mean that it is never rational to do what one desires because one wants to or to follow a rule because it is the rule. Nor do I mean that it is rational only when there is sufficient instrumental reason. In acting expressively the agent affirms the value both of the desire which constitutes him what he is and of the rule which constitutes his action what it is. To deem the gesture neither instrumental nor irrational, we need his good reason for the affirmation. Otherwise it is the idlest sleight of hand for sociologists to classify determined voters as *wertrational* economic men. So far Barrel is merely consistently selfish and Lock merely oversocialised. Neither is made more intelligible by dubbing his actions expressive.

Hence I prefer to keep to the notion of real interests, while recognising that it may be in one's real interest to affirm an identity. The case is the minimal one, that 'a is the best means to g' does not entail 'a is a rational action', since the inference requires that g be in the agent's real interest, which in turn is a matter of who he is. Since I shall not be more specific, we must be content with a formal statement. Catching up the earlier points, I propose that S acts rationally in doing a if and only if

(1) a is likeliest to realise g.

(2) It is in S's overall real interest to realise g.

(3) Conditions (1) and (2) are S's reasons for doing a.

Those willing to support me can now pass judgement on the lettuce problem. The economist's strategy is sound enough, since it seeks the candidate who best advances his real interests, whereas the sociologist affects not to judge the norms in terms of the interests of the citizens. But the economist ascribes rationality to a notional sort of atom who cannot have real interests, whereas the sociologist has at least the makings of a connection between the rationality of ends and the identity of the agent. Yet, for a *homo sociologicus* of the sort considered so far, the connection is that it is always rational to conform to the norms of one's culture, just because they are the norms. Those disliking both Lock and Barrel can therefore award the prize to Stock, on the grounds that he alone is a rational citizen. He is detached enough from the norms to make place for economic calculation but not so detached that he ceases to be essentially a citizen. Unlike Lock, he leaves a distance between himself and the role the Water Authority has scripted for him. He alone emerges as a rational person with an essential social identity and his prizewinning solution is to take as little notice of the Water Authority as a rational citizen should.

There is one further ambiguity to resolve, however, before Stock can claim his prize. Although the trio were picked at random from actual groups of people, they are not yet flesh and blood. In the abstract we prefer the man conceived as a citizen at a distance from the norms. But it does not follow that such a man will in fact abandon his flowers and save his lettuces. Sometimes he will act like Barrel, on the un-Barrelish grounds that the government needs to be provoked into enforcing a norm properly in the interests of all. Thus fervent humanitarians will sometimes refuse to give money to charity, because charities do just enough good to let the state shirk its responsibility to do more. Conversely Stock will act like Lock, when he finds the norms excellent or deems the national crisis urgent enough to forgo his distance for. Indeed the doctrine of collective responsibility depends on getting mutinous Stocks to act like Locks for the larger good. In the abstract, we conclude that the rationality of the ends justifies the means; that ends are rational insofar as they serve the real interests of the agent that real interests are to be gauged by making a true model of man; and that social science must take note in explaining no less than social ethics in justifying. But the model of man is one question and the rational way for Stock to act in a drought another.

Nonetheless I submit also that Stock was right to abandon his flowers and save his lettuces. Unlike Barrel, he is essentially a citizen and so party in principle to the enterprise of providing collective goods. Whereas Barrel thinks of himself as a shopper in a supermarket, free to spurn the amazing offers on the shelves and the appeal of the Spastics' box at the door, Stock sees a duty not to let the side down. Consequently Barrel cannot urge directly that it is rational for Stock to pay less for everything. Instead he must argue either that it would be rational for Stock to think of himself like Barrel or that even a citizen, who is essentially a citizen, is a fool to save water. Stock can then reply that he is essentially a citizen and so can find it rational to act expressively at small inconvenience. Against Lock, however, he contends that blind obedience is no virtue. It is indeed foolish to let used bath water drain into the sea or to add to the import bill for Dutch greenstuff. As an unsentimental contributor to the pluralist state, he offers up his thirsty flowers and keeps his lettuces. And so I picture the three of them riding into the sunset at the end of their debate, Barrel in the middle of the road in his well-washed Mercedes, Stock with a dusty saloon and a tankful of unleaded petrol, Lock about to be knocked off his bicycle into the ditch as a reward for saving energy too. But notice that it is not Stock on the bicycle. In the old dispute between herbivores and carnivores, Stock is a carnivore.

Meanwhile the seasons advanced, the rains came, the reservoirs filled and England enjoyed the wettest autumn for years. The Water Authority could still be heard shouting through the cascade that the drought was as serious as ever. But the Dunkirk spirit had gone from the papers, washed out by sight of the collective good being provided from on high. Lock felt cheated of his virtue, Stock mourned his lost chrysanthemums and Barrel reached for the salad cream. The saving of water had turned out both vain and unnecessary. But that was merely a quirk of fate and we are here to deliver the judgement of Reason.

Reprinted from R. Harrison (ed.) *Rational Action: Studies in Philosophy and Social Science.*
© Cambridge University Press 1979. Printed in Great Britain.

Internal and external reasons

BERNARD WILLIAMS

Sentences of the forms 'A has a reason to ϕ' or 'There is a reason for A to ϕ' (where 'ϕ' stands in for some verb of action) seem on the face of it to have two different sorts of interpretation. On the first, the truth of the sentence implies, very roughly, that A has some motive which will be served or furthered by his ϕ-ing, and if this turns out not to be so the sentence is false: there is a condition relating to the agent's aims, and if this is not satisfied it is not true to say, on this interpretation, that he has a reason to ϕ. On the second interpretation, there is no such condition, and the reason-sentence will not be falsified by the absence of an appropriate motive. I shall call the first the 'internal', the second the 'external', interpretation. (Given two such interpretations, and the two forms of sentence quoted, it is reasonable to suppose that the first sentence more naturally collects the internal interpretation, and the second the external, but it would be wrong to suggest that either form of words admits only one of the interpretations.)

I shall also for convenience refer sometimes to 'internal reasons' and 'external reasons', as I do in the title, but this is to be taken only as a convenience. It is a matter for investigation whether there are two sorts of reasons for action, as opposed to two sorts of statements about people's reasons for action; indeed, as we shall eventually see, even the interpretation in one of the cases is problematical.

I shall consider first the internal interpretation, and how far it can be taken. I shall then consider, more sceptically, what might be involved in an external interpretation. I shall end with some brief remarks connecting all this with the issue of public goods and free-riders, which is discussed by Hollis in the preceding paper.

The simplest model for the internal interpretation would be this: A has a reason to ϕ iff A has some desire the satisfaction of which will be served by his ϕ-ing. Alternatively, we might say...some desire, the satisfaction of which A believes will be served by his ϕ-ing; this difference will concern us later. Such a model is sometimes ascribed to Hume, but since in fact Hume's own views are more complex than this, we might call it *the sub-Humean model.* The sub-Humean model is certainly too simple. My aim will be, by addition and revision, to work it up into something more adequate: in the course of trying to do this, I shall assemble four propositions which seem to me to be true of internal reason statements.

Basically, and by definition, any model for the internal interpretation must display a relativity of the reason statement to the agent's *subjective motivational set*, which I shall call the agent's S. The contents of S we shall come to, but we can say:

(i) An internal reason statement is falsified by the absence of some appropriate element from S.

The simplest sub-Humean model claims that any element in S gives rise to an internal reason. But there are grounds for denying this, not because of regrettable, imprudent, or deviant elements in S – they raise different sorts of issues – but because of elements in S based on false belief.

The agent believes that this stuff is gin, when it is in fact petrol. He wants a gin and tonic. Has he reason, or a reason, to mix this stuff with tonic and drink it? There are two ways here (as suggested already by the two alternatives for formulating the sub-Humean model). On the one hand, it is just very odd to say that he has a reason to drink this stuff, and natural to say that he has no reason to drink it, although he thinks that he has. On the other hand, if he does drink it, we not only have an explanation of his doing so (a reason why he did it), but we have such an explanation which is of the reason-for-action form. This explanatory dimension is very important, and we shall come back to it more than once; if there are reasons for action, it must be that people sometimes act for those reasons, and if they do, their reasons must figure in some correct explanation of their action (it does not follow that they must figure in all correct explanations of their action). The difference between false and true beliefs on the agent's part cannot alter the *form* of the explanation which will be appropriate to his action. This consideration might move us to ignore the intuition which we noticed before, and lead us just to legislate that in the case of the agent who wants gin, he has a reason to drink this stuff which is petrol.

I do not think, however, that we should do this. It looks in the wrong direction, by implying in effect that the internal reason conception is only concerned with explanation, and not at all with the agent's rationality; and this may help to motivate a search for other sorts of reason which are connected with his rationality. But it is concerned with his rationality: what we can correctly ascribe to him in a third-personal internal reason statement is also what he can ascribe to himself as a result of deliberation, as we shall see. So I think that we should rather say:

(ii) A member of S, D, will not give A a reason for φ-ing if either the existence of D is dependent on false belief, or A's belief in the relevance of ϕ-ing to the satisfaction of D is false.

(This double formulation can be illustrated from the gin/petrol case: D can be taken in the first way as the desire to drink what is in this bottle, and in the second way as the desire to drink gin.) It will, all the same, be true that if he does ϕ in these circumstances, there was not only a reason why he ϕ-ed, but also that that displays him as, relative to his false belief, acting rationally.

We can note the epistemic consequence:

(iii) (a) A may falsely believe an internal reason statement about himself, and we can add

      (b) A may not know some true internal reason statement about himself.

(b) comes from two different sources. One is that A may be ignorant of some fact such that if he did know it he would, in virtue of some element in S, be disposed to ϕ: we can say that he has a reason to ϕ, though he does not know it. For it to be the case that he actually has such a reason, however, it seems that the relevance of the unknown fact to his actions has to be fairly close and immediate; otherwise one merely says that A would have a reason to ϕ if he knew the fact. I shall not pursue the question of the conditions for saying the one thing or the other, but it must be closely connected with the question of when the ignorance forms part of the explanation of what A actually does.

The second source of (iii) is that A may be ignorant of some element in S. But we should notice that an unknown element in S, D, will provide a reason for A to ϕ only if ϕ-ing is rationally related to D; that is to say, roughly, a project to ϕ could be the answer to a deliberative question formed in part by D. If D is unknown to A because it is in the unconscious, it may well not satisfy this condition, although of course it may provide the reason why he ϕ's, that is, may explain or help to explain his ϕ-ing. In such cases, the ϕ-ing may be related to D only symbolically.

I have already said that

(iv) internal reason statements can be discovered in deliberative reasoning.

It is worth remarking the point, already implicit, that an internal reason statement does not apply only to that action which is the uniquely preferred result of the deliberation. 'A has reason to ϕ' does not mean 'the action which A has overall, all-in, reason to do is ϕ-ing'. He can have reason to do a lot of things which he has other and stronger reasons not to do.

The sub-Humean model supposes that ϕ-ing has to be related to some element in S as causal means to end (unless, perhaps, it is straightforwardly the carrying out of a desire which is itself that element in S). But this is only one case: indeed, the mere discovery that some course of action is the causal means to an end is not in itself a piece of practical reasoning.[1] A clear example of practical reasoning is that leading to the conclusion that one has reason to ϕ because ϕ-ing would be the most convenient, economical, pleasant etc. way of satisfying some element in S; and this of course is controlled by other elements in S, if not necessarily in a very clear or determinate way. But there are much wider possibilities for deliberation, such as: thinking how the satisfaction of elements in S can be combined, e.g. by time-ordering; where there is some irresoluble conflict among the elements of S, considering which one attaches most weight to (which, importantly, does not imply that there is some one commodity of which they provide varying amounts); or, again, finding constitutive solutions, such as deciding what would make for an entertaining evening, granted that one wants entertainment.

As a result of such processes an agent can come to see that he has reason to do something which he did not see he had reason to do at all. In this way, the deliberative process can add new actions for which there are internal reasons, just as it can also add new internal reasons for given actions. The deliberative process can also subtract elements from S. Reflection may lead the agent to see that some belief is false, and hence to realise that he has in fact no reason to do something he thought he had reason to do. More subtly, he may think he has reason to promote some development because he has not exercised his imagination enough about what it would be like if it came about. In his unaided deliberative reason, or encouraged by the persuasions of others, he may come to have some more concrete sense of what would be involved, and lose his desire for it; just as, positively, the imagination can create new possibilities and new desires. (These are important possibilities for politics as well as for individual action.)

We should not, then, think of S as statically given; the processes of deliberation can have all sorts of effect on S, and this is a fact which a theory of internal reasons should be very happy to accommodate. So also it should be more liberal than some theorists have been about the possible elements in S. I have discussed S primarily in terms of desires, and this term can be used, formally, for all elements in S. But this terminology may make one forget that S can contain such things as dispositions of evaluation, patterns of emotional reaction, personal loyalties, and various projects, as they may be abstractly called, embodying commitments of the agent. Above all, there is of course no supposition that the desires or projects of an agent have to

---

[1] A point made by Aurel Kolnai: see his 'Deliberation is of Ends', in *Ethics, Value and Reality* (London and Indianapolis, 1978). See also David Wiggins, 'Deliberation and Practical Reason', *PAS*, LXXVI (1975–6); reprinted in part in *Practical Reasoning*, ed. J. Raz (Oxford, 1978).

be egoistic; he will, one hopes, have non-egoistic projects of various kinds, and these equally can provide internal reasons for action.

There is a further question, however, about the contents of S: whether it should be taken, consistently with the general idea of internal reasons, as containing *needs*. It is certainly quite natural to say that A has a reason to pursue X, just on the ground that he needs X; but will this naturally follow in a theory of internal reasons? There is a special problem about this only if the agent's needs are not taken up into his desires or motivations: if it is possible for the agent to be unmotivated to pursue what he needs. I shall not try to discuss here the nature of needs, but I take it that insofar as there are determinately recognisable needs, this is a possibility, and there can be an agent who lacks an interest in getting what he indeed needs. I take it, further, that that lack of interest can remain after deliberation; and that it would be wrong to say that such a lack of interest must always rest on false belief. (Insofar as it does rest on false belief, then we can accommodate it under (ii), in the way already discussed.)

If an agent really is uninterested in pursuing what he needs; and this is not the product of false belief; and he could not reach any such motive from motives he has by the kind of deliberative processes we have discussed; then I think we do have to say that in the internal sense he indeed has no reason to pursue these things. In saying this, however, we have to bear in mind how strong these assumptions are, and how seldom we are likely to think that we know them to be true. When we say that a person has reason to take medicine which he needs, although he consistently and persuasively denies any interest in preserving his health, we may well still be speaking in the internal sense, with the thought that really at some level he *must* want to be well.

However, if we become clear that we have no such thought, and persist in saying that the person has this reason, then we must be speaking in another sense, and this is the external sense. People do say things that ask to be taken in the external interpretation. In James' story of Owen Wingrave, from which Britten made an opera, Owen's father urges on him the necessity and importance of his joining the army, since all his male ancestors were soldiers, and family pride requires him to do the same. Owen Wingrave has no motivation to join the army at all, and all his desires lead in another direction: he hates everything about military life and what it means. His father might have expressed himself by saying that *there was a reason for Owen to join the army.* Knowing that there was nothing in Owen's S which would lead, through deliberative reasoning, to his doing this would not make him withdraw the claim or admit that he made it under a misapprehension. He means it in an external sense. What is that sense?

A preliminary point is that this is not the same question as that of the status of a supposed categorical imperative, in the Kantian sense of an 'ought' which applies to an agent independently of what the agent happens to want: or rather, it is not undoubtedly the same question. First, a categorical imperative has often been taken, as by Kant, to be necessarily an imperative of morality, but external reason statements do not necessarily relate to morality. Second, it remains an obscure issue what the relation is between 'there is a reason for *A* to...' and '*A* ought to...' Some philosophers take them to be equivalent, and under that view the question of external reasons of course comes much closer to the question of a categorical imperative. However, I shall not make any assumption about such an equivalence, and shall not further discuss 'ought'.

In considering what an external reason statement might mean, we have to remember again the dimension of possible explanation, a consideration which applies to any reason for action: if something can be a reason for action, then it could be someone's reason for acting on a particular occasion, and it would then figure in an explanation of that action. Now no external reason statement could *by itself* offer an explanation of anyone's action. Even if it were true (whatever that might turn out to mean) that there was a reason for Owen to join the army, that fact by itself would never explain anything that Owen did, not even his joining the army. For if it was true at all, it was true when Owen was not motivated to join the army. The whole point of external reason statements is that they can be true independently of the agent's motivations. But nothing can explain an agent's (intentional) actions except something that motivates him so to act. So something else is needed besides the truth of the external reason statement to explain action, some psychological link; and that psychological link would seem to be belief. *A*'s believing an external reason statement about himself may help to explain his action.

External reason statements have been introduced merely in the general form 'there is a reason for *A* to...'; but we now need to go beyond that form, to specific statements of reasons. No doubt there are some cases of an agent's ϕ-ing because he believes that there is a reason for him to ϕ, while he does not have any belief about what that reason is. They would be cases of his relying on some authority whom he trusts, or, again, of his recalling that he did know of some reason for his ϕ-ing, but his not being able to remember what it was. In these respects, reasons for action are like reasons for belief. But, as with reasons for belief, they are evidently secondary cases: the basic case must be that in which *A* ϕ's, not because he believes only that there is some reason or other for him to ϕ, but because he believes of some determinate consideration that it constitutes a reason for him to ϕ. Thus Owen Wingrave might come to join the army because (now) he believes that it is a reason for him to do so that his family has a tradition of military honour.

Does believing that a particular consideration is a reason to act in a particular way provide, or indeed constitute, a motivation to act? If it does not, then we are no further on. Let us grant that it does – this claim indeed seems plausible, so long at least as the connexion between such beliefs and the disposition to act is not tightened to that unnecessary degree which excludes *akrasia*. The claim is in fact *so* plausible, that this agent, with this belief, appears to be one about whom, now, an *internal* reason statement could truly be made: he is one with an appropriate motivation in his *S*. A man who does believe that considerations of family honour constitute reasons for action is a man with a certain disposition to action, and also dispositions of approval, sentiment, emotional reaction, and so forth.

Now it does not follow from this that there is nothing in external reason statements. What does follow is that their content is not going to be revealed by considering merely the state of one who believes such a statement, and how that state explains action, for that state is merely the state with regard to which an internal reason statement could truly be made. Rather, the content of the external type of statement will have to be revealed by considering what it is to *come to believe* such a statement – it is there, if at all, that their peculiarity will have to emerge.

We will take the case (we have implicitly been doing so already) in which an external reason statement is made about someone who, like Owen Wingrave, is not already motivated in the required way, and so is someone about whom an internal statement could not also be truly made. (Since the difference between external and internal statements turns on the implications accepted by the speaker, external statements can of course be made about agents who are already motivated; but that is not the interesting case.) The agent does not presently believe the external statement. If he comes to believe it, he will be motivated to act; so coming to believe it must, essentially, involve acquiring a new motivation. How can that be?

This is closely related to an old question, of how 'reason can give rise to a motivation', a question which has famously received from Hume a negative answer. But in that form, the question is itself unclear, and is unclearly related to the argument – for of course reason, that is to say, rational processes, can give rise to new motivations, as we have seen in the account of deliberation. Moreover, the traditional way of putting the issue also (I shall suggest) picks up an onus of proof about what is to count as a 'purely rational process' which not only should it not pick up, but which properly belongs with the critic who wants to oppose Hume's general conclusion and to make a lot out of external reason statements – someone I shall call 'the external reasons theorist'.

The basic step lies in recognising that the external reasons theorist must conceive in a special way the connexion between acquiring a motivation and coming to believe the reason statement. For of course there are various means by which the agent could come to have the motivation and also to believe the reason statement, but which are the wrong kind of means to interest the external reasons theorist. Owen might be so persuaded by his father's moving rhetoric that he acquired both the motivation and the belief. But this excludes an element which the external reasons theorist essentially wants: that the agent should acquire the motivation *because* he comes to believe the reason statement, and that he should do the latter, moreover, because, in some way, he is considering the matter aright. If the theorist is to hold on to these conditions, he will, I think, have to make the condition under which the agent appropriately comes to have the motivation something like this, that he should deliberate correctly; and the external reasons statement itself might be taken as roughly equivalent to, or at least as entailing, the claim that if the agent rationally deliberated, then, whatever motivations he originally had, he would come to be motivated to ϕ.

But if this is correct, there does indeed seem great force in Hume's basic point, and it is very plausible to suppose that all external reason statements are false. For, *ex hypothesi*, there is no motivation for the agent to deliberate *from*, to reach this new motivation. Given the agent's earlier existing motivations, and this new motivation, what has to hold for external reason statements to be true, on this line of interpretation, is that the new motivation could be in some way rationally arrived at, granted the earlier motivations, yet at the same time that it should not bear to the earlier motivations the kind of rational relation which we considered in the earlier discussion of deliberation – for in that case an internal reason statement would have been true in the first place. I see no reason to suppose that these conditions could possibly be met.

It might be said that the force of an external reason statement can be explained in the following way. Such a statement implies that a rational agent would be motivated to act appropriately; and it can carry this implication, because a rational agent is precisely one who has a general disposition in his S to do what (he believes) there is reason for him to do. So when he comes to believe that there is reason for him to ϕ, he is motivated to ϕ, even though, before, he neither had a motive to ϕ, nor any motive related to ϕ-ing in one of the ways considered in the account of deliberation.

But this reply merely puts off the problem. It reapplies the desire and belief model (roughly speaking) of explanation to the actions in question, but using a desire and a belief the content of which are in question. *What* is it that one comes to believe when he comes to believe that there is reason for him to ϕ, if it is not the proposition, or something that entails the proposition, that if he deliberated rationally, he would be motivated to act appropriately? We were asking how any true proposition could have that content; it cannot help, in answering that, to appeal to a supposed desire which is activated by a belief which has that very content.

These arguments about what it is to accept an external reason statement involve some idea of what is possible under the account of deliberation already given, and what is excluded by that account. But here it may be objected that the account of deliberation is very vague, and has for instance allowed the use of the imagination to extend or restrict the contents of the agent's S. But if that is so, then it is unclear what the limits are to what an agent might arrive at by rational deliberation from his existing S.

It is certainly a feature of the present account of deliberative reasoning (or rather, promissory sketch of such an account) both that it is vague, and that it is more permissive than would have been allowed by the sub-Humean. I do not think that these features could be or should be eliminated in a fuller account. There is an essential indeterminacy in what can be counted a rational deliberative process: it is a heuristic process, and an imaginative one, and there are no fixed boundaries on the continuum from rational thought to inspiration and conversion. Now to someone who thinks that reasons for action are basically to be understood in terms of the internal reasons model, this is not a difficulty. There is indeed a vagueness about 'A has reason to ϕ', in the internal sense, insofar as the deliberative processes which could lead from A's present S to his being motivated to ϕ may be more or less ambitiously conceived. But this is no embarrassment to those who take as basic the internal conception of reasons for action: it merely shows that there is a wider range of states, and a less determinate one, than one might have supposed, which can be counted as A's having a reason to ϕ.

It is rather the external reasons theorist who faces the problem at this point. There are of course many things that a speaker may say to one who is not disposed to ϕ when the speaker thinks that he should be: as that he is inconsiderate, or cruel, or selfish, or imprudent; or that things, and he, would be a lot nicer if he were so motivated. Any of these can be sensible things to say. But one who makes a great deal out of putting the criticism in the form of the external reason statement seems concerned to say that what is particularly wrong with the agent is that he is *irrational*. It is this theorist who particularly needs to make this charge precise: in particular, because he wants any rational agent, as such, to acknowledge the requirement to do the thing in question.

Owen Wingrave's father indeed expressed himself in terms other than 'a reason'. But as we imagined, he could have used the external reasons formulation; and this fact itself provides some difficulty for the external reasons theorist. This theorist, who sees the truth of an external reason statement as potentially grounding a charge of irrationality against the agent who ignores it, might well want to say that if Wingrave *père* put his complaints against Owen in this form, he would very probably be claiming something which, in this particular case, was false. But what the theorist would have a harder time showing would be that the words *meant* something different as used by Wingrave from what they mean when they are, as he supposes, truly uttered. But what they mean when uttered by Wingrave is almost certainly *not* that rational deliberation would get Owen to be motivated to join the army – which is (very roughly) the meaning or implication we have found for them, if they are to bear the kind of weight such theorists wish to give them.

The sort of considerations which, I fear loosely and sketchily, have been offered here strongly suggest to me that external reason statements, when definitely isolated as such, are false, or incoherent, or really something else misleadingly expressed. It is in fact harder to isolate them in people's speech than the introduction of them at the beginning of this paper suggested: those who use these words often seem, rather, to be entertaining an optimistic internal reason claim. But sometimes the statement is indeed offered as standing definitely outside the agent's *S* and what he might derive from it in rational deliberation, and then there is, I suggest, a great unclarity about what is meant. Sometimes it is little more than that things would be better if the agent so acted. But the formulation in terms of reasons does have an effect, particularly in its suggestion that the agent is being irrational, and this suggestion, once the basis of an internal reason claim has been clearly laid aside, is bluff.

If this is so, the only real claims about reasons for action will be internal claims. This idea, and the considerations that lead to it, obviously contrast strongly with Hollis's views, as expressed for instance in his discussion, in the preceding paper, of the water shortage. I shall not embark on any detailed criticism of Hollis's arguments, but it may be helpful, both to clarify my own view and to bring out the contrast in the positions, if I end by merely setting out a set of questions, together with the answers that would be given to them by one who thinks (to put it cursorily) that the only rationality of action is the rationality of internal reasons.

1. Can we define notions of rationality which are not purely egoistic?

   Yes.

2. Can we define notions of rationality which are not purely means–end?

   Yes.

3. Can we define a notion of rationality where the action rational for A is in no way relative to A's existing motivations?

No.

4. Can we show that a man who only has egoistic motivations is irrational in not pursuing non-egoistic ends?

Not necessarily, though we may be able to in special cases. (The trouble with the egoistic man is not characteristically irrationality.)

Let there be some good, G, and a set of persons, P, such that each member of P has egoistic reason to want G provided, but delivering G requires action C, which involves costs, by each of some proper sub-set of P; and let A be a member of P: then

5. Has A egoistic reason to do C if he is reasonably sure either that too few members of P will do C for G to be provided, or that enough other members of P will do C, so that G will be provided?

No.

6. Are there any circumstances of this kind in which A can have egoistic reason to do C?

Yes, in those cases (not Hollis's case) in which reaching the critical number of those doing C is sensitive to his doing C, or he has reason to think this.

7. Are there any motivations which would make it rational for A to do C, even though not in the situation just referred to?

Yes, if he is not purely egoistic: many. For instance, there are expressive motivations – these may be rather inappropriate in Hollis's case, but not e.g. in the celebrated voting case.[2] There are also motivations which derive from the sense of fairness. This can precisely transcend the dilemma of 'either useless or unnecessary', by the form of argument 'somebody, but no reason to omit any particular body, so everybody'.

[2] A well-known treatment is by M. Olson Jr. *The Logic of Collective Action* (Cambridge, Mass., 1965). On expressive motivations in this connexion, see S. I. Benn, 'Rationality and Political Behaviour', in S. I. Benn and G. W. Mortimore, eds., *Rationality and the Social Sciences* (London, 1976). On the point about fairness, which follows in the text, there is of course a very great deal more to be said: for instance, about how members of a group can, compatibly with fairness, converge on strategies more efficient than everyone's doing C (such as people taking turns).

8. Is it irrational for an agent to have such motivations?

In any sense in which the question is intelligible, no.

9. Is it rational for society to bring people up with these sorts of motivations?

In so far as the question is intelligible, yes. And certainly we have reason to encourage people to have these dispositions – e.g. in virtue of possessing them ourselves.

I confess that I cannot see any other major questions which, at this level of generality, bear on these issues. All these questions have clear answers which are entirely compatible with a conception of practical rationality in terms of internal reasons for action, and are also, it seems to me, entirely reasonable answers.

Ethical consistency

ROSS HARRISON

1   AIM OF PAPER

In this paper I wish to argue, or at least to suggest, that the notion of *consistency* has the same importance in both moral and non-moral cases; that it is perfectly feasible to regard moral judgements in a realist manner; but that moral judgements also possess certain properties which are normally attributed to judgements regarded in a non-realist manner.

2   PRELIMINARY

'The reasons for each of two inconsistent beliefs cannot in the end be the best possible reasons', wrote Bernard Williams just over ten years ago.[1] He held that the case was different for practical, or moral, judgements, and this paper is prompted by this suggestion of Williams that the notions of *consistency* and *reason* can be used to make a distinction between practical and non-practical judgements. I wish to start by mentioning Williams at the outset since I wish to make it clear that this is where I gained my interest in the question, and because the thesis which I shall be attacking in this paper is a rather crude and unsubtle account of his suggestion. However, because the thesis is rather crudely given, and because I would like to concentrate on the ideas in themselves without getting drawn into the additional complication of how far I am criticising Williams as such, I shall from now on not mention Williams as much as I strictly ought to. References to his work are given in the footnotes.

I would like to mention one other possible complication before beginning the argument. This is that I have already labelled the two kinds of judgements about which it is to be argued whether there is, or is not, a basic distinction in several different ways (moral/non-moral; practical/non-practical; beliefs/practical judgements) and in general it seems to be very

---

[1]   The quotation is from 'Consistency and realism' (PASS 1966), reprinted in *Problems of the Self*, p. 198. This is the central paper I am concerned with, but also of importance are two other papers reprinted in the same collection, 'Ethical consistency' and 'Deciding to believe'.

hard to state what these two types of judgements are if we wish to avoid either begging the question at the outset or else getting drawn into grotesque and unintended consequences. For example, to describe the two kinds of judgements as judgements of fact and judgements of value rather tends to presuppose that judgements of value are not judgements of fact, and so to beg the question against ethical realism. On the other hand, to describe the difference as being between action-guiding and non-action-guiding judgements either leads quickly to the conclusion that there is no important difference, or else forces one into the absurb result of denying that such judgements as 'the house is on fire' or 'this is poison' are not action guiding. Williams' own way of making the distinction, as between 'theoretical' and 'practical' judgements,[2] is similarly liable either to fail to make the intended distinction or to imply that 'there is a lexical ordering between liberty and average utility' is not a theoretical statement, or 'people who don't change down before hills ruin their engines' is not a practical statement.

I wish to avoid this problem in the rest of this paper by the simple device of declaring that it is not important. I shall myself describe the distinction as being between 'descriptive' and 'evaluative' judgements. I wish to do this, however, without any prejudice as to whether it is a distinction of kind, a distinction of degree, or a distinction of reason without any foundation in the reality of things. By 'evaluative judgements' I shall mean 'those judgements like "pain is wrong"', by 'descriptive judgements' I shall mean 'those judgements like "grass is green"'. If, in fact, these two referring expressions refer to the same set of judgements, then it will have been shown that there is not any real distinction; two different ways of referring to judgements does not by itself show that there is any difference in the judgements referred to.

3   THE THESIS WHICH WILL BE CRITICISED

The thesis under consideration holds that the notion of consistency has a crucially different rôle to play in the areas of descriptive and evaluative judgements; whereas it can be regarded as an ideal to be aimed at in both types of discourse, its lack in the evaluative area is not crucial in the way that its lack in the area of descriptive judgements is. This is connected with, or taken to imply, a difference in status between the two kinds of judgements from the point of view of realism; since descriptive judgements are understood realistically, consistency is essential if the judgements are not to be deficient in some way (i.e. false); however, if we may properly have a set of evaluative judgements which is inconsistent and yet which is not deficient in any similar way, then it follows that evaluative judgements

2   *Problems*, p. 203.

should not be taken in a realistic sense. Let me sum up this thesis in the claim that the best possible set or system of evaluative beliefs might well be inconsistent, while the best possible set or system of descriptive beliefs could not be. As Williams asserts, 'when two people come out with inconsistent assertions, there must be something wrong'.[3]

The idea that there is a crucial difference in point of consistency between descriptive and evaluative judgements is related to three other points of difference. The first is that evaluative judgements can be taken to be analogous to imperatives, and can also be usefully compared with systems of rules such as legal rules. Now, whereas it is obviously undesirable in itself for a legal system to have inconsistencies, or for a sergeant major to utter commands which it is impossible to follow, both these things might well occur in the system of rules or commands which was thought to be the most desirable system, taken as a whole. For if we evaluate such systems on pragmatic grounds,[4] that is according to how they fulfil our purposes, then such an inconsistent system may achieve more of our purposes (because, for example, it is simpler and easier to use) than a consistent one would.

The second related difference may be put in terms of the metaphor of the 'direction of fit' between words and the world.[5] At least in evaluative judgements of a normative character, appropriateness or satisfaction is achieved when the world fits the words. (I say that he ought to stop tormenting her, and he does); whereas in descriptive judgements, appropriateness or satisfaction is achieved when the words fit the world (he has stopped tormenting her, and I say that he has). I may, for my own purposes, try and twist the world into several incompatible directions at once and so, quite properly, have evaluative beliefs incapable of complete satisfaction; I can not, however, quite properly think that the world *is* twisted in these incompatible directions at once, and so properly have descriptive beliefs incapable of complete satisfaction.

The third difference is related to the second, and is about the amount of choice or control that I have over my judgements. If the world has to fit my words, then I am in control of the independent variable and, so it may seem, have full choice over what my judgements are to be. Whereas if my words have to fit the world, then my judgements are the dependent variable, and I only have control on them indirectly, in so far as I have control on the world. It may seem, therefore, that I am able to choose certain ends or ultimate purposes, and, given them, choose more immediate ways of realising them. But however definite I am about my purposes, it is

---

[3] *Problems of the Self*, p. 197.
[4] This and the other following points are all meant to be glosses on points of Williams'. This one appears, for example, on p. 198.
[5] For this see *Problems*, p. 203.

normally thought that I cannot choose to have descriptive beliefs as a way of realising them. For example, my purpose may be happiness, and I am sure that belief in God will make me happy; this does not by itself enable me to choose to believe that God exists.[6] Contrast this with the case in which my purpose is happiness, and I am sure that happiness consists in intellectual self-fulfilment; then it may seem that this is enough for me to choose to evaluate highly intellectual self-fulfilment. Descriptive beliefs, it might be argued, are less like actions than evaluative judgements; they cannot just be chosen because they are thought to be the best means to certain ends. The possibility of choice with respect to them makes another difference between factual and evaluative judgements.

4 ARGUMENT AGAINST THIS THESIS

The claim to be attacked, then, is that the best possible set or system of evaluative judgements might be inconsistent, but that the best possible set of descriptive judgements could not be. The chief argument for this supposition is that our reasons for adopting a set of evaluative judgements are pragmatic, and that inconsistency may serve our purposes as well as consistency. The trouble I have with this argument is that I think that the same reasons can apply in the case of descriptive judgements, and so there is not a disanalogy between the two cases. It is allowed in both cases, that is, that consistency is always good in itself, so that it would be better to have a consistent set of judgements than an inconsistent set, other things being equal; however it is argued that in the evaluative area this is just one ideal to be traded off against other ideals such as convenience in use, so that in the best possible system these other ideals may be satisfied at the expense of consistency. It seems to me that exactly the same could be said of a set or system of descriptive judgements. Again, consistency is thought to be good in itself, so that a consistent system is always preferable to an inconsistent system, other things being equal. However, I do not see why there might not be other ideals to be satisfied by a system of descriptive judgements, which again might come into competition with this ideal of consistency. Just as in the evaluative case, these competing ideals might relate to the conditions which would need to be satisfied before the system of judgements could be used. Here also considerations of simplicity might well come into conflict with consistency.

This is not to say that the truth itself could be inconsistent; however, to put it in a rather metaphorical way, the truth is not the judgements themselves but rather the end towards which they aim, or towards which

---

[6] Compare on this Pascal's wager; and Williams' paper 'Deciding to Believe' (*Problems*, pp. 136–51).

they are the means. It is not necessarily the case that a necessary condition on the end is a necessary condition on the best possible means of realising that end. So although the truth has to be consistent, it does not follow that the best set of judgements available to us, which are our means of attempting to realise this end, must also be consistent. We might gain more of the truth (realise more of our end) if we take a set of judgements which is inconsistent than take one which is consistent. This becomes even more obvious if the end is taken not just to be truth as such but also knowledge; for we may well possess more knowledge in a set of inconsistent judgements than a set of consistent ones. This is because the set of inconsistent judgements might be much better organised, so that individual judgements could be justified and predictions made with some confidence; the price of this being some simplification or idealisation which meant that the occasional inconsistency could also be derived. Suppose that we had two systems, A and B, which were both taken to be describing the world. A contains a series of mathematically related expressions which could nearly always be counted upon to make reliable predictions but which would occasionally, together with certain observation statements, deliver something of the form a and not-a. B is just a list, or conjunction, of a series of observations. Since B consists solely of singular statements describing events (or states at a time), it does not contain any inconsistencies. However, it might well contain less knowledge than system A and so, for all we know, less truth as well. In system B, the observations might all be wrong, and we would have no method of finding out; in system A, we can not only give justification or support to parts of the system that might come into doubt (by using the close relations between the parts of the system), but we can also use it to make reliable predictions and gain new knowledge. In other words, we have more expectations about a system of descriptive judgements than just consistency; we expect it also to realise such ideals as the justification of its parts, or the realisation of new knowledge. However, if there are more ideals than one, then it is possible for these ideals to come into conflict; and we may well feel that our ideals as a whole are better served by a system of judgements which sacrifices consistency in order to gain theoretical understanding or predictive power; but this is just to make the same kind of trade-off between ideals which it was supposed characterised evaluative judgements, and distinguished them from descriptive ones.

It might be objected to this that all this shows is that adopting an inconsistent set of judgements might be the best thing to do at a certain stage of knowledge, but that this could never be finally satisfactory. The claim of the thesis being attacked is not that all sets of descriptive judgements which it is reasonable to hold must be consistent, but rather that there is always something crucially unsatisfactory about an inconsistent set of descriptive judgements in a way that there is not with an inconsistent set of evaluative judgements. The claim, that is, is that we could not stop and be fully satisfied with an inconsistent set. I think, however, that this claim still does not distinguish between descriptive and evaluative judgements, although we must be careful what it means. It might just be the claim that consistency is an ideal, so that we could not be finally satisfied with an inconsistent set, in that in it one of our ideals was not satisfied. However, it has been acknowledged throughout that consistency is an ideal of both descriptive and evaluative discourse. If we take a moral example, in which it is thought that the right judgements to hold are inconsistent, such as the tragic dilemma cases,[7] then it might well be said that the person in the case was not finally satisfied, in that one of his ideals, consistency, was not satisfied; and this would still be true even though he thought that he had the most satisfactory set of judgements taken as a whole. To say that the inconsistent set, whether descriptive or evaluative, is not finally satisfactory in this sense is merely to say that there is at least one direction in which the system could be improved. This, however, is quite compatible with a system which does not realise this ideal being the best possible system. As Leibniz was at pains to demonstrate, the best possible system does not mean the best in every respect, but rather the best combination of respects, even though some of these respects may not be fully realised. A failure fully to realise the ideal of consistency may be a property of the best possible system.

If, therefore, the claim that an inconsistent set of descriptive judgements can never be finally satisfactory means more than that it just fails to realise every ideal of such a system (in which sense an inconsistent set of evaluative judgements is not finally satisfactory either), then it must be the claim that an inconsistent set can never be the best possible set. However, once we allow that there are several ideals to be satisfied in the descriptive case as well as the evaluative case, and once we have given the general outline of what a situation would be like in which we preferred to follow these other ideals (as in systems A and B above), then it does not seem obvious that an inconsistent set of beliefs might not be the best possible set. That is, that such a set might be not just the best set to have at a particular time, or from a certain limited point of view, but the best possible set to end up with. For we are concerned with human discovery of truth, and human acquisition of knowledge, and it may be the case that such human procedures are only possible if beliefs meet certain standards of simplicity and organisation. It

---

[7] The tragic dilemma case is the one particularly discussed by Williams in 'Ethical Consistency' (*Problems*, pp. 166–86). The case particularly discussed is that of Agamemnon and Iphigeneia; the central idea is that it is right for someone to hold in a full, rather than merely prima facie sense, two moral principles which came into conflict in a particular case. This would be shown, for example, by the person displaying regret that he had not followed one of them, even though he could not help but not follow one of them.

may well be the case that God has no need of a set of inconsistent judgements but, for human beings, the choice may be between an inconsistent science and no science at all; and if this is so, there is no need to think that inconsistency is a merely transitory property of the judgements we happen to hold at the moment. It might also be a property of the best possible set of judgements with which we finally end up.

This comparison between descriptive and evaluative judgements has taken place under the assumption that it is clear that the best possible set of evaluative judgements might well be inconsistent, that is, under the assumption that the Williams account of the tragic dilemma case is basically correct. This assumption might itself be questioned; that is, it might be thought that even for evaluative judgements the best possible system could not be inconsistent. In that case, a finally satisfactory treatment of the tragic dilemma case would involve letting one of the two competing moral principles over-ride the other (for example, by deriving them both from one single, independent, external principle). If this is felt about evaluative judgements, then it removes the point of the above attempts to establish an analogy in the case of descriptive judgements by showing how they also must match up to conflicting ideals. However, it removes the point of this analogy at the cost of allowing a different, and much more direct, analogy to be established between descriptive and evaluative judgements. For now it can be claimed that in neither case is inconsistency part of the best possible system. The thesis that there is a basic difference between the two cases only gets going because it proposes a rather special treatment of consistency in the case of evaluative judgements, a special treatment which the tragic dilemma case is meant to illustrate.

5 REALISM

It will be remembered that the difference between evaluative and descriptive judgements proposed in the thesis under examination was associated not just with a supposed difference in the reasons for consistency but also with such considerations as realism, choice of beliefs, and the direction of fit between words and the world. To take the latter first, it does not by itself seem to produce any clear disanalogy. For whichever direction of fit we are interested in, a lack of fit in a particular situation is a lack of fit, and so something which is in itself unsatisfactory. In both cases we may think that the lack of fit at particular points is justified by the overall fit of the system we prefer. This is just to repeat the point that the best possible set of judgements might not all be true (fit at every point). It is unclear, however, why this should matter if the direction is that we are attempting to fit words to the world and not matter if we are attempting to fit the world to words.

35

In both cases there is a breakdown in the realisation of our particular intentions which might be justified in the interests of the realisation of our overall intention.

It may be felt, however, that to keep making the analogy in this way misses the crucial point. This point is that if the direction of fit is from the world to words, as when we are attempting to describe the world, then this attempt can only be evaluated in a realistic spirit. Descriptions, that is, are evaluated according to whether or not they are true, and this depends upon whether they succeed in fitting a quite separate, mind-independent, world. This being so, inconsistency must be a defect, in that at least one of a set of inconsistent judgements must be false. The ultimate standards in this case, that is, since they involve the notions of truth and of independent reality, are closely concerned with the question of fit itself. The situation, it can be argued, is importantly different in the case of evaluative judgements. For although here we also have a lack of fit if we have an inconsistent set of judgements, this is not now of prime concern. For if we do not construe our evaluative judgements in a realistic spirit, then questions of fit cease to be important. The important constraints motivating the choice of judgements are pragmatic or moral; and these may well be perfectly satisfied by an inconsistent set of judgements. So it could be argued (and this, I take it, is the full Williams position) that it is misleading in the last section to claim that consistency is an ideal of both kinds of judgements; for although this is true, it is true in the two cases for quite different reasons. The importance of consistency for descriptive judgements is that inconsistent judgements cannot all be true; whereas the importance of consistency for evaluative judgements is that beyond a certain level of inconsistency a system of evaluative judgements becomes unworkable or impractible. This also demonstrates the difference with respect to whether this ideal needs to be realised. In the descriptive case, any inconsistency is automatically a deficiency, whereas in the evaluative case the inconsistency only becomes a deficiency when it arises above a certain level. If there is only a small amount of inconsistency, therefore, it can be held that a set of evaluative judgements possessing it is the best possible set (because possessing no deficiency) whereas a set of descriptive judgements could not be.

This may well seem to be the strongest way of putting the argument for the thesis I am opposing. It is not Williams' own way since this argument starts by presupposing a different realist status for factual and evaluative judgements and moves from there to a difference in consistency, whereas Williams wishes to move in the reverse direction, from difference in consistency to difference in realist status. This may be important, and in any case I do not see that this new way of putting the argument gets over the crucial point against the earlier version, which is that the best set for us of descriptive judgements may be a set which contains inconsistency. This point follows solely from realising that pragmatic considerations apply also to descriptive judgements, and is totally independent of the question of the realistic status of evaluative judgements. If, in addition, it can be urged that it is mere question-begging to suppose that evaluative judgements do not have a realistic status, then symmetry is totally restored. In both cases, and for the same reasons, there is something undesirable about inconsistency (inconsistent judgements cannot all be true), but in both cases this may be overweighed by consequential gains in simplicity or organisation.

Furthermore, without begging the question either way on the realist status of evaluative judgements, I think that the cases are perfectly symmetrical in that in both cases every single case of inconsistency matters. It is not true that for evaluative judgements inconsistency only becomes important when it arises above a certain level. On the contrary, every single case must have practical effects. It is undesirable to be caught in the kind of tragic dilemma cases which Williams describes, in which Agamemnon thinks both that he should and also that he should not save Iphigeneia. It is obviously desirable that our moral system should never deliver inconsistencies like this. So, quite apart from any presumptions about the realist status of evaluative judgements, the descriptive and evaluative cases are symmetrical in that every single case of inconsistency matters (and that other things may matter more).

The idea that inconsistency is of especial importance in the descriptive case is supported in Williams' treatment, I think, by a particular view about the nature of reasons for descriptive judgements. To requote the remark of Williams with which I began, he claims that 'the reasons for each of two inconsistent judgements cannot in the end be the best possible reasons'.[8] This, I think, only follows if we have a fairly strong commitment to a rationalist ideal, as in Leibniz or Spinoza, in which every judgement has a reason and all these reasons are consistent with each other (so that in the end we can take the one great consistent set of judgements, realise that they are therefore all clearly and distinctly perceived, and take them all to be true). If we think, as I suggested above, that this ideal might not be realisable at the human level, then this remark of Williams' ceases to be self-evident. I shall give an alternative view of the nature of reasons in section 7.

It may be thought that the onus is still on me to show that the kind of inconsistent moral views we have in the tragic dilemma cases is perfectly compatible with a realistic view of the nature of moral judgements, in which moral judgements are given truth-values. Given that analogous

[8] The quotation is from 'Consistency and realism' (PASS 1966), reprinted in *Problems of the Self*, p. 198.

inconsistency may properly exist in the area of descriptive judgements, which unquestionably have truth value or realistic status, this can be established easily enough. In the tragic dilemma case, not all the particular judgements we make can be true. However, it does not follow from this that they may not be the best set of judgements which we can have, granted that we are pre-eminently interested in establishing the moral truth of the matter. The moral principles which deliver them, that is, are the right moral principles even if they lead to problems on this particular occasion. Even though they could not all be true, they might nevertheless be the best ones to *believe* even if we are interested in nothing apart from the end of acquiring truth and knowledge in the moral area; they are the product of the right method of acquiring moral truth and knowledge.

Attributing realistic status to either moral or descriptive judgements is holding that what makes them true is independent of our thought of them. God, we may suppose, knows whatever this is directly, so that in his direct knowledge of the True, he knows also the Good. None of God's beliefs in either case are false; and so they are not inconsistent. However, for us, perhaps the best we can do (the best set of beliefs held for the best reasons) involves inconsistency. Human limitation prevents us getting the whole story; but this does not mean that what we do get may not be viewed realistically. We may think, because it is true, that fathers should care for their daughters and commanders care for their fleets. God knows, although we do not, how the inconsistencies to which this gives rise should be resolved in particular cases. Even if we can never remove the inconsistency, this does not mean that we are not able legitimately to think that there is a truth of the matter, inaccessible to us, nor to think that we are following the best possible means available to us of acquiring that independent truth. I conclude that there is nothing in the foregoing arguments which prevents our regarding moral, or evaluative, judgements in a realistic spirit.

6 CHOICE

The difference between factual and evaluative judgements may be felt to rest upon differences in the possibility of choice, itself dependent upon whether we are trying to fit the words to the world or the world to words. Let me agree that we can't choose our beliefs just like that, so that, just as by taking mere thought alone, I can't add one inch to my stature, so by taking mere thought alone I can't just come up with the belief that, say, God exists. The importance of this is that beliefs cannot be regarded like actions and chosen (at least in a certain decision-theoretic model) according to pay-offs. However great the possible gain, I can't just like that choose to believe that God exists. The trouble is, that I can't just like that choose to make a particular evaluative judgement either. However great the possible gain, I can't just choose to think that God is good, or to approve of Wagner's music. I can go through the motions of doing so (saying that I do, acting as if I do), but this is not the point, and in any case also applies equally to the descriptive and the evaluative area. It is also the case that, even if I can't choose the belief directly, I can choose to undergo certain processes which I know will result in having the belief (having my brain programmed; entering the monastery). However, this again applies equally to the descriptive and the evaluative area.

It may seem, however, that choice must come in somewhere in a way that separates the two kinds of judgements. For, it can be argued, people can obviously be evaluated for their evaluative beliefs (Hitler was a bad man because he thought that Jews were inferior), and it is surely wrong to evaluate, to praise or blame, someone for something that he has not chosen. Ought implies can not. I think this is right in that it is only when we are praising or blaming a person, rather than directly evaluating the belief itself, that questions of choice come in. However, here we may observe that people are also regularly praised or blamed for the purely descriptive beliefs that they hold. We blame Hitler, for example, for having mistaken descriptive judgements about race (such as about difference in blood). We blame the drug manufacturers for believing that thalidomide was a harmless drug. This is not to break the principle, or assumption, that we should not blame someone for doing something which he could not help doing (or for being in a state which he could not help being in). This is because, as was suggested above, even if we cannot choose beliefs directly, we can choose to operate processes which will result in new beliefs being acquired. The particular cases mentioned above were those in which we already knew which belief we wished to acquire. This, however, is not necessary: we can choose to operate certain processes because we think that they will result in our having the true belief, without having any antecedent idea of which belief that is. Such processes are the normal processes of scientific research, testing, observation, and so on. So we can blame people for having particular descriptive beliefs, because we can blame them for refusing to operate the processes which one should operate if one is interested in acquiring true beliefs. They choose not to test their beliefs, and so are blameworthy. We evaluate truth, that is, and so evaluate methods of acquiring it; which means that we may praise or blame people for operating, or refusing to operate, those methods. Evaluation of judgements, and evaluation of people for holding them, applies in the case of descriptive judgements as well as in the case of evaluative judgements.

7 GENERAL PRINCIPLES AND PARTICULAR APPLICATIONS

I said above that if inconsistency was tolerable or explicable, this depended upon a view of the nature of reasons. I think that an account can be given of the rôle of reasons which maintains the analogy between descriptive and evaluative judgements; which shows how inconsistency can arise; and which explains why inconsistency is not fatal. This is also necessary in that anyone with a tender logical conscience will have been worried by the claim that any use at all can be made of an inconsistent set of judgements in any area. For, it may be thought, if a set of judgements contains an inconsistency, then every other judgement follows from it, and so such a set can be of no conceivable use to us. The direct answer to this is that we are concerned with the beliefs themselves rather than the contents of beliefs, and it is not true that because someone believes an inconsistency he therefore believes everything. However, a more complete explanation than this of why inconsistency is tolerable is required, and such an explanation depends upon a fuller account of the nature of reasons.

If we take as our examples the kind of tragic dilemma cases described by Williams, then the inconsistency arises in the individual consequences of perfectly general beliefs which are not, in themselves, inconsistent. The inconsistency, that is, is not of the form involved in the judgement that one ought, and that one ought not, keep one's promises. The inconsistency in Agamemnon's case arises solely out of the impossibility, given the way that the world is on this particular occasion, of fulfilling the two moral precepts 'a commander ought to save his fleet' and 'a father ought to save his daughter'. There is no essential incompatibility between these two judgements taken in themselves. Similarly, it was implicit in my account of the two systems of description of the world, one highly organised but delivering inconsistencies and the other a case by case report of observations, that the inconsistency in my preferred candidate was also inconsistency in the particular applications of the central principles of the theory which were not in themselves inconsistent. In trying to apply our simple and powerful theory it occasionally gave inconsistent predictions or descriptions of particular cases; but these were thought to be tolerable because of the organisational power of the theory on other occasions, such power deriving from the essential consistency of the central principles of the theory.

The central principles, whether descriptive or evaluative, provide reasons for considering particular cases in particular ways. As such, in any operable system, they cannot be in themselves inconsistent so that (for example) pain could be taken as a reason for thinking that something was both a good and a bad thing, or decrease in acceleration a reason for thinking that something had both increased and decreased in mass. If there is inconsistency in the central principles ('mass is both increased and decreased by acceleration') then they cannot be used to provide reasons. However, if the central principles are consistent, then inconsistency may still arise in the particular cases to which they are applied. For the central principles provide reasons for considering particular cases in particular ways according to the descriptions under which these particular cases are subsumed. A case may fall under more than one description, one of which provides reasons for considering, or treating, it in one way, and another of which provides reasons for considering, or treating, it in an incompatible way. Hence inconsistency can arise at the level of particular cases. An operation, for example, causes pain in one way and alleviates it in another; it can therefore be considered to be both a good and a bad thing, although this does not mean that pain in itself is considered to be both a good and a bad thing.

This might still be felt insufficient to explain how inconsistency can arise and why it is tolerable. For, it might be said, how can it be the case that the central principles are consistent in themselves but only deliver inconsistency in particular cases. If something has inconsistent consequences, this shows that it is inconsistent in itself. The answer to this is that in both the descriptive and the evaluative cases, the relation between general principles and particular applications is not that the former provide logically sufficient conditions for the latter. General principles are not, for example, in the above account understood as being merely universal generalisations over particular cases. When it is suggested that pain is a reason for considering something to be bad, this need not be understood as asserting the generalisation that all cases of pain are bad. If it is understood in this way, of course, and if a particular case of pain (in an operation, say) is taken to be good, then the inconsistency in the particular case will indeed climb back into, and refute, the central principles. However, it can be understood in quite a different way, as meaning that pain is always a reason for considering something to be wrong. In this way it can be used consistently, that is always regarded as true, even if there are some events which are both cases of pain and are not bad. Similarly in the descriptive case. Something may properly be used as a reason even when there is only a (high) probability relation between it and the thing which it is a reason for; or we may think that the relations between our central principles of scientific theory and particular applications always allow some looseness of fit. Because there may always be other variables operating on particular cases than those we can consider or control, our central principles may not give us universal generalisations which apply to observable particulars. This again means that some inconsistency in the application of theory to these particular observable situations is possible without holding the theory to be in itself inconsistent.

In both the evaluative and the descriptive case, therefore, it is possible to take the central principles as being consistent in themselves and as providing reasons for considering particular cases in particular ways. This both explains how inconsistency can arise and also neutralises its apparently fatal effect. It also shows how it is possible in both cases to have an entirely realistic approach to the central principles, thinking that it is just quite simply true that commanders should look after their fleets and fathers save their daughters, in spite of the Iphigeneia case.

8   VERIFICATION AND MIND-DEPENDENCE

Up until now I have been trying to establish analogies between the descriptive and evaluative areas of discourse with respect to the topics of consistency, reasons, and realism. I would like to end by suggesting some disanalogies and making some rather speculative suggestions about them. Even if we accept that there is an analogous structure of central principles and particular applications in the two cases, I think that there may be an important disanalogy in the relative status of principles and particular applications with respect to their verification. In the evaluative case, central principles are more fundamental, in the descriptive case particular applications are.

When we think not just of the realist status (the possession of truth value) of descriptive judgements, but also of their epistemological status (how they are verified, or the truth value is established), then particular beliefs obviously have a primary importance. General beliefs or principles are verified (or falsified) by reference to particular beliefs, and this remains true even if there is a looseness of fit between them so that general beliefs are not just taken to be universal statements about observable particulars. We may hold 'force equals mass times acceleration' to be just as true as 'this balance now reads ab'; but we verify, or support, the former kinds of statement by means of the latter. We assume that we are more entitled to believe in the properties of particular objects or events than to believe in the interrelations of the properties themselves. What I am expressing here is the double empiricist claim that beliefs are justified by experience and that experience is of the particular (Hume: ''tis a principle generally receiv'd in philosophy, that everything in nature is individual').[9] So when we are concerned with the verification of beliefs describing the world, this verification proceeds by description of experience, and this experience is expressed in singular propositions ('this is red', 'this pointer reads 200', and so on).

By contrast, I think that it is plausible to claim that the epistemological

[9]   *Treatise*, 1.i.vii (Selby-Bigge, p. 19).

relation between general principles and particular judgements is different in the moral and evaluative cases. We could hold, that is, that we directly perceived the general rules or principles and, by means of them, justified our evaluation of the particular cases. If we wanted to hold, for example, that all, or most, actual cases of pain were bad, we could take it that this followed from the direct perception that pain was a bad thing, rather than that the perception that pain was a bad thing followed from the individual perception of the wrongness of many individual cases of pain. Of course, there are accounts of the nature of moral judgements (G. E. Moore-style intuitionism) in which the evaluative case is strictly analogous to the descriptive case. In both cases we just perceive the properties of individual objects and establish generalisations. But it is much less obvious that this has to be the order of verification in the evaluative area than that it has to be the order in the descriptive area; someone claiming to perceive directly that pain is wrong sounds a good deal less strange than someone claiming to perceive directly that force is mass times acceleration.

I have not, of course, produced much argument to show that there is a different order of verification between the evaluative and descriptive areas. I have just appealed to what I hope is the prima facie implausibility of someone dividing objects or events into those he thought good or bad (just as someone might divide them into large or small objects) and then only subsequently observing which other properties they possessed in order to establish correlations. Someone might of course arrive at the realisation that pain was a bad thing from observation of particular cases, but I think that it is more plausible to suppose that he does this because he observes, in each case, that it is bad because it is painful, rather than just observing a correlation between badness and pain. He is, I think, directly observing the reasons as reasons.

Let us suppose, in any case, that there is a different order of verification in the descriptive and in the evaluative cases. The question is what follows from this, particularly in respect of the realist status of evaluative judgements. What I think is the case, although admittedly this continues to be rather speculative, is that it does not have any direct, or automatic, consequence with respect to realism. It does mean, however, that evaluative judgements possess a property which is normally possessed by objects which are viewed in a non-realist manner. This is an essential generality. Ideal objects, mind-dependent objects, are general in the way that mind-independent objects are not; and if general principles are especially important in the evaluative case, dictating how the applications are to be described, then these applications are more general, more language-dependent, than is normally the case with a realist subject matter.

Let me try and explain this admittedly obscure notion. If we take the

43

existence of particular objects which are paradigmatic of realism, such as physical objects, then there can always be more said about them than in any particular set of descriptions. The individual is always more than it is described as being; language fails to catch up with the particular. By contrast, when we have objects which are mind-dependent, they are as they are described. If the ideology of a people results in the reification of a god, or of an economic entity, then it is in itself just as it is thought of or described; language captures it entirely. If the clicking of a gun makes me afraid, then there is more to that clicking than I can describe, or am aware of. If the unicorn in a dark room makes me afraid, then, since there is no real unicorn, the unicorn I fear is exactly as I describe it; if I don't think of its colour, for example, then it doesn't have a colour. This is what I mean when I say that non-real objects are essentially general in a way that real objects are not. They share the generality of language. They are as they are described in language.

If, then, there is a difference in verificationist status between central principles and particular applications in the descriptive and evaluative cases, so that central moral principles dictate how particular cases are to be viewed whereas central descriptive principles can be refuted by the particular instances, then evaluative judgements are general in a more fundamental way than descriptive ones are. The way in which a real particular outstrips language can be caught by the descriptive case, with its sensitivity to the particular, in the way that it cannot by the evaluative in which the inter-relations between central terms are crucial ('pain is a bad thing'). Evaluative judgements, therefore, seem to have a property which is normally only possessed by a non-realist subject matter. However, I do not think that the difference in verification has an immediate effect on the realist status of evaluative judgements. This would at least require the empiricist assumption that everything which exists is particular, that all truths are of the particular. Yet it is natural to regard mathematics realistically, as possessing truth value in virtue of something language-independent. Verification here, as in an axiomatic system such as Euclidean Geometry, starts at the level of central principles. The general elements are more fundamental than the particular applications of the geometry to the world. So I do not think that the different verificationist status of central principles in evaluative judgements by itself shows (or would show) that evaluative judgements should not be regarded realistically.

I do think, however, that one important difference between the factual and the evaluative cases does arise as a consequence of the different status for verification of central principles and particular applications. For, if both cases can be organised so that inconsistency does not appear at the level of the central principles themselves, but rather at the level of their particular consequences, then in the descriptive case inconsistency will appear at the more important epistemological level while in the evaluative case it will only appear at the less important level. Inconsistency in descriptive judgements may, therefore, have a damaging effect on the possibility of verification in a way that it cannot on evaluative judgements. In the latter we only lose some consequences, in the former we may lose the whole system. This might explain why inconsistency is regarded as more important in the descriptive than in the evaluative case.

I suggested above that inconsistency might arise in the best possible set of judgements, descriptive or evaluative, because this inconsistency was compensated by other gains. These gains could arise when the judgements were organised in a system, so that some of the judgements formed reasons for other judgements. Inconsistency could then be compensated by better, or simpler, organisation. The links of the central reason-giving principles to the individual judgements they generated gave benefits which made us wish to keep this structure of reasons intact even when it generated some inconsistency at the level of individual judgements. The additional problem which may arise when we consider verification is how the system can be established, or at least justified, at all. The verification in the descriptive case depends upon the individual judgements, so it is crucial that there is not too much inconsistency at this level, otherwise there will not be enough control on the selection of the central principles. In the evaluative case, our ability to establish the central principles is unimpeded by inconsistency at the individual level. We can therefore establish the system even if there is inconsistency in particular judgements. So inconsistency is here less important. This, however, has nothing to do with establishing any difference from the point of view of realism; it is simply a difference from the point of view of knowledge.

Wish-fulfilment

RICHARD WOLLHEIM

1. Every desire has *an object* and *a fate*.

2. Every desire is either *a desire to ϕ* or *a desire that p*. So much for the object of desire or (the same thing in other words) the structure of desire-sentences.

The fate of desire calls for a somewhat more elaborate classification. So: When the object of a desire is actualised, then, other things being equal, the desire is *satisfied*. When the object of the desire is not actualised and the desire remains active, the desire is *unsatisfied*. In more extreme cases, and where most probably the intervention of others is involved, the desire is *frustrated*. And I said deliberately 'and the desire remains active', for a desire, without being satisfied, may become *extinct*. Again, in more extreme cases it may be *extinguished*. A greater complexity is introduced when we recognise that a desire may become *transformed*: that is, a substitution may be carried out on its object, and what I have already said about the object of a desire should alert us to the fact that there is likely to be more than one place within the object where substitution can occur and thus more than one way in which desire may be transformed. So, a desire to ϕa may be transformed into a desire to ϕb or into a desire to ψa – or into a desire to ψb.

3. Freudian theory has supplemented the ways in which a desire's fate may be classified by pointing out that a desire may gain a kind of pseudo-satisfaction. The terminology for this isn't stable, and, since I want to characterise it in a way that will be neutral between two rival accounts of this fate, I shall propose my own. I shall call this fate '*gratification*'. And I shall introduce gratification, whose structure is more complex than that of the other fates, by means of a contrast with satisfaction. Thus:

my desire $\left\{ \begin{array}{l} \text{to } \phi \\ \text{that } p \end{array} \right\}$ *is satisfied*, other things being equal, iff $\left\{ \begin{array}{l} \text{I } \phi \\ p \end{array} \right.$

my desire $\left\{ \begin{array}{l} \text{to } \phi \\ \text{that } p \end{array} \right\}$ *is gratified*, iff it is for me as if $\left\{ \begin{array}{l} \text{I } \phi \\ p \end{array} \right.$

And what Freudian theory has added to this general characterization is two further propositions in amplification. The first, which is closer to general psychological theory, is that

(1) it is for me as if $\left\{ \begin{matrix} I \ \phi \\ p \end{matrix} \right\}$ when I effectively imagine that $\left\{ \begin{matrix} I \ \phi \\ p \end{matrix} \right\}$

and the second, which belongs really to abnormal psychology, is that:

(2) such effective imagination is an essential constituent of an infantile – hence also regressive – way of mental functioning.

So I now want to consider:

What is meant by effective imagination?

Or

How could the imagination be thus effective?

4. In order to answer this question – or these questions if there is plurality there – I shall first offer an analysis or reconstruction of the imaginative activity. This reconstruction is one that I have already proposed in an essay entitled 'Identification and Imagination',[1] and for that reason I shall present it here only in a compressed form.

My reconstruction has its point of origin in another reconstruction which has been fairly widely canvassed. This earlier reconstruction is, I think, very suggestive but ultimately turns out to be inadequate. As a reconstruction it bases itself on the analogy between imagination and acting, and it proposes that we should conceive of imagining the doings of oneself or of others as acting those doings over to oneself or internally. The inadequacy of the reconstruction comes from the fact that the analogy is not taken sufficiently seriously. My reconstruction depends on taking the analogy seriously.

The earlier reconstruction goes wrong because it does not take cognisance of the fact that the activity of acting is a *dependent* activity. To act is to fill a certain role, but, if this role is to be filled, then there are two other roles that must also be filled. Or if they are not filled, it is from the point of view of acting a relevant and anomalous fact that they are not. And there is, of course, nothing to prevent these roles being filled by one and the same person. The roles are that of the dramatist, who devises what the actor acts, and that of the audience who reacts to what the actor acts. Now if these roles are integral to that of acting, then a reconstruction of imagination on the analogy with acting must find a place for them too. There must be an internal version of the role of the dramatist, and an internal version of the role of the audience, and precisely what my reconstruction of imagination offers is a place for them.

[1] Richard Wollheim, 'Identification and Imagination' in *Freud: A Collection of Critical Essays*, ed. Richard Wollheim (New York, 1974).

5. What is the import of saying that the imaginative activity contains an internal version of the role of the dramatist, and an internal version of the role of the audience? I shall abbreviate these to internal dramatist and internal audience, and then proceed to characterise both roles. I shall do so largely negatively, by stressing what is not intended.

First: to postulate *an internal dramatist* is to make the point that in addition to the stream of imagining whatever it is, we also determine or initiate what it is that we imagine. But what is not intended is *either*

(a) that we invariably have a free hand in what we imagine. For instance, in at least one kind of imagining, once we have settled whom we imagine, then what we imagine about whoever it is becomes more or less fixed. We are constrained by that person's repertoire, where the repertoire itself is determined by beliefs and feelings that we have about that person. We are constrained by the repertoire – not, of course, confined to it.

or

(b) that if feels to us as though we were determining or initiating what we imagine. To say that we do determine or initiate what we imagine is to impute an activity to ourselves, but not necessarily a free activity or an activity in which we feel free.

Secondly: to postulate *an internal audience* is to make the point that the effect upon us of what we imagine is a part of the imaginative activity. This is not to say that what we imagine will invariably have an effect upon us – it may not – but if it does, this will be part of, as opposed to a consequence of, the imaginative activity. Of course, it is also possible that the imaginative activity will have consequences for us. But that will be the effect not of what we imagine but of the fact that we imagine it.

An example of this point may be helpful. Let us imagine that I engage in erotic daydreaming. I imagine myself involved in some complicated sexual activity with a woman. Now the effect of what I imagine – that is, the complicated sexual activity – will doubtless be – if that is, there is an effect – sexual excitement, and my point in postulating the internal audience is to assert that this sexual excitement will be part of the imaginative activity. However, later, I may reflect on the fact that I engaged in erotic daydreaming, more specifically that I imagined myself involved in some complicated sexual activity with a woman, and then I may feel guilty, alternatively I may feel pride in my lack of inhibition. But now the guilt or the pride will not be part of the imaginative activity, they will be consequences of it: they will be consequences of it because they are not the effect on me of what I imagined, they are the effect of the fact that I imagined it.

A word more needs to be said about the internal audience. For we may now make a distinction within the internal audience which corresponds directly to a distinction observable within the real-life audience. The distinction is that between the empathic audience and the sympathetic audience – I use both terms idiosyncratically – and in its primary application this distinction is to be explained in terms of the kind of reaction that the audience has to the character upon whom its attention is focused. Let us call that character 'the hero'. Then we may say that *the empathic audience* is that audience whose reaction to the hero is that it feels what he feels. Thus: if he feels terror, it feels terror: if he feels brave it feels brave; And *the sympathetic audience* is that audience whose reaction to the hero is that it feels in response to what the hero feels. Now the notion of 'feeling in response to what someone feels' is obviously more complex than that of 'feeling what someone feels' and for a start it presupposes a judgement on the part of the person who feels – in this case, the audience – about the person in response to whom he feels – in this case the hero. The judgement, let us assume, is either a favourable judgement or an unfavourable judgement and then the relationship of the audience's feelings to the hero's feelings can be set out thus: If the judgement is favourable, then if the hero feels terror, it will feel pity: if the hero feels brave, it will feel admiration. But, if the judgement is unfavourable, then, if the hero feels terror, it will feel delight: if the hero feels brave, it will feel terror.

The distinction between the empathic and the sympathetic audience can, I have suggested, be transferred to the internal audience. In other words, sometimes we may imagine something or other occurring, and the internal audience will be empathic: that is, if we are left at the end of the imaginative activity feeling anything, we will feel what the hero of the imagined happening felt, i.e. was imagined to feel. And sometimes we may imagine something or other occurring, and the internal audience will be sympathetic: that is, if we are left at the end of the imaginative activity feeling anything, we will feel in response to what the hero of the imagined happening felt, i.e. was imagined to feel.

Now, this is important because this distinction corresponds to another within the imaginative activity that reaches right down into the content of imagination. This further distinction I choose to express as that between the kind of imaginative activity in which we centrally imagine someone – hence peripherally imagine others, if there are others – and the kind of imaginative activity in which all those whom we imagine, all the *dramatis personae*, are acentrally imagined. For when someone is centrally imagined, the internal audience is empathic to him: and when everyone is acentrally imagined, the internal audience is sympathetic. And the rationale of this emerges when we see that centrally imagining someone is tantamount to imagining someone from the inside – the suitability of the former phrase over the latter lying in the fact that, though the less familiar, it has the greater explanatory value.

6. We may now return to the questions left hanging, and ask whether in this reconstruction of the imaginative activity we gain any greater insight into what could be meant by effective imagination, or how imagination could be so effective as to gratify desire.

As a first step to answering the question, let us try to lay down conditions that would have to be satisfied if it could be plausibly said that desire was gratified. Suppose that I desire to ϕ, alternatively that p, then for my desire to be gratified, or – what I have contended is the same thing – for it to be for me as if I am ϕ-ing, alternatively that p, it must be that I have

(1) the belief that I have ϕ-ed or that p

and

(2) the pleasure that I would get in ϕ-ing or at p.

On the relationship between these two I shall have nothing systematic to say. For instance, it might be held that (2) presupposes (1), in that the only way one could identify pleasure – that is, pleasure in this or at this as opposed to pleasure in that or at that – is through belief. For there would be no sense in saying not just that I was pleased, but that the pleasure I got was pleasure in this or at this unless I also believed that I was doing this, or that this was the case. My suspicion is that this is true but only above a certain level of complexity, and that one could identify certain elementary pleasures – those of taste or sex – without the corresponding beliefs. But nothing that I have to say is, I believe, affected by what position one takes on this point.

If, however, we accept these two candidates as the conditions of gratification, the question arises whether imagination can be so effective as to bring them about. And I think that my reconstruction of the imaginative activity should lead us to see how *in favoured circumstances* it can. My reconstruction does not, of course, permit us to see this straight off, but it shows us where to look.

For if we look on the one hand to the role of the internal dramatist, on the other hand to the role of the internal audience, we shall see, in each case, something to account for the power of the imaginative activity to bring about the two conditions necessary for gratification: that is to say, the relevant belief and the relevant pleasure. Where by talking of power, I mean only that the imagination will produce these conditions *in favoured circumstances*.

Let us look at each role in turn.

The relevant feature about the role of the internal dramatist is this: As I have said, the dramatist may well be constrained by the repertoire. There are certain things that, given who it is whom we imagine, we *must* imagine, and other things that we *just can't*. And the repertoire has its roots in reality. But, given that we *can* imagine such-and-such about whomever it is, the fact that this is counter-factual or opposed to reality is quite irrelevant. It will not, in other words, influence what I imagine. So what I imagine can fit in with not only beliefs that I actually have but also beliefs that I might, or might wish to, have: for instance, those beliefs which represent my desires as satisfied.

This point is worth staying with for a moment, since there is a ready way of misunderstanding it. The misunderstanding would consist in taking it as a merely verbal point: such as that we would no longer call the particular psychological activity 'imagination' if truth-directed considerations were that influential. But though this may be true, it is not the whole truth. For what it omits is the further fact that imagination has *the power* to reject such considerations: the considerations are not influential, but this is because they are not permitted to be influential. In other words, the point is trivialised to a verbal point by overlooking the fact that the imaginative activity is an *activity*: as such it takes place under a concept. And by saying that it takes place under a concept, I mean not only that it is described by that concept, but that it is regulated by that concept. And part of the regulative power of the concept under which imaginative activity takes place – that is, the concept of imagination itself – is that it repudiates or nullifies truth-directed considerations – at any rate, beyond a certain point. That imagination is in this way linked to the concept of imagination is something that we shall see to have further relevance for the understanding of wish-fulfilment.

Now I turn to the role of the internal audience and a feature of that role which makes its contribution to the efficacy of imagination or to imagination as gratification. It is this: If I imagine what I desire, then what the internal audience will feel – and hence what I will feel, if I feel anything – will be pleasure. That this is so can be seen by putting together two facts, both of which are complex. The first fact is this: If, on the one hand, I desire to ϕ, I shall anticipate that I will enjoy ϕ-ing; if, on the other hand, I desire that p, I shall anticipate that I will be pleased at p. (Nothing, of course, implies that these anticipations are, or are likely to be, borne out.) The second fact is this: If, on the one hand, I imagine the object of my desire when I desire to ϕ, I shall centrally imagine myself ϕ-ing, that is, the internal audience will be empathic and moreover empathic to me; if, on the other hand, I imagine the object of my desire when I desire that p, I shall acentrally imagine that p, that is, the internal audience will be sympathetic, and sympathetic on the basis of a favourable judgement. In the first case, then, the empathic audience will feel what I would feel: that is, pleasure. And in the second place the sympathetic audience will feel what one would feel towards something one judges favourably: that is, pleasure. So either way round, what the internal audience will feel will be pleasure.

Accordingly, consideration, first, of the role of the internal dramatist and, then, of the role of the internal audience shows how *in favoured circumstances* imagination may gratify desire. And now let me recapitulate what I have said with an eye to showing that the qualification is needed: that it is only in favoured circumstances that gratification ensues upon the activity of the internal sector.

Imagining that I am ϕ-ing or that p *can* generate the belief that I am ϕ-ing or that p, because, in so far as I engage in imagination, other beliefs which I may have and which run counter to these beliefs do not prevail. The internal dramatist need not be influenced by them. Nevertheless, I may simultaneously be aware of these beliefs and, even if they do not affect what I imagine, they may well affect what I believe. So when I imagine myself ϕ-ing or that p, I shall come to believe that I am ϕ-ing or that p *only if I am engrossed in the imaginative activity*.

Imagining that I am ϕ-ing or that p *can* generate the pleasure that I would get in ϕ-ing or at p because, in so far as the imaginative activity has an effect, the effect will be that of pleasure. This, i.e. nothing else, is what the internal audience will feel. But I have already made it clear that this last assertion is compatible with the internal audience's feeling nothing – with, that is, the imaginative activity having no effect on it at all. And to specify the circumstances in which the internal audience will feel something rather than nothing, hence pleasure, or in which when I imagine that I am ϕ-ing or that p, I shall experience the pleasure that I would get in ϕ-ing or at p, I shall once again make use of the phrase *that I must be engrossed in the imaginative activity*.

From which it follows that there is yet *another or third* use for this phrase: that is, to characterise in an overall way the favoured circumstances in which imagination will gratify desire – that is to say, in which imagination will bring it about for me as if I were ϕ-ing or as if p, whichever is desired.

7. To show that imaginative activity will in favoured circumstances gratify desire does not by itself account for wish-fulfilment. For wish-fulfilment is certainly conceived of by Freud as something more than fortuitous in its incidence. It is systematic, in at least the two following ways: that it occurs, or characteristically occurs, as part of a mode of mental functioning, and that it can to some degree or other be induced or put into operation.

How can this aspect of wish-fulfilment be done justice to?

More specifically, what further conditions should be placed upon the imaginative activity so that it ensures the favoured circumstances for its occurrence and hence is calculated to gratify desire?

RICHARD WOLLHEIM

There are two distinct conditions either of which might *prima facie* be adequate to account for the systematic character of wish-fulfilment. Both conditions are conditions upon the epistemic state of the wish-fulfiller. Furthermore these two conditions correspond to two distinct ways in which Freud himself conceived, or at any rate discussed, the phenomenon.

The first condition is that, when we imagine something or other, we should suppress the fact that we are merely imagining it: or that the concept under which, as we have seen, the imaginative activity invariably takes place should be suspended or repressed.

The second condition is that the imaginative activity should take place not merely under the concept of imagination but also under some more general view – or theory, as I prefer to say – of the mind, where this theory re-presents thoughts, indeed mental phenomena in general, as possessed of an exaggerated efficacy. According to this theory, imagination adjusts the world so that it conforms to its objects.

The first condition – the suppression of the concept of imagination – corresponds to what Freud says when he connects the notion of gratification with that of hallucination, or when he treats the dream as the exemplar of wish-fulfilment.[2] The second condition – that there should be an overarching theory of the mind – corresponds to what Freud says when he connects the notion of gratification with the 'overvaluation of psychic phenomena', and goes on to propose that wish-fulfilment is really a special case of 'the omnipotence of thoughts' – or, more precisely perhaps, our belief in the former derives from our belief in the latter.[3]

8. Where do we proceed from here? What I have so far done is this: I have shown how imaginative activity could produce gratification of desire: but only in such a way that its production would be coincidental. Accordingly I have presented two further accounts of how imaginative activity could ensure gratification, or how it could produce it systematically: each account proposing some further condition that needs to be appended to the imaginative activity to arrive at efficacy.

Both these two accounts come from psychoanalytic theory, and therefore a reasonable suggestion would be that they should be treated as alternative empirical hypotheses about the necessary and sufficient conditions for wish-fulfilment, and therefore choice should be settled on scientific considerations. Philosophy has nothing more to add to the argument.

2 Sigmund Freud, *Complete Psychological Works*, ed. James Strachey (London 1953–74), e.g. 1900a, vol. IV, pp. 121–34, vol. V, pp. 533–5, 564–72: 1908e, vol. IX, pp. 145–9; 1916–17, vol. XV, pp. 126–35, 213–27.
3 Freud, *Works* e.g. 1909d, vol. X, pp. 233–5, 298–301: 1912–13, vol. XIII, pp. 83–90: 1917a, vol. XVII, p. 139.

54

But this would be premature. For even if both accounts do come out of an empirical theory, it does not follow that they can be taken on trust as perfectly eligible hypotheses in this context. That is to say, it must be asked of each whether it is perfectly coherent in itself and whether it provides an adequate explanation of the phenomenon under consideration. In the following discussion I shall take these two questions together, and I shall regard both as falling within the purview of philosophy.

Before, however, I embark on an examination of these two accounts, I want to suggest – quite tentatively – a way in which they might be fitted into my reconstruction of the imaginative activity. Since both relate not to the nature of imagination but to concurrently entertained beliefs about the imaginative activity and what it is or isn't, they must reappear inside my reconstruction of the imagination as somehow higher-order phenomena. And I suggest that they might figure thus: they might figure primarily as claims, covert or overt, that the internal actor makes about what he is doing. On the first account, the actor tries to pass himself off as a real-life character rather than as an actor: his claim is covert. On the second account, the internal actor asserts that his acting will bring to pass the happenings he enacts: his claim is overt. And as a secondary feature of these accounts, it might be said that the corresponding claims that the internal actor makes about what he is doing are claims that he is encouraged to make by the way in which the internal dramatist conceived the part or role he prepared for him.

9. In some loose, but intuitively (I hope) obvious sense, the first account is weaker than the second. On the grounds of parsimony, this might seem to be in its favour. However, the difficulty I experience with the first account is this: that I do not see how it can explain what it professes to explain without becoming as strong as the second. Or, more accurately, without becoming as strong descriptively, though it would remain weaker explanatorily, which would presumably be against it.

Let me elaborate: I have claimed that all imaginative activity occurs under the concept of imagination. And it occurs under it, not just in the obvious sense that the concept is true of it but in the more interesting sense that the concept regulates it. Most importantly, the concept regulates it in that it prevents the inroad of truth-directed considerations. However, though the activity occurs under this concept, there is clearly no need that we should be conscious that it does, or that we should be conscious of the concept. Compare the way in which when we speak English, the concept of the English language is regulative but not necessarily conscious.

Accordingly, it is far from clear that the suppression of the concept of the imagination – which is all that the first account requires on its weakest interpretation – is really going to make the difference necessary for the imaginative activity to be systematically efficacious.

At this juncture it is natural to propose that the first account should be reinterpreted, and that the requirement, that the concept under which the imaginative activity occurs is suppressed, has more read into it. One such reading would be that the concept of the imagination is deleted in that it falls out of the conceptual equipment of the person. He altogether loses the distinction between phantasy and reality. This reading certainly fits in with certain things Freud says about wish-fulfilment, guardedly or unguardedly, but the case against it might be put by saying that it restores the systematic character to wish-fulfilment but only at the expense of making it a closed system. For it is now problematic how the person whose conceptual equipment altogether lacks the distinction between phantasy and reality could ever knowingly satisfy his desires. Given that it is clear how such a man could obtain wish-fulfilmcnt, it becomes correspondingly unclear how he could obtain anything else. And that is an unwanted outcome for the theorist of wish-fulfilment.

So yet another and stronger reading of the first account proposes itself. And that is that the concept of imagination is not deleted, it is retained, but that the person believes that what he imagines is also real. Now it seems to me that on this reading the first account can indeed explain what it is invoked to explain – that is, wish-fulfilment as a systematic phenomenon – but now it itself stands in need of explanation. For how does the person come by such a strange though useful belief? In other words, the first account has now attained that condition which I described a few minutes back by saying that it can only explain what it professes to explain by becoming as strong as the second account – or as strong descriptively as the second account though still explanatorily weaker. For the first account is now as strong descriptively as the second account in that it correlates wish-fulfilment with the belief that what is imagined is also real, but the second account also offers an explanation of how this belief arises. And that the second account does so is, other things being equal, its strength.

10. Other things being equal means, of course, in this context that there is some independent reason for postulating belief in that theory of mind to which the second account assumes subscription. Psychoanalytic theory claims that there is, though whether it also claims that there is reason for postulating it wherever wish-fulfilment obtains is, as I have indicated, less easily resolved.

At this point it is worthwhile spelling out the theory of mind in question, for it is more complex that I have so far indicated. I have two reasons for wanting to spell it out. One is that it will allow us to gauge better the goodness or otherwise of the explanation that the second account provides of the phenomenon of wish-fulfilment. The other is that it will accord us some insight into the motivation that psychoanalytic theory has for postulating, in circumstances other than wish-fulfilment, subscription to such a theory of mind.

Freud, as is well known, connected the theory in question with primitive man's belief in magic, and in doing so he might have given the impression that the theory conceived of the conjunction between an individual's thoughts and the events that, according to it, they occasion as brute. In other words, the theory seems to say that, when a man thinks that p, then p, and then to offer no kind of explanation, or even to suggest that no explanation could be provided, of this link. However, if we judiciously put together the various observations that Freud has to make on the score of the omnipotence of thoughts, it is possible to extract from them the rudiments of a rather richer theory. The distinctive feature of such a theory is that it intermediately proposes for the mental – that is to say, both for the mind and for its phenomena – a conceptualisation in corporeal terms. The infant or primitive man – or, we must add, regressive man – is led by the theory he embraces to think of his thoughts as some part of his body or, again, of his thinking as a particular piece of bodily functioning, and this conceptualisation provides us with an explanation of such a person's belief in the omnipotence of thoughts. For as he comes to attach, in accordance with developmental norms, an exaggerated efficacy to this part of the body or to that particular piece of bodily functioning, so he will correspondingly overvalue the psychic phenomena he has equated with them. So, for instance, in *Totem and Taboo* Freud says that primitive man sexualises his thoughts,[4] by which I take him to mean that for primitive man not only is thinking an object of sexual attention, it is also a form of sexual activity: and if he assigns unreal powers to his thoughts, it is because he has already assigned similar powers to his sexual activity.

And now let me turn briefly to the second reason for spelling out the theory of mind under which wish-fulfilment, on one account of the matter, falls. It was so that we could better see how subscription to it might be invoked to explain *other* regressive mental phenomena. And here I would like to append one remark.

Once we grasp the bodily conceptualisation of mental phenomena that underlies the belief in the omnipotence of thoughts, then we will immediately appreciate that any disturbance in the way in which the relevant part of the body or the relevant bodily function is apprehended will immediately show up in a related disturbance in mental functioning itself. An excessive

---

[4] Freud, *Works*, 1912–13, vol. XIII, p. 89.

sexualisation of the bodily item will result in a corresponding repression of mentality. And it is, interestingly, just along these lines that both Freud and Melanie Klein[5] and Bion[6] have suggested explanations of intellectual – indeed more generally mental – inhibition.

11. Let me in conclusion emphasise the point that the distinctive feature of this analysis of wish-fulfilment is not the connection between wishing and imagination but the fact that imagination as it occurs in connection with wishing occurs under the regressive or 'corporeal' theory of the mind. In saying that the connection between wishing and imagination is not the distinctive feature of my analysis, I have in mind the fact that wanting or desiring, of which wishing is, as it were, the half-brother, also requires imagination for its analysis. What, of course, it does not require – what indeed it rules out – is that imagination should occur under the corporeal theory of the mind. And since this more general link between desire and imagination gives some support to the analysis of wishing that I offer, I shall say something in amplification.

It is a powerful philosophical intuition that wanting or desiring has a very special connection with action. However, this intuition appears to be denied in the prevailing account of how action is to be explained: action is to be explained, or 'rationalised', by citing a conjunction of desire(s) and belief(s) belonging to the agent at the time of the action and currently causally efficacious.[7] For the explanatory schema to which this account gives rise – or any refinement of it necessary to afford due recognition to those elements which it ignores or underestimates, such as intention, or identification with desire – does nothing to indicate that there is a more intimate connection between desire and action than there is between belief and action. Given belief, desire is necessary, but, given desire, belief is necessary, and the two suffice. Are we then to abandon as illusory the powerful philosophical intuition, as I have called it, that one of these connections is special in a way in which the other isn't?

I think that we should not abandon the intuition, and one way of saving it is to introduce alongside the doing of an action the tendency to imagine doing some action. For, if doing an action requires desire and belief, desire suffices for the tendency to imagine doing an action. Of course, whatever action the desirer imagines doing is an action that he would do only if he had that belief which conjointly with his desire rationalises it. But he does

5 E.g. Melanie Klein, *Writings*, ed. Roger Money-Kyrle (London, 1975), 'A Contribution to the Theory of Intellectual Inhibition' in vol. I: 'Envy and Gratitude' in vol. III.
6 W. R. Bion, *Second Thoughts* (London, 1967), secs. 8, 9.
7 Cf. Donald Davidson, 'Actions, Reasons, and Causes', *Journal of Philosophy*, 60 (1963), pp. 685–700.

not have to hold this belief before he can imagine doing the action. Indeed, my suggestion is precisely that, even if he holds no relevant beliefs, there is some action or actions that he will tend to imagine doing, given his desire. Now, it is just this tendency, and the fact that it is connected with the desire in isolation from belief, that licenses us in thinking that, when the desire is conjoined with belief and an action follows from their conjunction, nevertheless the action is more intimately connected with the desire than it is with any belief. It is this, in other words, that justifies the original intuition.

So much for the connection between action and those desires which either lead to action or would lead to action if appropriate beliefs were held. But the intuition that desire is specially connected with action has, or has been implicitly taken to have, a wider application than this. It applies also to desires that do not lead to action because other desires outweigh them. But how does it apply to them? An obvious answer, which consists in advancing some such hypothetical as: If there were no desires that were stronger than them, and some relevant beliefs were held, then... (where this clause is filled in by a description of some action), is obviously deficient because it too puts desire and belief on a par. But suppose that we rewrite this hypothetical so as to take account of this objection, and then we get something like, If there were no desires that were stronger than them, then there would be a tendency to imagine... (and here, again, we get a description of some action), this still seems inadequate. For it seems to be the case that, even when a desire is outweighed, some kind of activity residually attaches to it. Now, again, an appeal to imagination, or to imagining doing some action, may supply the answer. For the struggle between conflicting tendencies to imagine different courses of action does not have to be analysed, whatever may be the appropriate analysis for conflicting tendencies to act in different ways, simply into hypotheticals. For the conflict between tendencies to imagine whatever it may be is itself likely to be represented in imagination.

However, this does not yet exhaust the kinds of desire that there are. Nor does it exhaust the case for connecting desire with imagination. In addition to desires that a man has a tendency to act on and to desires that a man would have a tendency to act on if it were not for other desires that outweigh them, there are desires that could not, or certainly would not in anything like normal circumstances, lead to action. Examples would be desires that someone else should act in a certain way, or desires that something should have come about in a now unalterable past. But just when the connection between desire and action seems to give out, that between desire and imagination – which, as we have just seen, could be used to explain that connection when it did hold – continues to hold. For anyone who has such desires will, surely, tend to imagine their satisfaction. He will tend to imagine another doing what he would desire him to do or things being as he would have desired them to be.

If I am right in all this, then the connection between desire and imagination is actually more fundamental than that between desire and action which, over a certain range of cases, masks it. And if this is so, it prompts another reflection on which I will end: that the intuition that desire and action are specially connected is really a refraction of the more profound intuition that, first, desire and change (including, of course, change in factors that might otherwise be expected to change things from what they now are) are specially connected; and, secondly, whereas action is widely connected with change, it is not universally connected with it, which is just what imagination is.

Holistic explanation: an outline of a theory

CHRISTOPHER PEACOCKE

I am going to argue that a certain common structure is exemplified by (i) the explanation of an agent's actions in terms of his beliefs and desires, and (ii) the explanation of the course of a person's experience in terms of his location in a spatio-temporal framework and the way the world is at various places within that framework. Within the length of a paper I can present only the broadest outline of a case. So I shall produce a series of somewhat dogmatic statements, for the detailed justification (and qualification) of which the reader must turn elsewhere.[1] Once we have a plausible case for the parallelism of structure of explanation in (i) and (ii), various disputed views in each area may be assessed according as the arguments for them are such that their analogues in the other area are *non sequiturs* or not. I will in the second part of this paper briefly suggest how certain radical interpretation procedures may be criticised in this way. There are at least three other issues upon which the parallelism can be brought to bear: the presence of certain kinds of 'deviant' causal chains in both the action and the spatial cases; the question of some kind of priority ordering amongst schemes of explanation that are holistic in the way I shall argue that the action and spatial cases are; and the related (but distinct) issues of holism and indeterminacy in the theory of meaning. These three issues I shall not be able to discuss here; but the observations in the application to radical interpretation will give a model for possible application of the theory to other issues.

I

Suppose we ask what actions we would expect to be performed by a person with a certain belief, say the belief that the ice is thin. It is an obvious and familiar point that every type of action that we might cite in answer to this question presupposes that the agent has certain desires: all of keeping to the edge of the pond, calling one's children away from the middle, answering

[1] The detailed arguments are given in a book *Holistic Explanation: Action, Space, Interpretation*, Oxford University Press, 1979.

61

queries in a certain way, may be absent and yet the belief be present if the agent has certain desires. So the answer to our question must be that no action types are necessarily associated with the possession of a given belief, independently of assumptions about the agent's desires. Clearly a similar condition holds for desires and actions: a desire cannot be expected to issue in any particular kind of action, independently of suppositions about the agent's beliefs.[2]

Now let us ask a corresponding question about location at a place and experiences: what experiences would we expect to be enjoyed by a person located at a certain place? Again, the answer must be none whatsoever, independently of suppositions about what it is like at that place. The irreducibility is of exactly the same kind as the one we first considered, if agents are replaced by experiencers, contents of attitudes by what it is like at places, and belief by location. Finally, to complete the quartet, we can note that no particular kind of experience can be anticipated by a person given simply that it is ϕ at a place p: to conclude anything from this, we need to know also the location of the person in the space. In the spatial case what these principles imply is the irreducibility of the concepts of location at a place and of its being ϕ at a place: they do not imply the existence of absolute space in a sense in which statements about places would fail to be supervenient upon statements about spatial relations.[3]

These irreducibility principles are true in each case because, respectively, actions are jointly determined by beliefs and desires, and experiences that are of the world are jointly determined by location in space and what it is like at that location. Expressed with maximal crudity compatible with making the point, we may state the principle by which actions are jointly determined thus:

it is *a priori* that for any p, ϕ and x, there are conditions C such that if person x believes that his ϕ-ing and only that will lead to its being the

---

[2]   These points can be expressed formally. The irreducibility of belief to kinds of action consists in the fact that

$\sim \exists g \quad \forall$ agents $x \forall p$ (believes $(x,p) \supset x$ performs an action of kind $g(p)$).

The irreducibility of desires correspondingly consists in the fact that

$\sim \exists g \quad \forall$ agents $x \forall p$ (desires $(x,p) \supset x$ performs an action of kind $g(p)$).

[3]   A formal statement of the irreducibility principles for the spatial case now shows them to be instances of the same schemata as the formal principles in the action case. Where 'p' now ranges over places, for the irreducibility of location we have:

$\sim \exists g \quad \forall$ experiencers $x \forall p$ (At $(x,p) \supset x$ has an experience of kind $g(p)$).

For a place having an objective property we have:

$\sim \exists g \quad \forall$ experiencers $x \forall p \forall \phi$ (ϕ $(p) \supset x$ has an experience of kind $g(\phi, p)$).

Here we may seem to have an asymmetry since the function g is binary and not unary as it was in the action case for both belief and desire. But if in the irreducibility principle for belief we had replaced 'believes (x, p)' by 'believes $(x$, if he ϕ's then $p)$' we could also there replace '$g(p)$' by '$g(\phi, p)$'. This restores symmetry.

case that p, and x desires that p, and x notices that these attitudes make it reasonable for him to ϕ, and conditions C obtain, then x ϕ's.

The qualifications needed here include those required to accommodate alternative means to a given end, varieties of strength of belief and desire and so forth. I will not trouble to refine the principle here, because the points I want to make apply equally to the more refined versions. The corresponding principle for the spatial case is:

it is *a priori* that for any p, ϕ and x, there are conditions C such that if a person x is located at place p and it is ϕ at p and conditions C obtain, then x has an experience as of its being ϕ.

These two principles, which for reasons that will emerge I will refer to as 'the *a priori* principles' of the action and spatial schemes, have a number of striking and connected properties.

The first such property is that the principles seem to be *a priori*, in the sense that application of the irreducible predicates they contain in accordance with these principles is constitutive of mastery of those predicates. By this I mean not that anyone employing the concepts of belief and desire, or location and the display of a property at a place, must be able to state or even knows these principles; but rather that any account that is as explicit as possible about what makes us apply these concepts to new cases and which omits these principles and offers some other account of their application, will either fail to apply or yield wrong answers in some conceivable new cases. The force of this claim lies in what it excludes. For instance, if it is true, then there can be no physical reduction of the concepts of belief and desire that omits the principle. Let us look briefly at this issue. Because of the point that Putnam has so strongly emphasised in the past, that creatures with many different internal physical constitutions may have the same beliefs, any putative physical definition of belief that p, for particular p, will have to have a higher-order character: it will have to define this state in terms of its role, much as we may hope to give a physical definition of what a valve is in terms of its role, while not denying the obvious truth that to be a valve is not to have any particular physico-chemical constitution. But there is nothing that stands to a belief as allowing only a one-way flow of something or other stands to a valve; there are no attitude-independent manifestations of the belief.

In saying that application in accordance with the principle is constitutive of mastery of the concepts, there are two claims that do not follow from that and which I am not endorsing. One is that knowledge of one's own beliefs and desires can only be inferential. Any reasonable version of the causal theory of knowledge should provide a liberation from the worry that, if one claims that such principles are so constitutive of mastery, then knowledge of them can be obtained only inferentially from their effects. When one knows of a desire non-inferentially, one's belief that one has that desire is caused by some state that is also the ground of the causal power that is operative in future circumstances when the desire is engaged; it is a case of a common cause leading to knowledge. The second disclaimer is that it is not maintained that these are the *only* principles so constitutive of mastery of the concepts; for instance nothing has been said yet about the ideal of consistency for beliefs, nor of the source of this ideal.

The second noticeable property of these principles is that although in some sense *a priori*, they also seem to have an explanatory status. It by no means follows from the *a priori* status of these principles that this explanation is not causal: indeed the explanation manifestly *is* causal in the spatial case. Our language in fact has words for just those events that are explained in the appropriate way under some description by the principles: 'intentional' in the action case and 'perceptual experience' in the spatial case. (This actually needs special qualification in the action case. I would myself argue for the view that intention cannot be defined in terms of belief and desire, and this is something that has no analogue in the action case. Nevertheless this does not make belief and desire irrelevant to the ascription of intention: what unifies such diverse intentions as that of driving to the concert hall and that of turning a button on a tuner is the desire to listen to music.)

It will help at this point to introduce some abbreviations. Let us call, in any case in which we have intuitively a scheme of holistic explanation, the sentences the truth of which is explained by the *a priori* principles of that scheme its *B-truths*; let us call the irreducible predicates occurring in the antecedent of its *a priori* principles its *E-concepts*, and let us call truths containing those predicates *E-truths*. Thus location of an experiencer at a place is an E-concept of the spatial scheme; a B-truth of the same scheme might be 'Peter is now having an experience as of the southern view of the Radcliffe Camera'.

I have not yet offered any justification for calling the action and the spatial schemes 'holistic', however much our intuitions may favour doing so. The justification cannot be simply the presence of the *a priori* principles themselves: for these are found also where we speak of functional ends. It is *a priori* that there are conditions C such that if object x has the functional end of placing or keeping object y in state G, and x's ϕ-ing is necessary and sufficient for y's being in state G, and C obtains, then x ϕ's. (Here x might be a thermostat, y a room and G the state of being at 70 degrees Fahrenheit.) Nor can the justification be the presence of *a priori* principles with a pair of concepts, not just one, in the antecedent distinctively associated with the kind of explanation in question: though the action and spatial cases do have such pairs, so do other examples: consider the pair of concepts *valve* and *valve-lifter*. It is true that in these examples the concepts apparently display the feature of second-order physical reducibility. This gives a reminder that the distinctively holistic feature must be something that accounts for the second-order irreducibility of the E-concepts of the action and spatial schemes.

The distinctive feature seems to be this. When we ascribe a belief to a person, this ascription has if, true, all kinds of ramifications and repercussions for our expectations about what that person will do in various circumstances; but it has these particular ramifications only because the person has other particular beliefs and desires. Similarly in the spatial case, given the information that a person is at a particular place, we will gain indefinitely many expectations about what courses of experience are empirically possible for him, courses of experience that correspond to different paths he may trace out through his space; but again we can form these particular expectations only because we have beliefs about what it is like at various places. The same holds for desire vis-à-vis belief and the occurrence of some event or the instantiation of some property at a place vis-à-vis the location of the experiencer. The element we have so far omitted in trying to state explicitly the source of the holism is the presence of intertemporal restrictions on the applications of the E-concepts. It is not surprising that there are not properties of the *a priori* principles that are distinctive of holistic schemes of explanation, for those principles are concerned only with the application of the E-concepts at a given time, not across time. In the action case, these intertemporal restrictions flow broadly from the notion of rationality: the changing pattern of beliefs and desires over time must be responsive in intelligible ways to the information reaching the agent through perception, conversation and all other sources of evidence. This constrains the temporally successive B-truths that may be explained by the scheme: the ascription of an attitude has the repercussions it does in the context of the other attitudes possessed by the agent because of the limitations it places on what sequences of B-truths are intelligible if the ascription is correct. In the spatial case, the intertemporal restriction is given by the requirement that the temporally successive B-truths explained by the scheme must concern kinds of experience that one would expect to enjoy at adjacent places, and not just any places in the space in question. (This is of course not to say that the detailed structure of the space – whether finite or infinite, for instance – is not a matter for *a posteriori* investigation.)[4] In the case of both schemes, we can identify something it is reasonable to call the *holistically connected components* of the scheme: things such that it is of relations between them that the

---

[4] Contrary to appearances, the argument at this point does not necessarily exclude *a priori* discontinous motion. All the argument requires is the principle that in any application of the spatial scheme, there be *some* restriction, perhaps to be discovered empirically, upon which places may be successively occupied. Unless there are some such restrictions, it is hard to see how the experiencer could have empirical reasons for supposing that he is at one rather than another of two qualitatively similiar places.

intertemporal restrictions speak. These relations are (i) the relations (of implication and so forth) between the contents of attitudes and (ii) the spatial relations between places in the action and the spatial schemes respectively. Just as it is the relations between the contents of beliefs, desires, and intentions that makes the application of the E-concepts in the action case interlock, so spatial relations between places produces interlocking of the application of the E-concepts in the spatial case. It is not an accidental feature of the scheme we apply that the spatial relations of a particular place to other places is part of the place's essence, just as a particular attitude non-contingently has a certain content.

How different does all this make holistic explanation from explanation in the physical sciences? The failure of one-by-one verifiability of applications of the E-concepts that results from the holism might be said to be matched on the side of the physical sciences by Duhem's thesis that observations can confirm only sets of hypotheses, and not individual sentences one by one. Though Duhem was thinking primarily of generalisations rather than predications of individual objects, it is hard to see why the kinds of arguments he presented could not be applied in the construction of cases in which one-by-one verifiability is impossible without theoretical assumptions about individual objects. Nor it is impossible that there should be in a physical science principles that are *a priori* in the special sense relating to mastery that I have specified, provided certain scientific magnitudes are introduced simultaneously in certain principles, and it is, as it may be, part of the theory that these magnitudes cannot be identified except by means of their satisfaction of these principles. This is already a recherché kind of case, but is there nothing differentiating our holistic cases from it in principle? I think there is. It is connected with a topic I have no room to discuss before moving on to look at radical interpretation, viz. the existence in schemes of holistic explanation of a familiar distinction between deviant and non-deviant causal chains. The reconciliation of the *a priori* and yet explanatory status of the principles of each scheme will naturally proceed by an account of the realization of beliefs and desires and perceptual experiences in states of matter; and different kinds of explanatory routes from the realising states to the B-truths of the scheme can provide a way of analysing the distinction between deviant and non-deviant causal chains. It seems in the nature of the physical case described that there would not be the possibility of a distinction between deviant and non-deviant causal chains.

II

Whenever one family of concepts is not reducible to another, the question naturally arises of how we are able to apply those concepts at all. Now the non-existence of a reduction is compatible with the existence of what I shall call a quasi-reduction; the interest of the notion of a quasi-reduction is that it is a means by which someone without prior knowledge of the detailed application of the E-concepts of a scheme of holistic explanation to particular objects may come to know truths stated using them. More precisely, to specify a quasi-reduction for a given scheme of holistic explanation is to specify some concept Q and some method M applicable to a set of truths stated using Q that meet the following conditions:

(i) Q cannot be possessed by someone with no grasp whatsoever of the given scheme of holistic explanation,

(ii) Q can be applied prior to knowledge of the truth of applications of the E-concepts of the scheme to particular objects, and

(iii) M takes one from a set of truths stated using the concept Q but not using detailed applications of the E-concepts of that scheme to a particular set of detailed applications of the E-concepts of the given scheme.

In effect Davidson claims that the concept of holding a sentence true, and his radical interpretation procedure using the Principle of Charity, function as the concept Q and the method M respectively of a quasi-reduction for some fragment of the scheme of action explanation in terms of beliefs, desires and sentence senses.[5] The same status is claimed by some for Ramsey's famous method for arriving at an assignment of subjective probabilities and utilities from an agent's preference ordering. It can hardly fail to be true that there is some interesting conclusion to be drawn from further thought about quasi-reductions, for the following cases exhaust the possibilities. Either there is some reason that a quasi-reduction must be available for any system of holistic explanation, in which case one must see why it must and what it might be in the spatial case; or a quasi-reduction is available in the action and propositional attitude cases and not in the spatial case, in which case the ground of this difference needs to be made explicit; or else an account of how a scheme of holistic explanation is applied in no way requires that a quasi-reduction be available. In the second part of this paper I will argue for that last possibility and will try to show that the arguments that have been offered for suggesting that the concept of holding-true can play

5   See 'Radical Interpretation', *Dialectica*, 1973; 'On The Very Idea of a Conceptual Scheme', *APA Proceedings and Addresses*, 1973–4; 'Belief and the Basis of Meaning', *Synthese*, 1974; and 'Thought and Talk' in *Mind and Language: Wolfson College Lectures 1974* (Oxford University Press, 1975: ed. Guttenplan).

a crucial role as the concept Q of a quasi-reduction are fallacious. My concern here is not with the method M that is applied to truths using the concept Q, but rather with the availability in advance (of detailed applications of the E-concepts) of those truths themselves. It should be noted incidentally that in arguing against such a quasi-reduction, we are not arguing against something that could be an account of how we could come to acquire the scheme: a quasi-reduction cannot in principle supply such an account, for that is excluded by the first clause in the definition of the notion of a quasi-reduction.

How then do we manage to apply the spatial scheme? It is clear that any sequence of experiences whatever could be regarded as produced by tracing a path in a space, in the severely limited sense that for any sequence of experiences whatever we could envisage an assignment of features at various times to places in a space and a route through that space that would yield those experiences. But it is also equally clear that very many such sequences of experiences provide in themselves absolutely no basis for saying that a change in experience results from a change of place by the experiencer rather than a change at a place of the properties displayed in the objective world. (Of course, the same question arises equally for constancy of experience.) One way of seeing how experience can give reasons for empirically drawing such a distinction is to construct a simple example.

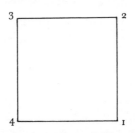

Let us imagine a space with just four relevant places, labelled 1 to 4, and ordered as in the figure. These places display observable qualities F, G, ..., L which are taken to be exclusive of each other. If one wishes to avoid any hint of discontinuous motion in this space, one may suppose either (a) that these qualities admit of variation in intensity, being most intense at the 'centres' 1, 2, 3, and 4, and fading at points between them, or (b) contingently the qualities have sharp boundaries. A segment of the history of such a world is given in the table below, the left-to-right ordering of entries on a given row representing the temporal ordering of occurrences of a quality at a given place, while occurrences represented in the same column are simultaneous. The line $\alpha\alpha'$ represents a possible experiential route through this world. In this world, regularity is provided by the cycles of qualities at each place; but there is nothing in the use to be made of the example that would prevent secular alteration in these patterns.

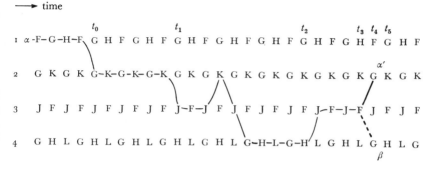

It seems that the sequence of experiences determined by $\alpha\alpha'$ is one which would in itself contain the materials for drawing the various major distinctions we are actually able to draw which involve the concept of location. It is plausible that someone with such a course of experience would by time t_2 have in his by then relatively small class of theories of the world the true description of the world, and it seems obvious that it is possession of a particular *empirical* theory of regularity that would permit him to conclude at t_5 for instance that at t_4 he had moved to place 2 rather than moving in the other direction to 4 or staying put at 3: for if he had followed route $\alpha\beta$ and been at place 4 at t_4 he could have experienced only F, H or G (at places 3, 4, or 1 respectively) at the next time t_5, and not K as he actually does. Once the theory is under way, we can also allow for hallucinations.

As against this general picture, it may be said that the empirical theory of regularity plays such a large role in distinguishing the place at which the experiencer is located only because we have deprived him of two resources that are usually available to us when establishing our location, *viz.* (a) our ability to move ourselves intentionally and (b) our ability to discover traces of earlier qualities at a place. Thus at time t_3 the experiencer might intentionally move himself towards place 2, or again at t_4 he may notice traces of quality K.

Both these suggestions are completely mistaken if they are meant to show that the experiencer would not then need to rely on a theory of empirical regularities. Anything the experiencer intentionally does or tries to do to move himself from one place to another needs to be independently ratified as doing just that, and so the experiencer must have some empirically confirmed theory that will ratify such actions as indeed producing change of place; the empirical theory of change at the four places is needed to do this. It is true that when an action has been discovered by the experiencer to move him, his doing so in some circumstances may allow him to draw distinctions he would not otherwise be able to make in those circumstances (a good example is the move from place 1 to place 2 in our world just before t_0): but it cannot provide a wholly independent source of evidence. This is even more obvious in the case of traces: to check that one feature is a trace of another, observation is useless unless one has the premise that one has remained at the same place. These replies to the objections from intentional movement and traces illustrate the compelling general claim that no qualitative feature of experience can by itself necessarily ensure any truth about the spatial provenance of that experience. This truth is just one of our earlier irreducibility principles in another guise.

A second essential component of our experiencer's ability to draw the required distinctions is his memory of his experiences, not only of which experiences he has had earlier, but also of their *order*: it is plain that possession of an exceptionlessly true theory of the world would not help him at all in establishing truths about his location if he remembered only his experience of the previous time interval, or remembered them all, but not their temporal ordering. There is a sense in which it is quite impossible for the spatio-temporal scheme of holistic explanation to be both well confirmed for the experiencer, and yet for him explanatory of only his present experiences; correspondingly there is a sense in which memory must be cumulative in a stronger sense than is given by mere accumulation of beliefs and memory images of one's past.

All of these observations upon the spatial case carry over to the action case. We can even formulate the observations for the action case in verbally parallel fashion. Any sequence of behaviour whatever is such that we *can* assign a pattern of beliefs, desires and sentence senses over time that would rationally explain it; but many of these sequences provide in themselves no basis for the distinctions we can draw between change of propositional attitudes and different attitudes already possessed becoming operative, or indeed change of sentence sense in some cases. Only empirical hypotheses about the stability of regularity of change of the propositional attitudes over time provides such a basis; and again, it is a regularity not in the facts explained, but in truths stated *using* the E-concepts of the scheme, that is in question. There is too an analogue of the remarks about memory: we cannot apply the action scheme to a creature without having reasons to believe that his past behaviour was of a certain kind, and this must include the order in which it occurred.

I now turn to the application to radical interpretation. The notion of holding a sentence true is thought to be appropriate for playing the role of a concept Q of a quasi-reduction because 'We can know that a speaker holds a sentence to be true without knowing what he means by it or what belief it expresses for him.'[6] It is no part of my position to deny that quoted claim; but it is part of my position to maintain that the kinds of circumstance in which we can know that a speaker holds a sentence to be true without knowing what he means by it or what belief it expresses for him in fact exclude the use of holding true as the concept Q of a quasi-reduction.

Now the concept of holding a sentence true has an analogue we should consider in the spatial case, that of being ϕ-located: a person is ϕ-located at a time iff he is at that time located somewhere at which it is then ϕ. It is also the case that a man can know that he is ϕ-located without knowing where he is or which place it is that is ϕ, as for instance on waking after having been transported during sleep and set down on the shore at Ithaca. In both cases this is possible because, in the cases that concern us,[7] the concept is fixed by an existentially quantified condition: for x to hold sentence s true is for it to be the case that for some p, x believes that p and s in x's language has the truth condition that p. (This is unspecific with respect to the p as ϕ-location is with respect to place.) But it also seems clear that one is able to know one is ϕ-located without knowing where one is or where it is that is ϕ only because one's experiences are of a kind previously obtained as experiences of an objective world, and to know that one was having such experiences one would need to have been operating in the past with some theory, however rudimentary, of one's path in an objective spatial world, with the ability to make particular applications of the E-concepts: to know where one is located and what it is like at that particular place. By this, I do not mean merely that one must in the past have had a general conceptual ability that has no specific connection with the present judgement 'I am now ϕ-located': on the contrary, I mean that one must in the past (or must now see that one was in the past in a position to) have judged that one was at a particular (a certain) place, and that that place was then ϕ, and that one's present experience is of a kind, (such as Odysseus' experience of the seashore) that one had when one knew oneself to be ϕ-located on more direct grounds of the kind we have already discussed.

Being an inductive inference, this step is naturally not *prima facie* invulnerable to various sceptical challenges: the point important for us at present is that it exactly parallels in the relevant respects the following kind of case involving propositional attitudes and holding true. Let us consider circumstances in which we know a man to hold a sentence true, on the basis

---

[6] 'Thought and Talk', p. 14; see also 'Radical Interpretation'.

[7] This caveat is presenting because strictly Davidson had defined holding s true as believing that s is true: and in this sense a man may hold true a sentence that is not in any language he understands. It is evident, however, that such holdings-true are irrelevant to belief ascription: I do not necessarily believe what is expressed by such sentences of Serbo-Croat as I hold true.

of honest assertion, but do not know what belief of his it expresses. We may know the sentence is held true because we know whenever he speaks in the straightforward tone of voice, he is speaking honestly, and we know, say, he speaks more quickly when trying to deceive, in a different tone when ironic, and so on; it just happens that on this occasion our speaker is using arcane vocabulary to his scientific colleagues. It seems clear in this case that our justification for our belief that the scientific sentence is held true must make reference to our earlier success in attributing beliefs on the supposition that such utterances are honest, just as Odysseus' justification for his belief that he is ϕ-located must make reference to earlier analogous successes. (In both cases of course it is not required that one remember which were the occasions on which such hypotheses proved successful: one needs only to know that there were such successes.)

If this is correct, we may say that an account, if one could be given, of how to determine a detailed application to objects of the E-concepts of a scheme, using truths about ϕ-location in one case and holding true in the other, would not supply a quasi-reduction: for these truths can be known only by someone with an ability to apply the E-concepts already, an ability the quasi-reduction was meant to deliver rather than presuppose. The sense in which holding true and ϕ-location may be said not to assume anything about detailed applications of the E-concepts, the sense which of course is ensured by the existential quantifiers in their definitions, is not a sense of failure to make assumptions that can be of help to the radical interpreter, or the man trying to work out a theory of his space *ab initio*.

So far I have discussed only one kind of case in which one can know that a sentence is held true without knowing what it means: that does not suffice to show there are not other kinds of circumstance in which there is a similar combination of knowledge and ignorance and in which the way the knowledge is reached does not preclude its use in a quasi-reduction. Some more general argument is needed to rule out that possibility.

Such a more general argument might run as follows. The central kind of evidence for someone's holding a sentence true is honest assertion. We can infer from the evidence of utterances that an assertion is honest, as Davidson himself notes, only if we 'know much about [the speaker's] desires and beliefs':[8] moreover it is not just knowledge of his believings-true and his desirings-true that we need. We need knowledge of such finely discriminated beliefs and desires such as the desire that one's interlocutor not be misinformed, the absence of any belief that he is countersuggestible, and so forth; and even the more realistic attribution of a general disposition to honesty requires a skeletal knowledge of the subject's beliefs and desires.

[8] 'Thought and Talk', p. 14.

It is a point Davidson has himself made time and again against Grice's programme reductively construed that finely discriminated propositional attitudes cannot be attributed to a language-using creature in advance of systematic interpretation of his utterances; here the point seems to come into play against his own use of holding true.

This argument is still incomplete. Certainly it cannot be avoided by saying that we could identify the incidence of holding true without any use of a theory of the agent's beliefs and desires at all:[9] that cannot be right, because holding true is a psychological concept. Nor would it be a defence to say that we could regard the ascription and testing of combinations of detailed propositional attitude ascriptions and interpretations as proceeding *en bloc*, any links between belief, desire, holding true and meaning functioning as constraints on the legitimacy of applying the whole package. This picture has a great deal of plausibility, but it is not one in which holding true is depicted as functioning as the concept Q of a quasi-reduction. On this conception, hypotheses about what is held true can be varied and tested by their consequences for action in the context of the remainder of the attitudes and interpretations held constant for the purposes of the test; and exactly the same is true of detailed propositional attitude and meaning ascriptions. But there is an intermediate position.

This is the position that while we need some knowledge of beliefs and desires in order to determine what is held true, the attitudes needed are not those for the ascription of which we need the interpretation of the very sentences whose interpretation the quasi-reduction involving holding true was meant to deliver.[10] There seems to be an objection of principle to this position. The following principle P seems to have great plausibility:

Someone can know what is is for something to be F only if he knows what it is for a particular thing to be F.　　　　　　　　　　(P)

This principle seems to be equally plausible whether the quantifier 'something' is interpreted objectually or substitutionally.

P applies to the case of holding true, for as we saw, that notion is defined by existential quantification; and it threatens a circularity for this intermediate position. Suppose the only account of what it is for someone who has a language to believe that p, for some detailed particular p, is given by the application of Davidson's radical interpretation procedure. Then in order to know what it is to hold something true, one has to

[9] Nor would it be a way that Davidson would want to take: in at least two papers he asserts that some advance knowledge of beliefs and desires is needed to identify holding true. See 'Thought and Talk', p. 14 and 'On The Very Idea', p. 18.

[10] Perhaps it is such a position Davidson has in mind when he writes 'we can tell when a speaker holds a sentence to be true without knowing...what *detailed* intentions do or might prompt him to utter it' (my emphasis): from 'Belief and the Basis of Meaning', p. 313.

know what it is to have particular beliefs (by principle P); and to know what it is to have particular beliefs in the case of a person with a language, one has to know what it is to hold a sentence true (by the nature of the radical interpretation procedure).

It might be replied to this objection that since there are many people with beliefs and desires, we can know what it is for someone for whose language we are constructing a meaning theory to have a particular belief because we know what it is for other persons to have particular beliefs. Now for this reply not to simply raise the same question again, presumably the important case is that in which these other people have beliefs but do not have a language. The reply would then be that we have enough of a grasp of what it is to have a belief from the languageless examples to know what it is to have a belief when the believer also has a language. But it seems that if this is true, it can only be so because belief plays some common role in both kinds of case, in conformity with certain general principles relating belief to the explanation of action. But if there is such a common role of belief, then for a person with a language, we can set out to find an empirically well confirmed theory of what beliefs he has that conform to this general role that belief has. So this imagined reply to the objection, if it succeeds in showing that a quasi-reduction is possible, shows too that what makes it possible also makes it not necessary.

These have been only sketches of arguments, and any fuller case needs not only to fill in the details, but also to consider a position according to which what we need in radical interpretation is an integrated quasi-reduction that delivers simultaneously all of desires, beliefs and sentence senses from some evidence available in advance of *any* of these.[11] Nevertheless consideration of the spatial case seems enough to suggest that insistence *a priori* that for any system of holistic explanation there *has* to be a quasi-reduction is an indication of an insufficiently radical holism.

[11] A case against one such integrated quasi-reduction is presented in the work mentioned in the first footnote to this paper.

Rational actors in macrosociological analysis

JAMES COLEMAN

STRATEGIES IN THE STUDY OF MACROSOCIOLOGICAL PROBLEMS

Several strategies have been employed in the study of problems in macro-sociology. (By 'macrosociology', I will mean the study of any social system, or portion of a system, which is larger than a small social group. This includes, but is not limited to, the study of whole societies.) To gain a sense of how theories with a conceptual base of rational actors address macrosociological problems, it is useful to distinguish them from other approaches to these problems.

One approach is that which describes regularities or laws in the functioning of social systems without accounting for these regularities by the mediation of purposes or goals on the part of persons. In sociology at the societal level, this approach is characteristic of Eisenstadt's or Parsons' studies of total societies. For example, Eisenstadt (1973) says, in analysing the lack of change in certain underdeveloped countries:

Again, in Durkheim's terms, in all these cases there took place a failure to establish and institutionalize new levels of solidarity, to make the transition from mechanic to organic solidarity, or from a level of low organic solidarity to a higher one, even though the older frameworks of solidarity were undermined by the growing differentiation and interaction between different groups and strata [p. 59].

Notice that these relationships, laws or regularities are not founded upon goal-directed action on the part of any actors, but are rather derived from observation of societies as units.

At a level below that of societies, the approach is exemplified by Smelser's theory of collective behaviour (1963), or my analysis of community conflict (1959). Smelser envisions the genesis of panics, crowds, and the like as similar to a production process, in which different elements such as a precipitating incident contribute 'value added' to the emerging product, which in the end is some form of collective behaviour.

A second approach is one in which no laws are sui generis at the social system level; all are derived from the action of individual persons. When there are laws or propositions stated purely at the social system level without reference to individuals, these laws are derivations from an individual-level

75

theory of action. That individual-level theory may be a theory of rational action, or it may be something different. Price theory in economics is an example of the former, for it is based on a model of rational actors confronting one another in a market. Psychoanalytic theories of culture, such as that of Abram Kardiner (1945), in which cultural myths and norms are based on fantasies which derive from certain unfulfilled needs of persons in the society, exemplify the latter.

I want to examine in this paper the second of the approaches described above: the approach in which all macrosociological laws are derived from a theory of action at the individual level. Further, I will confine myself to those approaches which are based on a theory of rational action. This is more than merely an exercise; I discuss this approach because I believe it offers more promise to the development of social theory than does any other. Thus in outlining the general properties of this theoretical approach, I will be outlining the directions that I believe social theory can profitably take.

What I will do in the paper is show just what approach can be taken in using rational theory for certain macrosociological problems. In each case, I will show derivations about macrosocial behaviour that can be made using this approach. Some of these derivations lead to predictions in accord with everyday observations about the functioning of social systems. Others, however, lead to predictions that must be tested by empirical research, since everyday observation does not provide an answer.

LEGISLATIVE BEHAVIOUR AND COLLECTIVE DECISIONS

The approach of rational theory to collective decisions in which each person has a vote and the outcome is decided by decision rule is this: Each voter is assumed to have a set of preferences among pairs of alternatives that are to be voted upon. These preferences are transitive: if A is preferred to B, and B to C, then A is preferred to C. Thus each has a preference order. Each casts his vote for that alternative which is highest in his preference order, among those to be voted on.

A classic theoretical problem of collective decisions which illustrates the relation between rational behaviour of individuals and the functioning of macrosocial systems is the Condorcet paradox, or stated differently, the Arrow impossibility theorem. The problem is this: individuals, acting rationally as described above, in a situation in which each casts a vote for an alternative outcome in an election, may not give an outcome that may be seen as rational for the collectivity as a whole. That is, voting by rational actors may give irrationalities at the systemic level. Kenneth Arrow has proved that is is not possible, under certain reasonable conditions, to create a decision rule that will prevent such 'systemic irrationality' (1951).

Rational actors in macrosociological analysis

Simple examples of the paradox may be constructed with three rational voters, X, Y and Z, and three alternatives, A, B, and C. If the preference orders are as indicated in Table 1 below, and the alternatives are to be voted on by pairwise elimination, then we find that:

(a) When A and B are voted on, the collectivity prefers A to B.
(b) When B and C are voted on, the collectivity prefers B to C.
(c) When A and C are voted on, the collectivity prefers C to A.

Table 1. *Preferences of three voters, X, Y, Z*

Preference order	X	Y	Z
1	A	B	C
2	B	C	A
3	C	A	B

Thus using this decision procedure, the rational actions of three persons provide collective outcomes which do not obey transitivity: A is socially preferred to B, B is preferred to C, but C is preferred to A. Depending upon which pair is voted on first, the outcome will be A or B or C. Arrow shows that it is impossible to find a decision procedure, short of dictatorial rule by one person, that will always preserve rationality at the systemic level.

This example, however, can illustrate a further point: that the macrosocial outcomes can be modified by expanding the range of behaviour allowed to rational persons. This seems intuitively appealing: rational persons in a collectivity are no more satisfied by collective irrationalities than is the theorist. Consequently, if they have additional resources, it seems understandable that they will attempt to use those resources to resolve the collective irrationality, not disinterestedly, but each to his own benefit. These actions may not always be successful, but sometimes they can be.

For example, in the above simple case, suppose each of these persons had outside resources, say in the form of money, each having an equal amount. But suppose that the outcome of the election of A, B and C was differentially important to them, that each would receive the amount indicated in Table 2 if the outcomes shown in Table 1 occurred.[1]

---

[1] I have expressed the utility of these outcomes in terms of money for convenience of exposition. However, it is not necessary to do so, but only to express certain preferences. The results which I will state below hold if: X has a transferable commodity D, and: X prefers outcome A to outcome B plus D; X prefers outcome A to outcome C plus D; Y prefers outcome A plus D to outcome B; Y prefers outcome A plus D to outcome C; Z prefers outcome A plus D to outcome B; Z prefers outcome A plus D to outcome C.

JAMES COLEMAN

Table 2. *Value of each outcome to each voter*

Outcome	X	Y	Z
A	$9	$2	$3
B	1	5	2
C	0	3	5

In this circumstance, the election is more important to X than to Y or Z: if X gets his first choice (A), he gets $8 more than if his second choice (B) occurs, and $9 more than if C occurs. However, for Y and Z, the outcome makes at most a difference of $3 to either of them.

Consequently, X can afford to take as much as $7 from his other resources to offer to Y or Z to vote always for A. This exchange would be profitable to either Y or Z; and in fact any amount from $3 up would be profitable to Z, and any amount from $4 up would be profitable to Y, even measured against their most preferred alternative. The result will be that the systemic outcome, no matter in what order the alternatives are voted on, will be A. The collectivity will exhibit rationality. A is collectively preferred to B, B is preferred to C, and A to C. Thus in such a situation, with an expanded set of resources, rational persons will act so as to overcome the irrationality at the systemic level. They are not always able to do so, but only because their resources are limited. Thus the source of Condorcet's paradox and Arrow's impossibility theorem lies not in something inherent about the shift from the individual level to the collective level, but in the limitations that casting a vote places upon individuals' expressions of interests. The systemic irrationality can always be overcome if the individuals have sufficient resources to express fully their interests, which a mere vote does not allow. Sometimes their additional resources are votes on other issues, rather than a private good, such as money in the example above. In such a case, certain instabilities are created (see, for example, Riker and Brams, 1973); nevertheless, the motivation to use this resource through vote-trading agreements exists, and in certain cases at least the instabilities may be overcome.[2]

[2] The general argument I am making can be seen by expanding the above example. Suppose there were a second issue on which Y felt intensely, as X does in the first, with the value of each outcome to each voter as follows:

	X	Y	Z
A'	5	0	3
B'	3	9	2
C'	2	1	5

Then X can offer Y an exchange of votes, to give outcomes A and B', making both better off than before, when A, B, C each have 1/3 chance of occurring, as do A', B', C'. But then Z can better that offer to Y, by offering an exchange to give C and B', making both Y and

78

These points would be academic, if they constituted merely a demonstration of some of the problems and complications in rational theory. But they lead to very specific predictions: that in such voting situations, rational persons will attempt to use outside resources, either private goods or votes on other issues, to obtain the outcome they prefer, and that they will do so in proportion to the importance of the outcome for them. That such attempts are widespread is evident by the legal proscriptions against the use of private goods (e.g., 'bribes' or 'payoffs') to influence the outcomes of legislative decisions, as well as the widespread use of vote exchanges (logrolling, promises of future votes) and political credit among legislators to influence outcomes. Thus rational theory leads to macrosocial predictions that are widely substantiated.

The approach can be generalised to systems of collective decisions and individual actions in which a set of actors is linked together by a number of events in which they have differential interests and over which they have differential control. We may think of such a system as a social system defined by the matrix of control of actors over events and the matrix of interests of actors in events. If the interests of actors in events are specified, and the control that each actor has over the outcome of each event, then it is possible to define both the value of an event in the system and the power of each actor to obtain outcomes he is interested in. Value is defined by the interest of actors in events, weighted by the actors' power; and power of an actor is defined as the control that the actor has of the event, each event weighted

Z marginally better off, and X much worse off. But then X can make both himself much better off and Z marginally better off by offering Z an exchange to give outcomes A and C'. Then Y can either offer X AB' or offer Z CC'. If he makes the former offer, the cycle repeats. If he makes the latter, then X can offer Y either AB' or CB', feeding back into the cycle at either point. The complete set of paths is

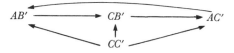

There are inherent instabilities, expressed in game-theoretic terms by the statement that the core of this game is empty. But we can go beyond that and note that if X, Y, or Z anticipate this cycle, then each will choose his second-best exchange (for X and Z outcomes A and C', and for Y, outcomes A and B'), because he will prefer that to the probability mixture $(1/3, 1/3, 1/3)$ of the other three outcomes in the cycle. If AB' is arrived at before AC', then because it is preferred by Y to the probability mixture of the other three, he cannot be enticed away, and it is stable. If AC' is arrived at before AB', then because it is preferred by both X and Z to the probability mixture of the other three, neither can be enticed away, and AC' is stable. The criterion of stability is of course weaker than the core, but nevertheless reasonable. Thus we can say that, even without side payments and unbreakable promises, the outcomes for this example would be A and B' with probability $1/2$, and A and C' with probability $1/2$. Of course, over the longer run, rational persons would also attempt to institute punishments to ensure that promises are kept, which would bring the collectivity even greater stability, and at generally higher levels of utility.

by its value. Thus this approach provides a way of arriving at a concept that has proved particularly elusive in sociology, the concept of power.[3]

Alternatively, if there are measures of outcomes of events and control over events, then in certain cases it is possible to calculate not only the value of events and the power of actors, but also to estimate the interests of actors in events.

I will not go into the technical details of this approach in the present paper, but will merely say that it assumes that the rational persons who are within the system will attempt to maximise their control over those events that interest them most, by giving up control over those events that interest them less. It describes a generalised exchange process for a social system defined by a set of rational actors and the events which they have control over and are interested in. It links together the individual-level assumptions (concerning interest, control, and maximising behaviour) and the system-level deductions (concerning outcomes of events, values of events, and power of actors).

THE STUDY OF FORMAL ORGANISATIONS

Formal organisations, such as bureaucracies, constitute an especially congenial locus for the application of rational theory, for they may be seen as the organisational instrument of a single person's purpose or will. They do not occur in nature, so to speak, but are formal constructions expressly designed to carry out a purpose. Max Weber, the first and most prominent theorist of formal organisations or bureaucracies, alternatively termed this form of social organization *rational* organisation. He conceived of the organisation, as it is ordinarily conceived, as a structure with a single purpose at the top, and with various bureaus, departments, and divisions, as parts of a machine designed expressly to implement this purpose. In Weber's theory, the persons who occupy positions in the organisation are merely cogs in the machine. What this means for our interest here is that they are not endowed with purpose or will. In contrast to the central will emanating from the top of the organisation, they are seen as implements or tools whose time, energy, and skills are employed in the service of the central organisational purpose.

In keeping with this general framework of ideas, much of the theory of bureaucratic organisation is a theory of managerial decision-making. For example, much of this theory has been developed in the disciplines of public administration and in schools of business, where the principal focus is on training managers. Herbert Simon, a major contributor to the field,

[3] This approach has been used in several empirical investigations. See El Hakim (1972), Hernes (1971), Walaszek (1973), Laumann and Marsden (1977), Marsden (1978).

exemplifies this well: his first publications (e.g., *Administrative Behaviour*, 1947) were written when he was in public administration; his later contributions (e.g., *Organisations*, 1958, with March) have been written in the context of the Graduate School of Industrial Administration, at Carnegie Mellon. These theories take either of two forms, either normative, prescribing to a manager the most efficient way of organising and running an organisation, or descriptive, describing how managers characteristically do make decisions and manage a complex organisations. Simon, in an early work (1947) expresses the normative version of this approach. He says, at the outset, 'Administration is ordinarily discussed as the act of "getting things done"... Principles are set forth for securing concerted action from groups of men' (p. 1). An example of the second is Cyert and March, who develop a theory of managerial decision-making at variance with the model of rational decision-making which aims to maximise an organisational goal such as profit. Cyert and March present evidence that managers act as problem-solvers, addressing successively problems which arise in the organisation in order of urgency. The managers, while still goal-oriented to the organisational purpose, act in somewhat the same way as does a fire department, putting out fires as they arise. This descriptive managerial theory is in keeping with a general notion that computational limitations, limitation of possibilities of search for alternatives, and organisational slack due to an unthreatening environment, militate against straightforward application of rational action, that is, full maximisation of utility (Cyert and March, 1963).

In much of this theoretical literature, though not all, the peculiarly human characteristics of the occupants of positions in the organisation play no part in the theory. The first moves away from that approach arise in taking these human characteristics into account in much the same way an engineer would do in taking properties of metals into account when designing a machine. For example, Dreyfuss (1952) in a paper which examines the structure of ranks, titles, and grades in business firms, shows how there is a proliferation of fine hierarchical distinctions among members of a department. The distinctions are not necessary, he shows, for structuring the duties of the various positions, but to serve as prestige-gradings which supplement salary differentials as rewards, and keep the occupants motivated to rise to the next higher grade, and not to combine against the employer.

Another example of this move from a strictly mechanistic theory of rational organisation is exemplified by the school of work known as human relations in industry, of which the best-known work is Roethlisberger and Dickson's *Management and the Worker* (1939). Beginning with the well-known Hawthorne experiment they examined how the social organisation among workers, affecting their psychological states, could be used to increase productivity. This work developed propositions about the relation between worker morale and productivity, propositions about how morale is increased or decreased by organisational factors, and propositions about the development of work norms.

In all this work, including as well the various works on types of incentive pay for workers, the conception of rational organisation was extended to take into consideration the psychological properties of persons who occupied positions in the organisation, although still from the perspective of the overall purpose of rational organisation. This (and something more) indeed was the plan of March and Simon's (1958) book, which began with the basic notions of rational organisation expressed by Weber and the earlier managerial theorists, and then extended the theory to take into account the fact that motivated social beings were occupants of positions in the organisation.

A critical stage in the development of theory of formal organisation beyond the 'human relations in industry' conception was provided by Chester Barnard (1938) with a theory involving 'inducements and contributions'. Barnard pointed out that an organisation was viable only so long as there was a mutually profitable exchange: inducements provided by the organisation to its employees sufficiently great to bring the employees to make contributions to the product of the organisation at such a level that those inducements could continue to be provided. In this conception of exchange, there came to be the recognition of multiple purposes, with each participant in the organisation being a rational actor engaged in an exchange of time, energy, and skills with the organisation in return for salary and other benefits.

This recognition of multiple interacting rational actors engaging in exchange opens up a pandora's box of theoretical possibilities. It also creates a difficult problem: if a bureaucratic organisation is to be seen theoretically as a system of social exchange, then there is danger of losing the original insights of Weber and others, predicated on the recognition that this is a *rational, constructed, purposive* organisation. For natural social organisation that grows up in physically proximate communities and in other areas of social life is appropriately seen as a system of social exchange, and if formal organisations are assimilated to that conceptual framework, there is a danger that its distinctiveness and the theoretical developments than can derive from that distinctiveness are lost.

There are some sociological analyses of behaviour within formal organisations that adopt the general exchange framework. But precisely because they do, they become something other than an analysis or theory of formal organisation. The best example of this work is Peter Blau's *Exchange and Power in Social Life* (1964). Blau shows how a large part of the occupational interactions among workers in an organisation's research laboratory can be described as an exchange of advice (from those seen as knowledgeable and from whom advice is sought) in return for deference (from the advice-seeker). This exchange, Blau shows, benefits both parties, providing prestige and power to the advice-giver and aiding the work of the advice-seeker. Thus within the laboratory, and by extension in other similar departments of bureaucracies, there develops an informal structure of power and prestige which affects the functioning of the department, and thus the organisation as a whole.

In this approach, the recognition of employees of an organisation as rational actors is complete. But the organisation as a rational actor does not enter; the organisation simply serves as the context or setting within which these persons carry out their exchanges and realise their interest. Similarly, George Homans, in his development of social exchange theory, examines behaviour of employees of organisations, and analyses that behaviour as consisting of mutually profitable social exchanges among those persons. Here too the formal organisation is merely the setting within which persons engage in exchange among themselves.

This is the current state of the theory of rational organisation. There continue the managerial decision-making theories which implicitly regard only the organisation, or its managers, as a single rational actor. At the other extreme are the theories of social exchange within formal organisational settings, in which the only purposive actors are persons in interaction, who happen to be employees of the organisation. At the same time, there is the recognition from Barnard onward, that the organisation as a rational actor can be seen as engaging in a specific type of exchange with each employee, also seen as a rational actor.

Without attempting to develop new theory, I will outline what I see as the appropriate theoretical directions from this point.

First, I believe that the central distinguishing feature of rational organisation is that it makes possible social transactions which go beyond two-person exchanges. This can perhaps best be seen in the simplest case, which is described in the law as *agency* and treated under the law of agency.[4] In the law of agency, there are three parties: the principal, the agent, and the third party. The principal wishes to engage in a transaction with a third party, but cannot do so himself, because of lack of time, skills, physical presence, certification, or another element necessary to the transaction. So

---

[4] The correspondence between principles of agency and rational organisation can be seen by that fact that some legal texts on corporation law include the law of agency as a section of that law, and by the fact that non-statutory law covering employer–employee relations is derived from the law of agency. See, for example, Conard, Knauss, and Siegel (1972).

he hires an agent, who carries out that transaction, not for himself, but *in the name of* the principal.

Here, then, is a situation in which a social transaction could not take place between two persons; a third was necessary. Thus a more complex structure is devised, in which the principal carries out a two-party transaction with a person who will become his agent, giving a salary commission to that person in return for that person's agreement to carry out a peculiar kind of transaction with a third party: one in which the agent uses his time and skills to effect the transaction, but in which the transaction itself involves resources of the principal and is carried out in the interests of the principal.

This is an 'artificial' or 'constructed' form of social organisation. As the result desired by the principal becomes more complex, more agents, some employing their skills interdependently with others, are necessary to accomplish the result, and the principal must establish the appropriate organisational structure and carry out 'employment' transactions with a person to fill each position in the structure.

Once taking this as an overall perspective, we can then conceive of organisational theory as involving several interdependent components. One component involves the set of exchanges made with the persons who are to be employed as agents; another is the structure of interactions (it is not precisely correct to call them exchanges, as I will explain shortly), among the agents (who may be conceived as occupants of positions in the organisation) involved in carrying out the organisation's purpose; a third is the spontaneous set of social exchanges which spring up between various agents (or employees) and are affected by aspects of the organisation structure.

The first of these components is that pointed to by Barnard in his discussion of inducements and contributions. The second involves creating a structure of authority, responsibility, of duties by the occupant of one position to another, which will produce the product of the organisation. Note that because each occupant is receiving a payment from the organisation, these interoccupant relationships are not to be conceived of as mutually profitable exchanges. The most primitive form of theory covering this component is classical bureaucratic and managerial theory; the more sophisticated is that which recognises that occupants of positions have certain psychological attributes which affect their performance. The third component of the theory is the sort of work carried out by Blau and Homans, referred to earlier.

What makes such theory particularly difficult is the interdependence between these three components of the theory. The nature of the transaction between the organisation and the agent will, by the kind of contingency it creates for payment of the agent (e.g., commission, salary, long-term contract, piece work) bring to differing degrees and in different ways the agent's interests into the interactions involved in the organisational structure itself. At one extreme, if the only contingency is performance acceptable to a supervisor, the employee (or agent) need put in only an acceptable level of time, effort, and skill, and the theory need only to take into account physiological properties of the employee (as for example, in the organisational theory known as 'Taylorism' [see Taylor, 1911], which gave rise to time and motion studies, and efficiency experts). At the other extreme, the contingency is so closely tied to the organisational goal that the employee realises his personal interests only to the degree that his actions benefit organisational interests (as, for example, is true as a first approximation for pure commission salesmen). At this extreme, the organisational theory, as well as the designer of the organisational structure, must develop a sophisticated system of exchange within the organisation, since, at this extreme, the organisation is a pure system of exchanges. Such organisational theory has never been developed, and it may be impossible to construct a rational organisation composed only of interactions which meet this criterion. Nevertheless, at the level of divisions within a rational organisation, such theory has been developed, originating with the practice of Alfred Sloan of General Motors. Sloan developed the notion that each division of General Motors should interact with other divisions on the basis of its own interests and its own 'profit': the Chevrolet division should decide to buy components from within or outside the corporation depending on where it could obtain the best buy; and the component and service divisions should not 'serve' the end product divisions, but should price their components and services as they would to an outside competitor, and receive payments from the division that purchased them.

Such a structure of mutually profitable exchanges is more feasible in certain parts of an organisation than others, and more feasible in broad divisions than in small units within them; the degree to which it can be extended throughout a rational organisation, and all they way down to the individual level, in theory and in practice, is an open question. It constitutes a kind of ultimate goal for theory and practice of rational organisation, a point at which rational organisation would be as self-sustaining at each module as is informal social organisation based on two-party exchange – for in such a structure no longer is the organisation as a rational actor (the principal in law of agency) required to engage in payments to employees, since their compensation arises directly from the transactions in which they engage as they work.

At this extreme of the second component of organisational theory, the third component, of which I used Blau's work as an example, becomes superflous, as it is absorbed into the second component. To the extent that the second component falls short of this goal, the third component, the informal two-party exchanges among persons within an organisation, constitutes a distinct social system, which interacts with the formal structure of the organisation. In such a situation, theoretical work is required to describe the character of this interaction, and its effects upon the functioning of the formal structure.

What I have tried to do in this section is to outline just how a theory of rational behaviour has been used in the study of formal organisations, how that use has enlarged as the conception of organisational employees as themselves rational actors has become incorporated within it, and what are the next steps in the development of the theory. The area is a particularly interesting one, because it involves the explicit construction of a supra-individual or corporate actor, designed to be rational.

TRANSFER OF CONTROL IN COLLECTIVE BEHAVIOUR

One class of social phenomena which has proved especially difficult to study and especially difficult to account for theoretically is that generally known as collective behaviour: mobs, panics, riots, manias, and similar evanescent phenomena. All these phenomena are marked by what is called 'social contagion', or social influence on a widespread scale. The only difficulty with viewing such behaviour as consisting of social contagion is that this description has a mystical quality of inevitability. It has no purposive element which can allow prediction of the conditions under which social contagion will be widespread and the conditions under which it will not.

However, we may turn the matter around, so to speak, and look at it not as social contagion from A to B, but as a transfer of control from B to A, and as a transfer which is made rationally. Then the way is paved for asking the conditions under which large numbers of persons in social proximity will make extensive transfers of control over their behaviour to one another.

I will use only one type of collective behaviour to illustrate the way in which this reconceptualisation can aid analysis. This is what Roger Brown, in a comprehensive examination of collective behaviour (1965) calls escape panics. The prototype is the panic which sometimes (but not always) occurs in a crowded theatre when there is smoke and someone yells, 'Fire!' What is necessary to explain is not only why a panic sometimes occurs, but also why, in apparently similar situations, it sometimes occurs and sometimes does not. The situation is unstable; behaviour can go either way, into a frantic rush for the exists, with possible jamming, or an orderly movement.

Such a situation is obviously one in which many persons are acting as if they were one – a situation in which there is a high degree of contingency of each person's behaviour on that of each other person (or alternatively, on what is perceived to be the behaviour of the crowd as a body). This is merely another way of saying that persons in a crowded theatre have made extensive transfers of control over their behaviour to others in the crowd or to the crowd as a unit, they take their cue from others' actions. But by what considerations can it be said to be rational to make such extensive transfers of control?

To answer this question, it is necessary to see what a person in a crowded theatre can expect as outcomes if he does transfer control to others and what he can expect if he does not. If he does not transfer control to others, then he must decide for himself whether there is a fire; not depending on others, he must find the exits himself, and he must decide, independently of what the others do, whether to file slowly toward an exit, or to rush toward one. If he does transfer control to others, he accepts others' judgement of whether there is a fire, he lets others' action guide him toward an exit, and he rushes or files out, depending on what others do.

The transfer of control can be viewed as broken down into parts: transferring control of judgement about whether there is a fire, transferring control about the judgement of where exits are, and transferring control about the decision about whether to rush or to file quietly. The rational considerations involved in the first two include one's location, one's experience with others' judgement compared to one's own, and similar factors. These do not lead to strong predictions, but only to those like the prediction that children will more likely transfer control than will adults, and those in sight of an exit will less likely transfer control to others' judgements than will others.

However, the question of transferring control over the decision to rush or file out can be looked at systematically. It is useful first to see what kind of benefit (i.e. escape from harm) he can expect under each combination of his actions and others' actions:

	Others' action	His action	Consequence	Benefit
1	Rush	Rush	Likely trap and death	Low
2	Rush	File out	Very likely trap and death	Very low
3	File out	Rush	Probable escape	High
4	File out	File out	Possible escape	Medium

He is worst off if others rush and he is determined to file out slowly, and best off if everyone else files out slowly and he rushes past them (so long as they continue to be orderly). He is almost as well off, however, if he files out with the others, when they make an orderly exit. He has, then three alternatives: he can rush out, independently of what others do; he can walk out slowly, independently of what others do; or he can transfer control to others, rushing if they rush and filing out if they file out.

It is clear that if he knows that the others' actions will be unaffected by his own (that is, they have not transferred control to him), then he is better off to rush, independently of whether they rush or file out: if they rush, he is less likely to be trapped if he rushes as well, and if they file out, and are unaffected by his actions, he is more likely to escape as well if he rushes. But if others *have* transferred control to him (or to the crowd as a whole, using his or anyone else's rushing as a signal of what the crowd's action will be), then it is not so apparent what is best for him to do. If he rushes when others are filing out ((B) above), then, rather than making a probable escape, he may transform the situation into (1), where all rush, leading to likely entrapment and death. If he begins to file out, on the other hand, he may cause or help cause others to file out as well, making the situation a (4), and greatly increasing his chance of escape above that of (1).

The alternatives facing him, and the rewards they bring, may be stated in a game-theoretic matrix, in which he is one player (A) in the game, and the crowd is another (B). The matrix is shown below, with rewards for him at the lower left of each cell, and rewards for the other at the upper right. The condition in which both he and the crowd transfer control is regarded as one in which they both file out, though each is ready to rush if the other gives indication of doing so.

Payoff matrix for escape panic

		Player B				
		Transfer control		Rush		File
Transfer control		med		low		med
	med		low		med	
Rush		low		low		very low
	low		low		high	
File		med		high		med
	med		very low		med	

This is a symmetric matrix; both players are in the same situation (we ignore here the fact that Player A is a person and B is the crowd). An inspection of the matrix will show that no one alternative dominates (that is, none gives a higher or equal payoff than any other action for every possible action of the other), but that one alternative is dominated. The alternative of filing out is no better than transferring control if the crowd transfers control or files out unilaterally, and is worse if the crowd rushes.

Thus this bottom row can be eliminated from consideration. But, because of symmetry, this means the third column can be eliminated as well. The alternatives remaining are to transfer control to the other, or to rush. Inspecting this 2 × 2 matrix shows that transferring control dominates rushing for both player A and player B. That is, it is rational for him to transfer control to others in an escape panic, filing out in an orderly fashion, but beginning to rush at any signal the crowd will rush.

The situation is unstable because any untoward action of anyone, even accidental stumbling, can suggest to at least one person that the crowd will rush, leading him in turn to rush and the others to take that as an even stronger signal that the crowd will rush. Thus, although the pair of alternatives shows the same reward as does the pair 'file-file', the structure is more unstable since it can easily lead to a situation in which everyone is rushing. In a somewhat different setting, but one which is structurally analogous, this solution is one proposed by military strategists: to establish an automatic response which cannot be overridden and that will be tripped by a nuclear missile from the opponent; and to let the opponent know that this has been done. [The latter action is comparable to Player A's informing Player B that he has taken the action in the top row. This makes it rational for Player B to take only the left or right action, but not the centre one (unilateral release of missile).]

There may, however, be a defect in the game-theoretic analysis I have carried out: if the upper-right-hand cell is unstable, then there are grounds for arguing that the payoff in this cell may be seen by player A to be lower than in the lower-left cell. This would invalidate the above analysis, and still leave him in a dilemma about what action to take. In that case, there is not a game-theoretic solution, but it is possible to see what he would do if he knew that others were taking each of the three alternatives. If he knew that others would file out independently of him (right column), for example if he were in a hidden portion of the balcony, or it is a bank panic in which he knows others do not know of the panic), then his rational action is not to move slowly, but to rush, as Table shows. If he knows that others will rush independently of him (i.e. in a bank panic where others do know of the panic), then his only alternative is to rush (or to transfer control, which, if he knows the others will rush, is the same thing). Thus if in his eyes the others' actions are not contingent on his own (that is, they fall in either of the two right-hand columns), his rational move is to rush. In contrast, if he sees that others have transferred control to him (left-hand column), then it is rational for him to file out or to rush so long as others do, but not to rush unilaterally. Notice also that if he has another alternative action, that of attempting to induce the others to transfer control to him, then it is rational for him to do that and then to file out and do so conspicuously.

This last analysis leads to non-obvious predictions at the macro-level. It predicts that for these persons who are in a position to feel that others' behaviour is not contingent on their own, and in those panics (such as bank panics) where the behaviour of each is not visible to others, each will rush. It also predicts that those persons highly visible to others, who feel that others have transferred control to them, will not rush, but maintain order, not for the benefit of others, but *because it is in their own interest* that the crowd is quiet. Also the analysis predicts that in a situation with an established hierarchical structure of leadership or authority, there will be, for purely self-interested reasons, less chance of a panic than in a situation which is egalitarian.

SUMMARY

I have attempted in the present paper to use three examples of areas in which rational behaviour models at the level of individual persons can prove fruitful for macrosocial problems. These are collective decisions such as are made in legislatures, formal or bureaucratic organisation, and collective behaviour such as in panics. The rational models used in the first two involve exchange for mutual benefit, while in the third the rational behaviour explored is unilateral transfer of control over action to another person.

REFERENCES

Arrow, Kenneth. *Social Choice and Individual Values*. New York, 1951.
Barnard, Chester I. *The Functions of the Executive*. Cambridge, Mass.: Harvard University Press, 1939.
Blau, Peter M. *Exchange and Power in Social Life*. New York: Wiley, 1964.
Brown, Roger. *Social Psychology*. New York: Free Press, 1965.
Coleman, James. *Community Conflict*. Glencoe, Ill.: Free Press, 1957.
Conard, A. F., Knauss, R. L. and Siegel, S. *Enterprise Organisation*. Mineola, NY: The Foundation Press, 1972.
Cyert, Richard M. and March, J. G. *A Behavioural Theory of the Firm*. Englewood Cliffs, NJ: Prentice Hall, 1963.
Dreyfuss, Carl. 'Prestige Grading: A Mechanism of Control', in R. K. Merton et al., *Reader in Bureaucracy*. Glencoe, Ill.: Free Press, 1953.
Eisenstadt, S. N. *Tradition, Change and Modernity*. New York: Wiley, 1973.
el Hakim, Sherif, M. 'Collective Decisions in a South Saharan Village', Baltimore: Johns Hopkins University, 1972, unpublished PhD dissertation.
Hernes, Gudmund, 'Interest, Influence, and Cooperation: A Study of the Norwegian Parliament', Baltimore: Johns Hopkins University, 1971, unpublished PhD dissertation.
Kardiner, Abram. *The Psychological Frontiers of Society*. New York, 1945.
Laumann, Edward, O. and Marsden, Peter, V., 'Collective action in a Community Elite: Exchange, Influence Resources, and Issue Resolution', in *Power, Paradigms, and Community Research*, Robert J. Liebert and Allen W. Imersheim (eds.) ISA; (Sage Publications Inc., Beverly Hills, Calif., 1977), pp. 199–250.

Marsden, Peter, 'Community Leadership and Social Structure: Bargaining and Opposition', Chicago: University of Chicago, 1978, unpublished PhD dissertation.

Mayer, P. J. *Max Weber and German Politics*. Faber and Faber, 1943.

Riker, W. H. and Brams, S. J. 'The Paradox of Vote Trading', *American Political Science Review* 67 1973, pp. 1235–47.

Roethlisberger, F. J. and Dickson, W. J. *Management and the Worker*. Cambridge, Mass.: Harvard University Press, 1939.

Simon, Herbert. *Administrative Behaviour*. New York: Macmillan, 1947.

Smelser, Neil. *Theory of Collective Behaviour*. New York: Free Press 1962.

Taylor, Frederick, W. *The Principles of Scientific Management*. New York: Harper, 1911.

Walaszek, Zdzislawa, 'Structural differentiations and Social Decisions: An experimental Study', Baltimore: Johns Hopkins University, 1973, unpublished PhD dissertation.

Rational choice and political principles

ALBERT WEALE

'Capitalism borrows much from the perfectly general logic of choice' (Joseph Schumpeter: *Capitalism, Socialism and Democracy* p. 182)

Frequently, in public policy, objectives conflict. The control of inflation may create higher unemployment; the maintenance of standards in the social services may restrict local autonomy; the protection of the public interest may require the suspension of constitutional liberties; or the pursuit of economic equality may inhibit efficiency. Faced with conflicting objectives how is a public official to select policies which reflect the right mix of objectives? By how much, for example, should efficiency be reduced in order to achieve greater economic equality?

One way of dealing with this problem is to incorporate all public policy objectives within a utilitarian maximand. Equality is to be pursued to the point at which the marginal increase in satisfactions for any one member of society achieved by redistribution equals the marginal increase for anyone else, and is at least as great as the marginal increase that could be attained for all persons by an increase in productive potential. Similarly other utilitarian prescriptions could be derived for other policy conflicts. Provided one had sufficient evidence one would then have a determinate set of solutions for all problems of policy conflict.

The objections to a utilitarian approach of this sort are well-rehearsed, but are none the worse for that. I find the substantive ethical objections – that the employment of a utilitarian calculus in public policy produces some highly counterintuitive and objectionable results – less appealing than the methodological arguments. The calculus in question requires that we be able to incorporate all public policy objectives into a single index of value. Not only has no one invented a utilitometer which would do the job adequately, there is no reason to think that there would be a consensus on the relative weightings to be given to the value of alternative consequences which would inevitably be required to programme a utility machine. For this reason alone utilitarianism is inadequate.

This difficulty with the utilitarian approach can be summarised by saying that it fails to register the way in which conflicting principles are regarded as ultimate values in political discussion. To the extent to which principles do conflict with one another, decision-makers must find some method of weighing the relative value of different principles. But this does not entail, what utilitarianism presupposes, that there exists a single scale of value in terms of which the actual principles employed in political discussion can be measured. When, for example, the Home Secretary introduces anti-terrorist legislation which effectively abridges the rights of citizens on arrest, his policy might be analysed as an attempt to maximise a function of the common good on some unique scale of value. But from the way that decisions are discussed it is more accurate to regard the policy as an instance of the need to weigh the two ultimate, if incompatible, principles of the government's duty to maintain individual rights and its duty to protect the public interest. In effect this is simply to point out that policy decisions are taken on the assumption of a plurality of values, where conflicting principles are not reconciled by their being subsumed under higher level principles.

Although utilitarianism fails to capture this aspect of political argument, it does at least offer a decision procedure, if only in outline, for solving problems of value conflict. To possess such a decision procedure is an attractive feature for a theory of political principles. The question therefore arises: is there an alternative way of conceptualising choice among political principles which also possesses this feature of offering a decision procedure in cases of policy conflict? The aim of this paper is to see whether the modern economic theory of consumer and allocational choice, if applied to choice among competing political objectives, provides an answer to this question. I shall therefore be concerned with the question of whether the outlines of a decision procedure can be formulated within which policy conflicts can be handled, in the same way that utilitarianism offered the outline of such a procedure. I shall be turning to the economic theory of choice, because as a remote off-spring of utilitarianism it promises much in this respect.

The thesis for which I shall argue is that not only does economic theory provide a relevant decision procedure, but that its procedure is also neutral between competing objectives, in so far as the choice of policy goals is made by an official or representative in a democratic political system. Conflicts of principle may be resolved by democratic representatives or officials in accordance with the logic of economic choice without thereby biasing the selection of objectives towards certain types of principle. I do not mean to imply by this thesis that the use of economic rationality will not lead officials to revise their statement of objectives on occasions. But revisions of this sort will only occur provided they were previously committed to policy objectives inconsistent with the values on which the policy was supposedly based. Any bias that exists in the use of this decision procedure, therefore, will be one producing a better fit between policy objectives and political values; it will not introduce a bias between political values.

The underlying explanation of this presumed value neutrality is that the modern account of economic choice is simply a special case of the general logic of choice. Schumpeter's remark[1] that capitalism borrows much from the perfectly general logic of choice illustrates this relationship well. His point was that in so far as capitalism was an efficient mode of production this was so because its institutions allowed rational decisions to be made about the allocation of scarce resources. Other institutions might replace those of capitalism, but in so far as they were efficient, they would make similar decisions on resource allocation to those made in a capitalist system. The same logic of choice applies in each case. The merit of capitalist institutions, for Schumpeter, was that they allowed wide scope for rational decisions to be made about resource allocation. But the concept of rationality was logically prior to that of the institutions within which choices were made. It is, then, an open question as to whether this rationality can be transferred from economic to political institutions.

II

It will be useful in discussing the difficulties which arise in using the economic concept of a rational decision procedure to set down briefly its basic elements. The economic theory of consumption rests on the following propositions. A consumer acts rationally if, in the selection of his commodity basket, he selects that mix of commodities, such that he would prefer no more of one item of consumption at the expense of the loss of another item of consumption. Why should this be regarded as a rational choice procedure? Suppose a consumer selected a basket of commodities such that a specified increase in one item would be preferred to a specified decrease in another item. Then not to substitute the former increase for the latter decrease is acting inconsistently with one's preferences. One could attain a more preferred consumption position by making the switch. The same logic can of course be applied, *mutatis mutandis*, to allocational decisions in production. If a greater return can be achieved by switching productive resources from one use to another, then it is irrational not to make the switch, provided always that one prefers higher return to lower. So, for both consumption and production, the logic of choice leads to a set of directions which a rational agent should follow.

In order for the economic criterion of choice to work successfully two

[1] J. Schumpeter, *Capitalism, Socialism and Democracy* (London: Unwin, 1943) p. 182.

assumptions need to be made about the preferences of individuals confronted with a choice problem. The first of these assumptions is that the individual in question should be able in principle to express a preference over all available choices, and, in particular, with consumption choices, the individual should be capable of stating his preference between different mixes of commodity bundles. Unless the consumer is able to do this, there will clearly be instances where it is impossible to say what a rational choice would be, since it will not be possible to know whether the substitution of one item of consumption for another is consistent with the attainment of the consumer's most preferred position. The second assumption that requires to be made about preference orderings is that they are transitive, so that if an individual prefers x to y and y to z, it is assumed that he prefers x to z. If this assumption is not satisfied it will not be possible to make a rational choice among alternatives, since there is no way of knowing whether the attainment of any one alternative is consistent with a persons's most preferred position. With intransitive choices over triples of options, for example, any one alternative will come out arbitrarily as either most preferred or not most preferred, since, although it will be preferred to one item which is preferred to the third, the third item itself is preferred to the original item. Hence there will be no way of making a rational choice, consistent with the attainment of one's most preferred position.

When the objects of choice are public policy objectives, rather than economic commodities, the form in which these two assumptions must be satisfied changes, although their substance remains the same. The first assumption, the requirement of connectivity of preference, assumes the following form. For the intended outcome of any policy decision, it is known whether that outcome satisfies the conditions of the political principles in question or does not satisfy them. So there must be no outcome which is indeterminate in respect of whether it satisfies a principle or not. Public officials must know, therefore, whether a policy will increase or decrease inequality, promote or hinder the public interest, or reduce or maintain local autonomy. They must then be capable of formulating preferences over these outcomes. The assumption of transitivity, the second element in the definition of rational economic choice, requires a consistent ranking in accordance to the degree to which principles are instanced in a social stage. So if social state x satisfies a principle α more than y, and y satisfies α more than z, then x is to be preferred to z, other things remaining constant.

If these two assumptions are satisfied in the case of a particular choice over policy objectives, then we can state the rule of rational choice for a public official. A public official will act rationally if he chooses to implement policies whose intended outcome is such that any other intended outcome is less preferred. Where a public official is faced with a number of conflicting

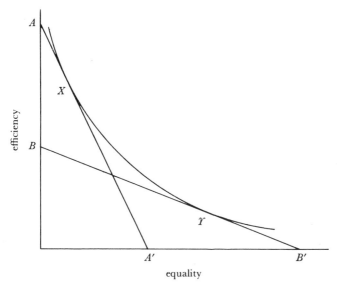

Figure 1

objectives, not all of which can be implemented simultaneously then a rational choice will be one in which the policy mix is such that there is no objective within the set of implemented policies which is less preferred than an objective outside the set. A public official chooses rationally therefore between competing objectives when his policies reflect the relative value assigned to the attainment of one goal by comparison with another. At present nothing is said about the source of these relative evaluations, though, as I shall point out, defining such a source involves problems for the thesis of value neutrality. So far, however, all that is being maintained is that it is possible to describe a decision procedure for public officials that is analogous to economic, and in particular consumer, choice theory.

In order to illustrate this approach it will be useful to consider a special case, where there are only two conflicting objectives. The reason for considering the two values case is that the technique of rational choice can be cast in the form of a graphical presentation, as Barry[2] once pointed out, by the use of indifference curves. An indifference curve represents different combinations of objectives all of which are equally preferable to a decision-maker. There will of course be an infinite number of such curves for any two values choice, corresponding to the different combinations available in

---

[2] B. M. Barry, *Political Argument* (London: Routledge, 1965) pp. 5–8.

the scope of choice. One such curve is illustrated in Figure 1, with two accompanying 'possibility curves', AA' and BB', representing the available opportunities for acting in accordance with the decision-maker's stated preferences. In this hypothetical case AA' and BB' represent two distinct choice situations. In the case of AA' the optimum mix of policies would occur at X, placing a relatively high emphasis on efficiency at the expense of equality, given the available opportunities for acting in accordance with stated preference. For BB' the optimum mix occurs at Y, where the emphasis is reversed. Both of these are optima, relative to the available alternatives, because no other point on the line touches the indifference curve, and so, by assumption, is not equally preferable to that particular combination.

There are several advantages to be gained by thinking of political choice in these terms. Firstly, we do not have to assume that the alternative objectives are evaluated by reference to some notion of utility under which the different principles are subsumed. The indifference curve simply represents the relative evaluation of policy objectives made by a decision-maker. Secondly, the approach provides a subtler notion of consistency than is usual in the logical appraisal of normative judgements. The example shows that the same relative evaluation of equality and efficiency will yield different recommendations, depending on the circumstances. The final recommendation will depend both on the evaluation of the alternatives and on the available opportunities confronting the decision-maker. So, whereas it is common enough to think that different evaluations may be required in different circumstances, the method of indifference curve analysis shows how the *same* evaluation will produce *varying* results depending on the circumstances.

Despite these advantages there are drawbacks in the applications of indifference curve analysis to the case of political choice. One such difficulty is that there is no reason to think that one can in practice have sufficiently detailed empirical knowledge to draw the possibility curves accurately.[3] There are severe estimation problems involved in determining in what ways and by how much increased economic equality reduces economic growth. To move from economic policy to other areas of public policy only increases these estimation problems. No coherent measurement scheme has been devised for quantifying constitutional liberties or the public interest, and in the absence of such a scheme, not much can be said that is meaningful on the relationships that hold between them.

Aside from these technical difficulties, there is also the problem that, as presented, the indifference curve technique suggests that decision-makers cannot posit a lexicographic relationship between one value and others. Clearly, however, many sophisticated political positions do rest on the idea

[3] Cf. M. Lessnoff, 'Barry on Rawls' Priority of Liberty' *Philosophy and Public Affairs* **4**, p. 113.

that there are some values or principles which should always take priority over others, most usually that a concern for individual rights ought to override considerations of the public interest. So in this respect the thesis I am proposing seems to fail from the start, since the indifference curve technique, as an instance of economic logic, precludes certain political positions from being considered. However, appearances here are deceptive. There is nothing in the technique itself to exclude the idea of lexicographic orderings, so that one value always takes precedence over another. Certainly the use of indifference curves in such cases may seem a little odd, since in order to represent a lexicographic priority the indifference cure will have to run parallel to one of the axes, possibly over its whole length. But the implications of this oddity are not at all clear. It may simply emphasise in graphical form the strong assumptions that have to be made if one is going to hold to a political theory in which some principles do exhibit lexicographic priority over others. What such odd indifference curves show is just how insensitive such political theories are to changes in the circumstances in which one implements one's objectives.

Finally, in outlining how this decision analysis might apply to political principles, it will be useful to say something on the way in which choice among policy objectives relates to choice among policy instruments. This will also serve to illustrate how the technique may in practice be applied to the study of public policy. The economic analysis of decisions rests upon the requirement that the decision-maker can state his relative preference between available alternatives, where it is not necessary to assume that the decision-maker in question is maximising some subjective quantity of utility. However, it is possible to interpret choice among competing objectives as though the decision-maker were maximising a subjective utility function. Clearly, however, there is no need to assume that only one such utility function will adequately account for the behaviour. The function must of course be consistent with the observed pattern of choice, but any one function from the set of linear transforms which are so consistent will do the job as well as any other. A more important point in this respect now arises in connection with the policy instruments that a public official must use in order to attain his policy objectives. Objectives like equality and efficiency must be translated into statements about the size and distribution of income and wealth, and other objectives, such as those relating to standards in the personal social services, must be couched in such terms as the number of residential places for children or the elderly. Corresponding to the subjective utility function for policy objectives, therefore, there will be an objective function to be maximised stated in terms of tangible policy goals, where these goals are thought to be attainable by the use of certain policy instruments.

ALBERT WEALE

If goals are specified and relative evaluations known, then it is possible
to use various optimisation techniques to work out the best deployment of
policy instruments. Such techniques would include linear programming,
where the aim is to calculate the deployment of instruments or resources
in order to maximise total weighted output of different products – for
example in a firm which has machinery to bake either white or brown bread,
and where the returns vary according to the pattern of output that is chosen.
However, in public policy analysis it is often useful to reverse the logic of
this procedure. That is, we assume that the decision-maker is maximising
output and is deploying his available resources in an optimum fashion.
Then, by a process of inverse linear programming we can calculate the
implicit valuation of competing goals. A good example of this approach is
provided by Lavers'[4] study of the implicit valuation placed on various
categories of patients in hospital. Given that one knows what medical
resources different types of patient consume, it will be possible to calculate
the relative weight which a hospital administrator attaches to the treatment
of, say, ulcer patients as against hernia patients. It is then possible to ask
the administrators in question whether these relative weights really are
consistent with the actual evaluations. If they are, then the technique has
shown that they are employing resources in the best way possible; if they
are not, then one can search out the source of the inefficiency. What this
example shows, in particular, is that the assumption of rational choice by
public officials in their decisions may be valuable, even when in practice
their decisions may not conform to the behaviour the analysis presupposes.
Often the divergence from patterns of rational choice in public policy will
be just as interesting as conformity.

The analysis of actual decisions is normally undertaken as a preliminary
stage to attempts to improve policy choice. At the stage of recommendations
for improvements the concept of rational choice is used as a normative idea,
and not simply as an analytical tool. The question can be raised, therefore,
as to whether it is adequate as a normative device. In particular does its
use implicitly commit one to certain values at the expenses of others? To
answer this question I shall state and criticise three arguments in turn
which suggest that it does.

III

Economic theories of choice presuppose that all alternatives can be ranked
by an agent relative to one another. However it is sometimes argued that
not all political values can be ranked with one another. I shall call this the

---

[4] R. J. Lavers, 'The Implicit Valuation of Forms of Hospital Treatment', M. M. Hauser
(ed.) *The Economics of Medical Care* (London: Unwin, 1972) pp. 190–205.

100

'incommensurability thesis'. If the incommensurability thesis is true, then the thesis of this paper is false: if some values cannot be ranked against one another, then the logic of economic choice will not be a value-neutral way of representing conflicting public policy objectives. In the nature of the case some value choices could not be adequately represented in such a form.

The incommensurability thesis is not easy to state. It is used to assert very different positions. A list of some of the positions it is used to assert are as follows: (i) the relation holding between some values or principles is lexicographic; (ii) it is false to say that a loss in one value can always be compensated by an increase in another value; (iii) it is not possible to devise a consistent value-scheme, given the fact of moral or policy conflict; (iv) it is not possible in every moral or political theory to deduce within the theory reasons for preferring one choice to another; (v) it is not true, from the fact that people make a choice in instances of moral and political conflict, that from their choices a coherent value-system can be inferred.

None of these propositions alone entails or is entailed by the others on their own. Yet they are often wrapped up together, and presented as a bundle constituting an alternative to the conventional wisdom asserting that values are commensurable. So far as the present argument is concerned, some claims of the incommensurability thesis can be disposed of rapidly. The economic theory of choice allows lexicographic orderings, so claim (i) fails. The related claim (ii) asserts that a lexicographic ordering prevailing across some range of a pair of values, will not occur across all possible ranges. This claim can be questioned, and some pertinent doubts have been raised concerning its truth.[5] But since it requires weaker claims than claim (i) it too falls against the present argument.

Claim (iii) is more difficult to formulate. One way of stating it is as follows. Suppose a political or moral theory requires an agent to implement, in some circumstances, two policies, which are incompatible. A consistent value system would have to assert that one policy ought not to be implemented, since it was incompatible with the policy which ought to be followed. Proponents of claim (iii) deny this conclusion. They assert, instead, that though one may not be able to perform one of two actions, either of which one ought to perform on its own, it does not follow that one does not have a duty to perform both.[6] Duties hold even which they cannot be simultaneously fulfilled. Only in this way, it is claimed, can we adequately explain feelings of regret in such circumstances. So the notion of consistency, on this account, cannot be transferred from the logic of assertions to deontic logic. However generally valid this claim is, it does not touch upon the

[5] J. Griffin, 'Are There Incommensurable Values?' *Philosophy and Public Affairs* **7**, pp. 39–59.
[6] B. Williams, *Problems of the Self* (Cambridge: CUP, 1973) pp. 166–86 [and see the third paper of this collection – *ed.*].

central argument of this paper. In one sense, indeed, it reinforces its central assumptions, since there is a clear parallel between the claim that duties hold, even when they cannot be implemented consistently with other duties, and the claim that desirable objectives in public policy conflict. In each case the natural requirement to impose upon the moral agent is that he makes the best choice from the range of conflicting considerations with which he is presented. This recommendation is independent of the status one assigns to the policy goal which is not pursued. The economic theory of choice is concerned to provide an analysis of what it is for a public official to choose the best mix of policies in such circumstances. It does not imply a particular thesis about the logical status of the considerations on which he fails to act.

Claims (iv) and (v) are left therefore. Combining them together seems to produce an argument against the economic theory. In order to see this, consider the way in which the incommensurability thesis is normally denied by those who reject its claims. The usual way in which the incommensurability thesis is rebutted is simply to point out that consumers, and policy-makers, have in the end to make a choice. To choose is to express an evaluation. Since people can and do make choices between difficult alternatives, this fact is normally taken to be sufficient proof of the claim that even 'incommensurable' values can be made commensurate. However, this rebuttal will not work against the incommensurability thesis stated in the form of claims (iv) and (v). To begin with, there are reasons to deny that reliable inferences can be made from acts of choice to the structure of a person's value system. The simplest example is that of indifference, where no choice behaviour will yield grounds for holding that someone is indifferent between two alternatives. Either someone will choose one of the alternatives, in which case the choice will be taken to indicate strict preference, or he will oscillate in his choice over a sequence of decisions, in which case indifference will be empirically indistinguishable from changes of mind. So the incommensurability thesis can correctly rest on the claim that there is no direct inference from choice to evaluation. Conjoined with the intuitively plausible claim that there are some political theories which only yield partial orderings over policy alternatives, the value-bias of the economic theory of choice seems set to follow automatically.

In order to block off this attractive-looking argument appeal must be made to the fact that the thesis of value-neutrality is stated only in respect of public officials in democratically responsible governments. The purpose of this restriction is to provide some special grounds for the legitimacy of making inferences from actions to values. The inference may be cut in the case of private individuals, whose choices may not express their attitudes. However it cannot be similarly cut for public officials, since their public position requires them to be accountable for their actions. Public officials cannot claim that there is some sense in which their actions do not reflect their values, since democratic institutions require policy action to be a test of what values the official is promoting. So, whereas the blunt assertion that persons must choose between alternatives provides no reason in general for holding that values can be treated as commensurable, the same point when applied to public officials does carry weight. Unless it did the concept of democratic accountability would be rendered nugatory. This means that the need for choice over conflicts of public policy implies that alternatives can be completely ordered; the concept of democratic accountability further requires that the complete ordering implied by the fact of choice over alternatives must be justifiable by appeal to a set of considerations or reasons developed within a political theory. Although claims (iv) and (v) of the incommensurability thesis may hold of private individuals, the concept of the democratic accountability of public officials implies that they cannot hold for instances of public policy choice. With this conclusion intact an economic decision procedure can be used by public officials operating within a political theory. Their public position will require them to satisfy the conditions under which the economic analysis is applied.

IV

A second set of objections to the economic approach stem from the claim that the notion of maximising the attainment of a goal is not an idea fundamental to social or political principles. Indeed there are ethical intuitions deeply embedded in some social and political attitudes by which maximising the value of some goal is thought to be intrinsically undesirable. An example is the 'statistical lives paradox', discussed by Schelling.[7] This paradox is instanced on those occasions on which sums of money are spent, say on a rescue from a mining disaster or on curative medicine, when the same sum of the money spent on preventive measures would save a greater number of 'expected' lives. That is, more lives would be saved even when the number of lives in question is appropriately discounted for the uncertain operation of the preventive measures. It would seem rational, if maximising the value of saved lives were all that mattered, to switch the money from its present use and spend it on the preventive measures. Yet in practice decision-makers seem reluctant to make this switch. Saving the lives of those in present danger seems to have more value than the saving of future, statistical lives.

This example convincingly shows that there are occasions on which decision-makers will not act so as to maximise the expected value of lives

[7] T. C. Schelling, 'The Life You Save May Be Your Own' S. B. Chase (ed.) *Problems of Public Expenditure Analysis* (Washington: Brookings, 1968).

saved, even when one might expect that they would. The interpretation of this result is less certain, however. One possibility is quite simply that decision-makers act irrationally in such circumstances. Alternatively the example suggests that maximising the expected value of lives saved is not the only value which decision-makers pursue, and some value is attached in itself to known present lives. Either way the significance of this result is uncertain for the problem of rational choice among political principles. It should be possible to determine, from empirical evidence, what weight is being attached to present as against future lives by the same process of inverse linear programming used by Lavers. Decision-makers can then be regarded as behaving as though they were maximising a function based on these relative weightings. This at least would be an adequate representation of the behaviour, and would presumably be the only foundation on which their decisions could be given a justification.

I am, moreover, rather unwilling to allow ethically controversial instances decide the correct way of representing political choice. Difficult cases make bad counter-examples. It would seem preferable to find an alternative way of representing principles, and see how that fared in competition with the maximising view. One such alternative is presented by Nozick[8] who suggests that political principles be regarded as *side-constraints* on action rather than as *goals* to be maximised. On this account a government should not act so as to maximise some collective goals, but simply to enforce individual rights. In acting in this way it is subject to certain constraints, namely that it should not violate individual rights in the performance of its tasks. But the existence of these side-constraints in no way entails, according to Nozick, the claim that public policy makers are to maximise some function of a goal.

How are we to choose between the view that political principles are to be represented as goals to be maximised and the view that they are to be thought of as side-constraints on otherwise ethically undetermined actions? In particular, does the selection of alternative accounts involve a commitment to different values, so that, whichever account we choose, the relevant conception of choice will only represent certain value systems? Nozick thinks that each account does presuppose substantive ethical choices. He argues that a side-constraints view recognises that each person is an individual, who ought not to be used to promote an overall social good. Utilitarianism, and similar goal-directed views, are, Nozick claims, unable to recognise this truth. To demonstrate this point he cites an imaginary example of the type often used to 'disprove' utilitarianism. Suppose that we have to kill an innocent person in order to prevent a mob rampaging through an area and violating the property and other rights of a large number of people. According to Nozick a goal-directed view of principles, like utilitarianism,

[8] R. Nozick, *Anarchy, State and Utopia* (Oxford: Blackwell, 1974) pp. 30–42.

might well license the killing of the individual, whereas the side-constraints view would not. This shows, Nozick supposes, that a side-constraints view of principles has an inherent tendency to respect individuality, as well as being an accurate representation of the process of 'liberal' value choices.

It is indisputable that there is a substantive difference between political theories which are rights-based, and therefore have a principle of respect for individuality underlying them, and political theories which use a criterion of collective welfare as the basis for making choices. A real example, to parallel Nozick's imaginary one, of how these differences emerge is that of the allocation of scarce life-saving medical equipment. A cost–benefit criterion, based on the aim of maximising social welfare, will allocate the equipment to the most economically productive patients. A rights-based principle, however, would recognise a common right to life for all patients, and would use decision-procedures – random selection suggests itself – which reflected this approach.[9] So, whatever the substantive merits of the two theoretical approaches, they will yield contrary policy prescriptions in particular instances. The principles they embody are neither intensionally nor extensionally equivalent.

However it is misleading to express this difference in the form of a logical distinction between different types of political principles in terms of side-constraints versus goals. Rights-based conceptions of social choice may be cast in a goal-directed form. In effect this proposal simply requires that we return to the earlier conception of lexicographic relations between principles. The point then becomes that one should aim at some goals before implementing policies to promote other objectives. On occasions these goals might be negatively defined, so that in Nozick's example one would aim to avoid punishing the innocent before protecting the property rights in the community at large. But there is no reason in general to think that lexicographically prior goals within a political theory will always be negatively defined. Nor is there any reason to believe that a deontological conception of ethics cannot be cast in a goal-directed form. After all, Kant's second formulation of the categorical imperative, which is supposed to underlie the side-constraints view, is stated as a goal-directed conception of morality: persons are to be treated as ends in themselves, and not merely as a means to further ends. Although Kant's formulation can be interpreted as ruling out certain considerations as admissible in the making of social choices, it can be understood simply to imply a restriction on the range of goals agents are entitled to pursue.

If there is no logical distinction between conceiving political principles as goals or as side-constraints, is there an argument from convenience for

[9]   Cf. J. F. Childress, 'Who Shall Live When Not All Can Live?' R. M. Veatch and R. Branson (eds.) *Ethics and Health Policy* (Cambridge, Mass.: Ballinger, 1976) pp. 199–212.

making the distinction? Does the concept of a side-constraint express an important feature of political principles which is relevant for the under-standing of contemporary political arguments? One way in which this weaker thesis might be upheld is to point out that many of the goals which political theories require to take lexicographic priority, like the protection of constitutional liberties, are established features of some political systems. The concept of a side-constraint, when applied to a political principle, may then underline the view that such principles, and the practices they imply, are such settled features of the conviction and habits of the bulk of the members of certain political societies that they are not strictly matters for policy choice. No policy would be pursued in such a community if it violated these principles. As an expression of this point, the side-constraints conception of principles makes a valid claim. However, this claim will hardly affect a thesis about the way that matters which are subjects of policy decision should be handled. Moreover, it is rarely the case that principles and practices are so settled within a political community that occasional policy choices would not have to be made which affect what is otherwise taken for granted. And where the taken-for-granted does come up for question, choices will have to be made on an estimate of the relative importance of the settled practice against the policy goal with which it conflicts.

The weaker thesis, that the distinction rests on convenience, might also be maintained if the side-constraints in question were thought to take the form of negative rights held by persons, prohibiting interference with their actions though not requiring positive assistance by others. The idea here might be that the function of political principles was simply to set limits to the actions agents might undertake in pursuing their own plans, but not to prescribe any elements of those plans themselves as might be implied by the notion of a positive duty to help others. The difficulty with this form of the weaker thesis is that such a distinction cuts across the more general distinction between a utilitarian and a Kantian conception of political principles. In particular, there is no argument from the requirement that principles have the form of the categorical imperative to the conclusion that the corresponding rights are negative in character. As Kant[10] argued, the formula that persons should be regarded as an end in themselves must be taken to imply the existence of some positive rights. For in order that the conception of a person as an end in himself has its full effect upon an agent, that person's ends must become, at least in part, the agent's ends as well. Fully to act in accordance with the categorical imperative, therefore, one must recognise some positive duty to promote the goals of others, and not

---

[10] I. Kant, *Groundwork*, translated as *The Moral Law*, H. J. Paton (London: Hutchinson, 1948) pp. 92–3.

merely a negative duty to refrain from interfering with others. So on the Kantian conception principles do not simply figure as the limits on an agent's action, they must also figure in that agent's purposes as well. There is no general feature of the form of political principles which would constitute the argument from convenience on which the side-constraints view might rest.

The implications of this analysis primarily concern the way in which some forms of state activity are interpreted. If the Kantian argument carries through, then individuals will have positive rights of assistance from others. It is wrong therefore to conceive of all forms of compulsory economic redistribution by the state as a violation of Kantian autonomy, as Nozick is prone to do. Economic redistribution is not a method by which the state uses one person as a means to benefit another person; it is rather the enforcement of a positive right. Compulsion on the duty-bearer is therefore no more a violation of Kantian autonomy than any state activity to preserve individual rights. To suggest the opposite is to hold to the view that rights enforcement as such violates autonomy. None of this implies, of course, that any existing pattern of redistribution conforms to Kantian requirements. What those requirements are is a matter of substantive ethical judgement. This analysis does imply, however, that the goal-directed form of redistributive and other public policies is not incompatible with a Kantian conception of principles with its rights-based conception of social choice.

A related, but distinct, problem is also raised by Nozick's example of the conflict between an individual's personal rights and the property rights of others. It is the question of how far the right to be protected from harm extends, and whether the right should be enforced even against innocent third-parties. In Nozick's example the problem takes the form of whether it would be justifiable to violate an individual's rights in order to protect the property rights of other members of the community. The fundamental problem here is that the rights which have been assigned to the members of a community conflict in practice with one another. It is not that there is a strict inconsistency in the rights' assignment. It is possible that the two sets of rights could be maintained, without them coming into conflict. In practice, however, the rights conflict because protecting a group of people from an intended violation of their rights involves abridging the rights of an innocent third-party. So in this second-best situation, some principle is required to decide upon the rights to be maintained, just as some principle is required to set the limits to the right of self-defence, which is similarly occasioned by an intended rights' violation. One way of interpreting the notion of side-constraints is as a substantive ethical judgement about what state officials should do in these circumstances. For the side-constraints view implies that state officials should not themselves violate rights, even when they intend by so doing to protect a larger set of rights. The only way that such a policy can be rationalised would seem to be in terms of a fundamental moral difference between the consequences of acts and the consequences of ommissions, in cases where the consequences were identical. Whether such a difference could be firmly established without appeal to a moral authority is an open question.[11] Even to have established the difference, however, would not show that it could not be incorporated into the policy goals of the government. It would merely show that such a goal should have lexicographical priority over attempts to enforce rights.

In general, and except in the case of public officials acknowledging a fundamental difference between acts and omissions, it is inherently implausible to view the state as simply bound by a set of side-constraints. The state, even on a minimal view of its functions, is at least concerned with the goal of rights enforcement. To suppose therefore that public policy should not be formulated in goal-directed terms leads to an inconsistency with the assumptions on which the state's activity is to be justified. If rights enforcement is seen to be a basic function of the state, then a goal-directed view of public policy automatically follows. To justify their activity public agencies have to maximise some function of rights enforcement.

This conclusion holds despite the apparent counter-examples which might be urged against it. The most obvious of these are cases where competitive rights are exercised by two or more individuals.[12] One of two men may have the right to a pound note which they are both chasing in the wind, provided he reaches it first, without it being the task of a rights' enforcement agency to ensure that one of them gets the note. However, it does not follow from this example that it is wrong to say that the goal of the public agency is maximising rights enforcement, since to suppose that either or both of the men have a right of possession over the note is to misdescribe the rights they have, namely that of appropriation subject to competition. It follows from a correct description of the case that, once someone has appropriated it, then a public agency should maintain his possession. But, before then, provided it regulates the competition, it is performing its enforcement tasks adequately.

Although it is plausible to think of public agencies as maximising some function of rights enforcement, there is no reason why any particular function should be chosen, within the financial and other constraints available to the state. An obvious conflict is whether one should seek to maximise the average level of rights enforcement by minimising the average number of violations or whether one should equalise the risk of rights

---

11 See J. Bennett, 'Whatever the Consequences' *Analysis*, **26**.
12 Cf. H. L. A. Hart, 'Are There Any Natural Rights?' *Philosophical Review*, **64**, pp. 175-91. Reprinted in A. Quinton (ed.) *Political Philosophy* (London: OUP, 1967) p. 57.

violations by maximising a function of equal rights enforcement. This problem occurs regularly in the allocation of police resources to the patrolling of different areas.[13] Wherever variations in crime rates lead to unequal marginal effectiveness of the same police resources the optimum deployment of resources becomes a problem. In particular the conflict between equalising the risk of crime and minimising the average risk of crime means that whatever function one seeks to maximise will involve an implicit choice between those two goals. However, the view that the maximisation of some specified benefit entails the implicit specification of the value of alternative distributions of benefits is clearly false in such cases.

It is equally misleading to say that in the allocation of scarce police resources some people's rights may be over-ridden in order to produce some overall social good. Since the problem of optimum deployment only arises because the means of rights enforcement are scarce relative to the objectives to be achieved, some people will inevitably run the risk of not having their rights enforced. Some mechanism will be needed to decide how to distribute that risk. Once the distribution has been decided, however, it seems only rational to achieve the desired objective in the most effective way possible. This is simply to say, however, that the notion of maximisation refers to the implementation of previously chosen values, and is not itself tied to any values. For this reason the economic theory of choice still retains its value neutrality when applied to public policy decisions.

v

A third set of objections to the proposed decision procedure concerns the difficulties encountered in seeking to institutionalise the approach. It might be urged that the formulation of objectives it requires, with the relevant specification of trade-offs, presupposes a paternalistic set of institutions. The only people who will be able to formulate objectives in this way are full-time public officials, not those citizens who will be affected by the policies which result. Consequently, policy-makers will not simply be deciding on some optimum mix of policies in the light of goals previously specified to them by citizens, but will themselves be in a position to impose their own preferences in the formulation of public policy. This process may not be regarded as undesirable, but it would hardly be compatible with the claim that the proposed model of rational choice was value-free.

In effect judgements about the paternalism of a set of institutions rest on second-order decisions about decisions. In particular they rest on claims about the way in which public policy should be formulated, and the type

---

[13] Cf. C. S. Shoup, 'Standards for Distributing a Free Government Service: Crime Prevention' *Public Finance*, **19**, (1964) pp. 383–92.

of institutions that are appropriate for making central policy decisions. To criticise a set of institutions, including rational choice requirements on a set of institutions, as paternalist is to presuppose a certain schedule of value preferences. In systematising such preferences, therefore, attention needs to be paid to the trade-offs implicit in the criticism. It is perfectly possible to prefer institutions which take decisions with a certain popular style to institutions which have a different style, even though the resulting decisions may be less successful or well-formulated. Yet, while such choices are possible, they seem themselves to involve the same elements that we found fitting the rational choice model for first-order decisions. A choice has to be made between competing objectives. Value has therefore to be attached to the outcomes of these intended objectives, and policies adopted which accord with the relative evaluations which decision-makers have assigned to these outcomes. Since the choices are second-order, some outcomes will be linked to others – by preferring one objective a person is thereby committed to other objectives. Despite these complications, it looks as though the same process of rational choice can encompass the criticisms of paternalist institutions, although it was thought to require some form of paternalism when applied to first-order decisions.

Occasions for constitutional choice rarely arise in practice. So the opportunity for citizens to express democratically their second-order preferences over alternative types of institution are too infrequent to see whether the anti-paternalist outlook is widely shared. Given this problem, one approach is to formulate institutional criticism in terms of the outcome of a hypothetical constitutional contract of the sort developed by Buchanan and Tullock.[14] Here the aim is to hypothesise what choices would be made by citizens who have to make second-order decisions about constitutional arrangements, where the choices are made subject to varying degrees of uncertainty about any particular individual's future constitutional role and function. The intention then is to use the results of this hypothetical exercise to justify or support particular schemes of constitutional criticism or reform. In such an approach, a notion of rational choice must of course be used, since otherwise there is no method of formulating the reasoning leading to the hypothetical contracting parties' converging on a particular set of political institutions. So, in as much as this hypothetical device underlies projects of constitutional criticism, the approach is just as dependent on the notion of rational choice as was the original formulation of the problem in terms of the need to reconcile competing, first-order objectives. At least one approach to constitutional criticism, including the criticism that constitu-

[14] J. M. Buchanan and G. Tullock, *The Calculus of Consent* (Ann Arbor: Univ. of Michigan Press, 1962).

tional arrangements are paternalistic, presupposes therefore the possibility of rational choice among alternative outcomes.

Second-order constitutional choices will range over alternatives, where it is known that the decision-making structure itself will influence the type of decision that will be made. The group maximand, which the process of collective decision-making produces, will itself be influenced by the type of institution in which the decision is made. A particular example of institution affecting maximands in this way occurs in the worker-managed firm. It can be shown that such firms will not have as their maximand an increase in the profitable use of labour, since this goal conflicts with the maximisation of the average income of its members. In the conventional firm the manager has an incentive to take on extra workers up to the point at which their productivity equals the cost of taking them on. Although this marginal productivity rule reduces average incomes, where there are declining returns to scale, it maximises profits which are, in the conventional theory, the explanation for entrepreneurial behaviour. However, there is no reason why workers in a worker-managed firm should maximise profits, since with declining returns to scale the employment of extra workers will reduce the returns per head available for wages. So in practice one finds that worker-managed firms tend either to under-utilise available labour, or impose significantly worse working conditions on new members by comparison with old and established members.[15]

This is merely one example, though a very striking one, of the relationship between institutions and the decisions they produce. Other relationships exist. One important set, for instance, is that between voting rules in a political constitution and the degree of economic redistribution implemented under that constitution. Unlike the case of the worker-managed firm, however, analysis here is much less developed, so that it is difficult to say anything generally meaningful about it. However, whatever relationship exists, it would clearly be relevant to appraise it when considering constitutional choice. So the evidence suggests that there are no grounds for abandoning the economic theory of choice when considering second-order decisions about the institutional relationships of a society. Moreover, there is no reason to think that, within the choice constraints imposed by the particular form of an institution, the economic model of choice provides an inappropriate method for taking decisions. Some principles of public policy may thereby be excluded from consideration in particular cases. But this will be the result of the previously taken institutional decision, not the result of a commitment to techniques of rational choice.

[15] P. J. D. Wiles, *Economic Institutions Compared* (Oxford: Blackwell, 1977) pp. 70–1.

VI

So far the three objections to the economic theory of rational choice among principles have been concerned with the conception of political values required by the theory, or with the difficulties of institutionalising the approach. A further difficulty, however, arises from the notion of rational choice presupposed in the theory, which is sometimes asserted to be defective.

To understand this objection, it is useful to look at the elements of a standard decision problem. Typically such problems have three elements: (1) the set of alternatives open to choice; (2) the relationships that determine the pay-offs as a function of the alternative chosen; (3) the preference ordering among pay-offs. In respect of all three it has been asserted that the classical concept of rational choice makes assumptions which are too strong for the actual information and computational capacities that human beings possess. Not all the alternatives can be known, nor can one estimate reasonably all their probable consequences. Moreover, the classical approach requires the decision-maker to have a preference ordering over all available alternative consequences. By contrast with this 'global rationality of economic man' an account of rationality is needed in which such strong assumptions are not made. Rather than requiring that choices be optimal, we should simply require that they be satisfactory. 'Satisficing' becomes the goal of decision processes.[16]

In one respect at least this objection does not touch upon the thesis of this paper, since that can be stated in a weak form to assert that where the classical model of rational choice is applicable, then no value bias will enter into one's choice simply by the use of that procedure. This revision is not in fact as drastic as it may sound. Its point can be illustrated by a specific example. Since the war British macroeconomic policy has been dominated, until recently, by the inflation/employment trade-off. The aim has been to find an acceptable balance between the rate of inflation and the rate of unemployment. However, one important aspect of this problem has been that the feasible combinations have shifted.[17] For any given rate of inflation a higher level of unemployment was needed to prevent an increase in the rate. It would therefore be a mistake to think that one could formulate one's mix of objectives to cover the whole of the post-war period at one go. Some scope must be given for developing feed-back on the development of the policy, and changing one's objectives as the feasible combinations changed. However, for any given feasible combination it still makes sense to think in global terms, and to ensure that one is making a decision with a complete evaluation of the alternatives.

[16] H. A. Simon, *Models of Man* (New York: Wiley, 1957) pp. 241–73.
[17] S. Brittan, *Steering the Economy* (Harmondsworth: Penguin, 1971) pp. 464–5.

Moreover, there are reasons for thinking that the revised model of rational choice, in which satisficing becomes the goal, is inadequate of itself as an account of choice. To see why, it is useful to introduce an example discussed by Simon.[18] The example is that of an organism searching for food in its environment. In this example Simon suggests that the rational strategy is for the organism to survey within its field of vision for food and when food is sighted to proceed to it and eat, leaving time to rest before the next occasion on which the need to eat arises. There should, by implication, be no need to determine an optimum sequence of eating routines or make any other choices than that of proceeding to the closest batch of food.

The trouble with this prescription for rational choice is that it is unable to cope with situations in which genuine problems of choice arise. Rather than present an account of choice, it offers an account of behaviour based simply on a patttern of stimulus and response, in which once the object of wanting is sighted the organism behaves in a specified way. It is clear, however, that such procedures cannot cope with situations in which genuine choice arises. For example, if there is the slightest suspicion that batches of the food are contaminated then a choice will have to be made about whether simply to eat the food or whether to test for contamination, possibly at the loss of the food itself. In other words a theory of rational choice must take account of agents as information processors and evaluators as well as information gatherers.

The point of the satisficing model which I take to be well established is that it is not always possible, or desirable in view of the time and energy it consumes, to rise above a sequence of decisions to check whether the best decision is being made at any one time in the light of the other decisions which are to be taken. However, it does not follow from this truth that it is never appropriate or useful to rise above a process of incremental decision-making to see whether one is taking a consistent series of decisions. It is widely recognised now in public policy that the impact of each government programme is not discrete and self-contained but inter-related with other programmes.[19] Clearly, decisions under the social security programme will have an impact on the personal social services, and these in turn will be related to decisions in housing and education. Because these programmes are institutionally separate, with the policy-makers in each field located in different departments, it does not make sense for the inter-relationships to be examined continually. However, neither does it make sense not to take a global view on occasions, and within the limited resources available to examine the inter-relationships of policy. Since problems like maintaining the quality of urban environments do not come separately, there is no reason always to separate the review of policies that

[18] *Op. cit.* p. 262.
[19] Cf. Central Policy Review Staff, *A Joint Framework for Social Policies* (London: HMSO, 1975).

ALBERT WEALE

are directed to those problems. And in this process it is useful to have a clear statement of the relative importance of the objectives one is trying to pursue, in order to avoid the wasteful deployment of resources. The occasions on which this exercise of determining relative weightings can be carried out may be infrequent. There are, however, reasons for thinking that frequency in this case is not an adequate measure of how valuable the procedure can be.

VII

In conclusion I should like to mention one problem with developing the economic model further in this field. In what I have said so far, the idea has been implicit that policy-makers are choosing between certain options. No allowance has been made for the fact that choices have to be made not only between intended outcomes but also between objectives where there is some uncertainty about what outcomes are likely to result. In considering how far the idea can be applied to the study of public policy, therefore, some attention should be paid to the question of how far uncertainty affects the nature of the decision process. One important respect in which the model is changed, for example, is that choices are no longer made between specified alternatives, but between outcomes with a probability range. Some attention has therefore to be paid to the value presuppositions implicit in the criteria for choosing among risky alternatives. This discussion would clearly involve the controversial question of what constitutes a rational decision under uncertainty or risk. For that reason alone it belongs not with an attempt to construct the outlines of the economic approach to political decisions, but instead to a particular theory of such an approach. At present I wish merely to maintain the theses I have sought to develop in this paper. The economic theory of rational choice offers a coherent approach to the analysis of conflicts in public policy objectives. Alternative account of political principles which suggest that they are either incommensurable or have a non-maximisation structure are inconsistent or irrelevant. There is no value bias in the use of the technique for first-order decisions, though the use of the technique may reflect the bias of different institutional methods of making collective decisions, which may themselves be the subject of second-order choices. Even if the technique cannot be applied continuously to separate public policies, its use on occasion may be a sensible way to avoid wasteful duplication of government effort. In short, the economic theory of rational choice, when used as a decision-procedure in cases of public policy conflict, does what few other intellectual techniques do: it produces both light and fruit.

Informational analysis of moral principles*

AMARTYA SEN

This paper is primarily concerned with developing a structure for informational analysis of moral principles. This includes analysing (i) the influence of moral principles on the usability of available information, as well as (ii) the influence of availability of information on the applicability and acceptability of moral principles. The paper is motivated by the belief, which is defended, that the informational perspective provides a useful approach to the understanding and use of moral principles.

While the presented structure is quite general, the moral principles with which this paper is chiefly concerned are those relating to what is often called 'social morality' (e.g. the pursuit of social justice rather than of personal abstinence). The illustrations reflect this emphasis.

1 MORAL PRINCIPLES AS INFORMATIONAL CONSTRAINTS

A moral principle, in its application, uses certain types of information and ignores others. Concentrating first on the latter, it is possible to view a moral principle as a requirement to *exclude* the use of certain types of information. These types of information are excluded in the sense of not being permitted to have any influence on judgements that fall within the scope of that principle. And when the principle is 'complete' in that its domain is wide enough to cover all the judgements under consideration, then the information in question is rendered totally 'inadmissible'.

Consider, for example, the utilitarian rule for ranking alternative social states or outcomes. This 'outcome utilitarianism' is a common feature of different versions of complex utilitarian structures, e.g. 'act utilitarianism' and 'rule utilitarianism'. The rule that social state x must be at least as good

* I am most grateful to Professor Richard Wollheim and other members of the Philosophy Department of University College, London, for their very helpful comments and criticisms of three lectures given there during January and February 1977, based primarily on an earlier draft of this paper. The version of this paper presented at the Thyssen Philosophy Group meeting in September 1977 contained a 'Technical Note' in the form of an appendix, which included proofs of some assertions made in the text, and also some additional material. For reasons of space the Note has been deleted.

as social state y if and only if the personal welfare sum in x is at least as large as the personal welfare sum in y can be applied to any pair of social states. The informational exclusion that this rule implies can be broken down into a number of separate exclusions, each corresponding to some principle with a narrower scope. Each of these exclusions can also be deduced independently from other – more limited – principles. Here is a list of types of information, among others, that are excluded from use by utilitarianism in ranking a pair of social states x, y. More limited principles that achieve the individual exclusions are mentioned in brackets; they have been chosen from the literature on collective choice theory,[1] and these limited principles are, of course, all satisfied by the utilitarian grand principle.

1. Any information about the alternative social states going beyond their description, e.g., the history of how the current choice situation came about ('end-statism').

2. Any information concerning social states other than x and y ('independence of irrelevant alternatives').

3. Any information going beyond the personal welfares in the social states x and y ('welfarism', a stronger version of 'neutrality').

4. Any information about the identity of persons vis-à-vis the personal welfare functions, viz, who has which welfare function ('anonymity').

5. Any information on personal identity specifying whether a person enjoying a certain welfare level in x and a person enjoying a particular welfare level in y happen to be the same person – no matter who ('strong anonymity', going beyond 'anonymity').

6. Any information about the welfare of any person who happens to be indifferent between x and y ('elimination of the influence of indifferent individuals', involving a type of 'separability').

7. Any information regarding interpersonal comparison of welfare *levels* as opposed to the comparative magnitudes of their welfare *differences* between x and y ('cardinal unit comparability').[2]

In applying the utilitarian rule of ranking social states, none of these types of information can have any role whatsoever.[3] Furthermore, if the utilitarian rule is to be applied to all problems of morally ranking social states, then

---

[1] For technical presentations and discussion of these and related conditions, see Sen (1977).

[2] As was noted before, this is not a complete list. For example, restriction 7 can be strengthened since utilitarianism is concerned only with the sum of the differences and not with their exact distribution. Note also that the restrictions are not all independent. Restriction 3 implies restrictions 1 and 2, and with a slight modification restriction 5 implies restriction 4.

[3] This does not, of course, imply that the *phenomena* that lie behind the inadmissible information cannot have any effect on the judgements. They indeed can have indirect effects through their influence on variables such that information on them is admissible. What is asserted is that no judgements will be affected by the *information* concerning these phenomena as such.

all of this information will be inadmissible evidence in any judgement on the relative position of social states.[4] While the principles identified with respect to these respective exclusions are, in fact, typically proposed and justified on simple ethical grounds, they have the effect of guaranteeing the corresponding informational constraints.[5]

The utility-based version of the 'maximin rule' related to Rawls's 'difference principle' also has the effect of imposing constraints 1 to 6 fully.[6] But it replaces restriction 7 by ruling out instead the use of information regarding welfare *differences* ('ordinal level comparability', instead of 'cardinal unit comparability').[7]

In contrast, the principles of rights based on the Marxian theory of value, including the moral rejection of 'exploitation', remove constraints 1, 2 and 3, but involve a tightening of the other constraints concerning the use of personal welfare information.[8] Nozick's (1974) 'historical' theory of rights would do the same, but there are differences in the types of current and historical information that would be allowed to influence the judgements (viz., a class of 'entitlement' information dealing with ownership, production and transactions – including inheritance – as opposed to dated labour vectors for Marx).

2   INFORMATIONAL AXIOMATIZATION OF MORAL PRINCIPLES

Informational constraints, then, can be derived from moral principles. But can moral principles be derived from purely informational constraints also? In a formal sense this is an impossibility. No matter how tight the information constraints are to derive a certain principle p, there are at least two other principles that are not excluded, viz., (i) recommending the exact opposite of what principle p does (anti-p), and (ii) recommending that all

---

[4] Utilitarianism can be used also to rank *actions* or *institutions* (as opposed to ordering social states only), and this would involve additional informational constraints of a somewhat different type (see section 8 below).

[5] Some of these principles – and others – act as additional informational constraints when combined with each other; on such compound constraints, see Sen (1977).

[6] This does not apply to Rawls's (1971) own use of maximin in his 'difference principle', since he introduced the convention of judging personal well-beings in terms of holdings of primary goods. In this sense, the 'difference principle' is non-welfaristic, violating restriction 3, but it can be seen as imposing additional constraints ruling out the use of direct psychological or behaviourist information on personal welfare levels.

[7] See Sen (1970, 1974b) and d'Aspremont and Gevers (1977). Note that this constraint and Restriction 7 are as close to being *frankly* informational constraints as any we have got in the list.

[8] However, for a more 'mature' stage of socialism, Marx (1875) himself proposed the principle of distribution according to 'needs', concentrating more on welfare information than on rights based on labour contributions, which he described as a form of 'bourgeois rights' (pp. 21–3).

alternatives be accepted as being equally good (universal indifference). Anti-p has exactly the same information requirement as p, and universal indifference has no information requirement at all. With the same informational constraints as imposed by utilitarianism (including restrictions 1–7 above), the anti-utilitarian rule of *minimising* the utility sum can be used equally effectively. And the possibility of adopting the 'lazy' morality of declaring *all* alternatives to be *equally* acceptable is always present without making any informational demand.

Thus, the relationship between moral principles and informational constraints is, strictly speaking, a one-way connection. However, the informational constraints may narrow the field of moral principles so severely that some relatively innocuous non-informational axioms may lead to an axiomatic derivation of the moral principle p. For example, for particular configurations of personal welfare values, both the anti-utilitarian principle and the universal indifference rule are inconsistent with the Pareto Principle (viz., violate the rule that if everyone is better off in x than in y, then x must be socially ranked above y).[9] Informational axioms may not be able to do the whole job, but they can do most of it, so that some simple non-informational axiom (or axioms) can complete the derivation.

There is, however, no compelling reason for entertaining a general preference for using informational constraints over other types of restrictions in the axiomatic derivation of a principle. It is a matter of judgement as to how best to combine informational restrictions with other conditions to arrive at a particular principle eliminating all its rivals.[10] The effect of emphasising informational constraints is to draw attention to a relatively practical consideration, viz., what information is, in fact, available. This is notably more sensible in some contexts than in others.

It may be remarked that there can be quite distinct motivations underlying the use of informational constraints in axiomatic derivations. In an axiomatisation aimed at presenting the 'best face' of a social principle, using an informational constraint that is 'natural' in the particular context has an obvious merit. On the other hand, in presenting a 'warts and all' view, there is a good deal to be said for using informational constraints that blatantly throw away obviously relevant and available information (provided, of course, the constraints happen, in fact, to be *implied* by the

---

[9] I am, in fact, not persuaded that the Pareto principle is as innocuous as it looks, and have indeed argued to the contrary (in Sen (1970, Chapter 6, and 1976)), but it is certainly among the most widely accepted conventions.

[10] For examples of various mixtures of informational and non-informational axioms in axiomatic derivation of social welfare rules, see Sen (1970, 1977), Hammond (1976, 1977), d'Aspremont and Gevers (1977), Maskin (1978), Deschamps and Gevers (1978), and Roberts (1976), among other contributions.

principle). For understanding a principle, axiomatisations with both types of motivation seem to have something to contribute.

Finally, it may be noted that the typical 'impossibility theorems', starting with Arrow's (1951) classic General Possibility Theorem, are also based on combining informational constraints – explicitly or (more often) by implication – with non-informational requirements. The relatively narrow class of principles that manage to make do with constrained information are all shown to violate the mild properties of 'reasonableness' that are also demanded, and so one ends up empty-handed.

In Arrow's particular case, information on personal welfare is admitted in the particularly poor form of giving no usable interpersonal comparison information, nor any cardinal information of welfare differences even for a given person. This is combined with *implicitly* ruling out (through the combination of unrestricted domain, independence, and the weak Pareto principle) the possibility of using virtually any information other than that of personal welfares, coming very close to 'welfarism'. Then some very mild conditions of reasonableness eliminate the rules that could live in such an informational famine. One achievement – among others – of Arrow's remarkable theorem is the elegant elimination of the usability of various types of information by combining principles that apparently demand other – rather mild – things, posing a challenging problem of 'who done it'.[11]

3 INFORMATIONAL DEPENDENCE, ADEQUACY AND EFFICIENCY

The discussion in the first two sections has concentrated primarily on the influence of moral principles on the use of available information. Attention may now be shifted to the influence of availability of information on the effectiveness and acceptability of principles as well as the interactions of the influences involved (sections 3 to 7).

Consider the problem of applying a number of moral principles to ranking a set X of alternative social states. The ranking need not be a complete one even with all the information that one might seek: some principles can rank some pairs but not others. (For example, the principle that sex discrimination must be stopped leaves unranked any set of social states in which such discriminations are equally present.) A principle that can rank all pairs of alternative social states from X given the necessary information may be called a *complete* principle for X. Utilitarianism is such a complete principle. So is maximin, or the lexicographic maximin rule (even though the 'difference principle' in Rawls's (1971) system is not,

[11] See Sen (1977).

because of the constraint imposed on its applicability by the principle of liberty).[12]

Even a complete principle may not, however, generate a complete ranking of X since the information may be inadequate to rank all the social states vis-à-vis each other. For example, if no information regarding interpersonal comparisons of welfare is available (all welfare comparisons being confined to the same person), then the utilitarian rule will be able to place one social state above another if and only if the first is Pareto superior to the second, i.e. if and only if someone is better off and no one worse off in the first state than in the second.[13]

It is reasonable to want that as more information becomes available, the ranking generated by a principle could expand but will certainly never contract. This requirement of *monotonicity* will be satisfied if an assertion is not made until there is enough information to make the assertion; a pair will be ranked one way or the other *only when* the available information is sufficient to order the two by the use of that principle.

Given monotonicity, the ranking produced by any principle with complete information is as extensive as it can ever be, and this ranking R_p will be called the *full ranking* of X by principle p. As noted before, this full ranking may or may not be complete.

It is, of course, perfectly possible for a principle to generate its full ranking even when there are obvious gaps in the information that one could seek. Indeed, for each principle only certain types of information are needed, and the absence of the rest makes no difference at all.

The information available is *adequate* for a principle p applied to a set X if it is sufficient to generate the full ranking R_p. *Many* alternative information availabilities may have this characteristic of adequacy for a given principle. If the available information is adequate and furthermore if there is no other adequate information situation that contains strictly less information, then the available information may be called *efficient* for that principle. Informational efficiency is a rather important concept since comparisons of principles in terms of acceptability is not independent of their respective information requirements, and efficiency characterises the least amounts of information that are adequate.

The idea of 'complete' information is itself an artifact of convenience, since one can always think of more factual questions to ask. The line is drawn rather arbitrarily in any given problem bearing in mind the set of principles

[12] Rawls (1971), in fact, asserts the 'priority' of liberty on the basis of the acceptability of this priority in the hypothetical original position (pp. 541–8). For a powerful disputation of the argument leading to this assertion, see Hart (1973). However, even when the principle of liberty does not have priority, the scope of the difference principle will be limited by its competing claim.

[13] See Theorem 7*1 in Sen (1970, p. 107).

under examination. The full ranking of a principle is taken to be a generated ranking such that no additional information could extend it in any way. For obvious reasons our concern will be not so much with completeness of information but with its adequacy and efficiency.

4 CONSISTENCY AND CONFLICTS

For a moral principle to be treated as consistent it must always generate rankings that have some consistency property. A requirement of *internal consistency* is that each generated ranking must be 'transitive' (if x is at least as good as y, and y at least as good as z, then x must be at least as good as z), and 'reflexive' (each x must be regarded as at least as good as itself – a condition that is, I suppose, better regarded as a requirement of sanity rather than of consistency in any sophisticated sense). Formally, therefore, each such ranking must be what is called a quasi-ordering: transitive but not necessarily complete.

A requirement of *external consistency* may also be imposed dealing with the 'compatibility' (i.e. no contradiction – direct or indirect) of the different rankings generated by the same principle under different assumptions of informational availability. The different rankings must be consistent *with each other*. This is an important requirement, but it can be shown that monotonicity and internal consistency together *imply* external consistency.

Finally, there is the problem of consistency *between* different moral principles. Two principles are *fully consistent* over X if the full rankings generated by the two are compatible with each other. This could be because the two principles have non-overlapping domains so that they cannot be in conflict over any X (e.g. 'when there is food shortage it should be equally shared through a system of rationing' and 'when there is food surplus some should be stored for future generations'). Or alternatively, their domains may be potentially overlapping, but over the particular set X of social states in question, this overlap may not occur (e.g. 'sex discrimination should be abolished' and 'racial discrimination should not exist' may not conflict in a particular choice where cases of sex discrimination always go hand in hand with cases of racial discrimination).

Even when two principles are not fully consistent for a given X, they may be so for a particular informational situation. Consider the utilitarian principle and the lexicographic version of maximin (leximin, for short).[14] With no information on interpersonal comparisons of personal welfares,

---

[14] Leximin declares x to be better than y if and only if *either* the worst off person in x is better off than the worst off person in y, *or* the worst off persons in x and y are equally well off but the second-worst off is better off in x, *or* the worst off persons are equally well off in x and y, and so are the second-worst off persons, but the third-worst off is better off in x, *or*...and so on. See Sen (1970, p. 138).

both generate a ranking exactly the same as the Pareto relation, failing to rank any pair of social states involving a conflict of interest. There is clearly no conflict between the two principles in this case.

Second, given information on interpersonal comparisons of levels only without comparability of differences (i.e. ordinal level comparability), leximin generates a complete ordering of X but the utilitarian rule generates only a partial ordering (formally the 'Suppes relation'),[15] which is subsumed by the complete ordering produced by leximin. No conflict again.

Third, if there is information for comparisons of units of personal welfares so that magnitudes of gains and losses can be commonly scaled, but absolute levels of personal welfare of different persons could not be compared (cardinal unit comparability), then the utilitarian rule will generate a complete ordering while leximin will simply produce the Pareto relation which will be subsumed by the utilitarian complete ordering. In none of these cases, therefore, will there be a conflict between utilitarianism and leximin. Conflicts could occur only when the information structure is richer with respect to *both* types of interpersonal comparisons of welfare.

Similarly, if information on interpersonal comparisons is limited, conflicts between welfaristic principles such as utilitarianism and leximin on the one hand and non-welfaristic principles (including historical ones) may become rather rare, and the same applies when non-welfare information (including historical data) happen to be rather limited.

The tradition of implicitly assuming complete information and considering the possible incompatibility of the full rankings of different principles tends to detect conflicts when one may or may not exist. When two principles have rather different information requirements (as given by efficient information sets), then the fullness of the ranking of one has no implication that the ranking generated by the other must be full also. In the absence of such a *primitive conflict* involving subsumed information sets, one principle can generate a full ranking without necessarily running into conflict with the other even when *full consistency* is violated. It is easily checked that for the usual 'rival' principles, primitive conflicts are very rare indeed.

The absence of conflicts between principles can represent one of three distinct possibilities:

(i) the nature of the principles are such that their domains can *never* overlap;

(ii) while the domains are not always non-overlapping, they happen not

---

[15] According to the 'Suppes relation', x is at least as good as y if there is a one-to-one correspondence between the persons such that everyone in x is at least as well off as his corresponding person in y (see Suppes (1966), and Sen (1970, chapter 9)). This subsumes the Pareto relation: everyone in x being at least as well off as himself in y.

to overlap over X, or, even if they do, their respective full rankings are, in fact, compatible;

(iii) while the full rankings over X are not compatible, the actual rankings in the given information situation are so.

5 METARANKINGS

In an earlier paper (Sen (1974a)), it was argued that moral views could be expressed more adequately by specifying a ranking of rankings of social states than by simply selecting one particular rankings of social states.[16] This device of 'metarankings' will be used now. The different rankings generated by the different principles for any given availability of information will be ranked in terms of the metaranking reflecting overall judgements of their acceptability.

The metaranking Q will be taken to be a quasi-ordering (transitive but not necessarily complete) of all possible quasi-orderings of the set X of social states under consideration. Many – indeed most – of the quasi-orderings of X would, in fact, be incomplete, and in ranking them it would have to be assumed that choosing such an incomplete quasi-ordering implies accept-ance of not being able to say anything on the relative merits of unranked pairs. A more complete ranking, thus, has an advantage *if* it articulates the real moral preferences, but if it goes counter to those preferences a less complete ranking may, in fact, be preferred since saying nothing may be better than asserting wrong things.

There is, therefore, no presumption that a more complete ranking is better. While more information leads to an extension rather than contraction of the ranking generated by a principle (the monotonicity property), there is thus no guarantee that more information will make the ranking produced by a principle more attractive. It would, of course, be a sad characteristic of a principle to generate worse rankings as more and more information became available. A principle such that its full ranking is worse than some less-than-full ranking generated by it with limited information may be described as being *negatively inclined*. In contrast, a *positively inclined* principle is one for which not only does the above not take place, but its full ranking is, in fact, at least as good as every ranking generated by it with incomplete information. (These two do not cover all possibilities, since there could be the intermediate case of the full ranking being non-rankable vis-à-vis some less-than-full ranking.)

There is nothing at all perverse in a principle being negatively inclined. Consider, for example, a moral system that is primarily 'Rawlsian' in the

---

[16] For critical discussions of the proposed framework, see Watkins (1974) and Baier (1977), and the replies that follow.

apocryphal sense of being geared towards utility-based 'leximin' – indeed inducing a metaranking the top element of which is the leximin order. Let the principle under examination be the utilitarian rule. The full utilitarian ranking is not much valued, since it makes lots of wrong placings as seen from the 'Rawlsian' perspective. However, if the information on inter-personal comparisons of welfare happens to be of the ordinal level comparability type, then the utilitarian rule will simply generate the Suppes quasi-ordering. This may well be valued more in the 'Rawlsian' system than the utilitarian complete ordering, since the Suppes quasi-ordering is a subrelation of the leximin ordering. Then utilitarianism is a negatively inclined principle in the 'Rawlsian' moral system.

However, while the Suppes quasi-ordering may be superior to the utilitarian full ranking in the 'Rawlsian' system, it must clearly be inferior to the complete leximin ordering. So while more information may have a negative effect on the use of the particular principle of utilitarianism, more information is far from harmful, in this case, for the *set* of principles as a whole, since it becomes possible to obtain the full leximin order from it. A set of principles is a *positively inclined set* if, for every less-than-full ranking generated by some principle, there is a full ranking of some principle – not necessarily of the same principle – that is at least as good. It is a characteristic of the richness of a set of principles that it be positively inclined, even though such rich *sets* would typically include negatively inclined *principles*. (With a 'Rawlsian' moral metaranking, it is, I suppose, a reasonable condition of 'richness' to include the 'Rawlsian' best, viz., leximin.)

6 METARANKING INFORMATION AND ALTERNATIVE MOTIVATIONS

A metaranking does, of course, have informational requirements also. It may, therefore, appear a bit absurd to rank rankings derived under alternative assumptions of informational availability by using a metaranking the informational requirement of which is left unspecified. The fact is that various alternative approaches are possible depending on the motivation of the exercise.

In judging the rankings generated by a set of principles under given informational availabilities, one approach is to use exactly that much information and no more. The metaranking based on the same information may be usefully employed to judge principles without any greater knowledge of facts but possibly using more sophisticated values than the principles in question may allow. Some principles are hardly more than simple slogans, and others – while more sophisticated – may still incorporate a great deal of informational wastefulness.[17] These weaknesses come out most sharply in a limited information situation, and alternative principles could be judged in terms of their performance without assuming any more information than has gone into the generation of rankings based on these principles.

An alternative approach is to assume more complete information in the formulation of the metaranking than in applying the principles to produce rankings of X.[18] In this approach the judgements are made with greater information to see how the principles fare with less: sight is used to check how the blinds perform. This is really in the nature of an experiment, applying the principles with deliberately less information than happens to be available to get an idea of the performance of principles under low-information conditions, which may, in fact, arise on other occasions. One can enrich the range of experiments by taking up hypothetical situations with data specification in great detail and then seeing how the different principles fare when some of the data are deliberately withheld. In *judging* relative performance, all the data may be taken to be available.

7 THE ACCEPTABLE AND THE BEST

The set of principles generates a corresponding set of rankings of X for any given information situation. If such a ranking is regarded as no worse than any other ranking in the set, according to the metaranking, then the principle generating that ranking is regarded as being *acceptable* for that information situation relating to X. There may, of course, be several such acceptable principles between which the metaranking is unable to discriminate (since the metaranking is a quasi-ordering and may be *neither* 'strict', i.e. antisymmetric, *nor* complete).

A principle may be called *self-supporting* if it is acceptable in every efficient information situation for that principle. If a principle is not self-supporting then even in some situation that is informationally exactly 'cut out' for it – being adequate and not wastefully so – it will still end up being rejected.

A principle that is acceptable with complete information, i.e. with information that is adequate for all principles, is *maximal*. If, in addition, that principle generates a full ranking that is not merely not worse than any

[17] It can be argued that the muteness of traditional welfare economics in making welfare comparisons arises largely from its use of principles that are based on utility information only, combined with the assumption of non-existence of most of such information. The consequence is not merely the inability to use utility information beyond some very elementary statements, but also the failure to make judgements based on non-utility information, which can have a fair amount of appeal.
[18] It is, of course, also possible to assume *less* information than used in the generation of rankings by principles, but I have not been able to think of a good reason for doing such an exercise.

other full ranking but in fact at least as good as all such full rankings, then the principle is *optimal*. The distinction between maximality and optimality arises from the possibility that the metaranking can be strictly incomplete: a ranking can, then, be acceptable by virtue of its not being 'beaten' by any other ranking even though it is not agreed that it is at least as good as all the others. It can be proved that if there is any optimal principle at all, then *all* maximal principles must be also optimal.[19]

Maximality, including the special case of optimality, is concerned with a situation in which there is no informational limitation. It is often taken for granted that it is such full-information comparisons that bring out the true 'ethical' appeal of a principle. There is indeed a sense in which a maximal principle – and more clearly an optimal principle – could be described as being ethically 'best'. But a principle being best in this sense does not guarantee its being acceptable in a particular information situation, for it may be eminently rejectable given the information at hand. The usefulness of principles has to be judged in terms of the informational context, and here the best can indeed be the enemy of the acceptable.

It can also be shown that a principle that is not self-supporting cannot be best (in the sense of being maximal or optimal) for a positively inclined set of principles. Being self-supporting is, thus, also passing a qualifying round to maximality (or optimality). But, of course, a principle that is not self-supporting could still be acceptable if information happens to be particularly limited.

Finally, tests of acceptability can be altered by permitting the possibility of applying *combined* principles when they have no conflict with each other. This possibility of combining exists not only when the principles are *fully consistent* in the sense that their full rankings are compatible, but also when their full rankings might conflict but the rankings generated by them in a given information situation happen to be compatible. If such combined principles are then admitted in the set of principles to be compared in a given information situation, these *enriched comparisons* may considerably alter the acceptability of pure principles. Indeed, a pure principle such that the ranking generated by it is not worse than any other pure rankings may now get dominated by some combined principle the ranking produced by which is superior. The notions of maximal and optimal principles are similarly modified when such enriched comparisons are permitted, though in this case the combinable principles must be fully consistent.

The possibility of combining is particularly important when some of the principles have a very narrow domain but are very persuasive over these domains. They may rank rather low in the context of ordering a much wider domain included in X, because of being silent on a great many comparisons.

---

[19] This result is a consequence of Lemma 1*d in Sen (1970, pp. 11–12).

But since they are likely to be compatible with other principles with a narrow scope dealing with other types of comparisons, combining them may be both feasible as well as effective in generating highly valued rankings of X.

8 STATES AND ACTIONS

The discussion so far has been entirely about ranking alternative social states. But an exactly similar analysis can be applied to ranking a set of actions as well. The principles in question could be those dealing with actions, generating rankings of a set X of actions. The metaranking will rank the rankings of the action set. The information in question will deal with all aspects of the actions that might conceivably be relevant to judge them, dealing with consequences of actions but also with any other aspects that could influence judgements on the choice of actions. The notions of informational adequacy and efficiency as well as of acceptability, self-support, maximality, optimality, etc., would remain unaffected with the alternatives in X redefined to be actions rather than social states.

It may, however, be relevant to ask in the context of this reinterpretation as to whether the notion of consistency of a principle should not be modified. Indeed, it could be argued that while a binary relation is natural for comparing the moral worth of social states, the proper concept for assessing a set of alternative actions is that of a *choice function* (specifying a non-empty subset of acceptable alternatives in each non-empty set of actions chosen from the universal set X). This translation can certainly be done and the concepts used could be correspondingly adapted, though I shall not attempt to do this here.

It is, however, worth remarking that certain fairly elementary conditions of consistency imposed on a choice function tend to make it representable by a binary relation with the standard regularity properties. Thus the difference between the choice function approach and that of binary relations is not altogether clear, and much depends on how we assess those conditions that yield binariness.[20]

[20] The literature on this is vast. In addition to the investigation of conditions that are necessary and sufficient for representing a choice function by a binary relation and for guaranteeing that the relation has certain specified regularity properties, there is also the more basic problem of *interpretation* of a binary relation 'derived' from a choice function. Alternative ways of 'derivation' exist; for interesting examples, see Hansson (1968), Herzberger (1973), Kanger (1976) and Schwartz (1976). This remains an important open question for the formal structure of informational analysis of moral judgements, especially of actions.

9 WELFARISM, CONSEQUENTIALISM AND END-STATISM

One type of informational constraint that was referred to in Section 1 was given by 'welfarism', whereby in ranking social states all information other than those about the welfares of the persons involved are excluded from use. This is a common characteristic of much of traditional welfare economics, and applies to such diverse principles as the utilitarian rule and leximin. I have tried to argue elsewhere (viz., Sen (1970, 1977)) that welfarism cannot even begin to accommodate values of liberty (such as freedom from interference in certain 'personal' matters), nor can it capture some of the important notions of egality (such as 'equal pay for equal work'). A welfaristic principle will have no direct use for the non-welfare information that is available, despite their relevance to these values.

Since utilitarianism and leximin have also been criticised recently for their end-state characteristics (see Nozick (1974)) and their consequentialism (see Williams (1973)[21]), it is useful to enquire how welfarism relates to end-statism and consequentialism.

Utility information about the individuals involved is only a part of the total information about end-states, so that an exclusive reliance on the data on personal welfares or utilities in these states implies an exclusive reliance on end-state data, but not the other way round. In this sense welfarism is informationally more restrictive than end-statism applied to evaluation of outcomes, and welfarism can be disputed without questioning the reliance on end-state data.

It might appear that a similar contrast must hold between consequentialism and welfarism, since consequences on personal welfares must be included among the total consequences of an action. But, strictly speaking, consequentialism and welfarism have no connection with each other at all, since the former is concerned with judging actions (and institutions, laws, practices, etc.), while the latter is aimed at ranking social states. The statements

(i) actions must be judged exclusively in terms of social states resulting from them, and

(ii) social states must be judged exclusively in terms of personal welfares in those states,

do not imply anything about each other. Welfarism is an informational restriction on the problem of ordering states (with which we started) and

---

[21] Bernard Williams is, in fact, concerned primarily with utilitarianism, though his general critique of consequentialism would apply to leximin as well. Since Rawls's theory of justice involved a great deal more than leximin, as was pointed out earlier, the question as to whether that theory is consequentialist or not is quite a different issue.

consequentialism that on the problem of ordering actions (which was introduced in the last section). Of course, if we were to assert both (i) and (ii), then actions too would be required to be judged only in terms of their personal welfare consequences. Indeed, utilitarianism asserts both and is thus both welfaristic and consequentialist,[22] and thus in that moral approach the two characteristics are combined. (However, when we characterised utilitarianism as a principle for ranking social states in section 1 – what was called 'outcome utilitarianism' – there was no occasion to go into its consequentialist aspects.)

An illustration might bring out the contrasts. Suppose we are told in comparing two social states x and y that the personal welfare numbers of the two persons involved, viz., 1 and 2, are $(6, 2)$ in x and $(5, 4)$ in y.[23] Utilitarianism would prefer y to x. So would maximin and leximin. So would virtually any standard criterion of 'equity' since person 1 is better off than 2 *no matter whether* they are in x or in y (2 being the worst-off person in both situations),[24] added to the fact that 1's loss in moving to y from x is small in comparison with 2's gain.

So far nothing at all has been said about the nature of x and y in any respect other than information concerning personal welfare values. A non-welfaristic principle may demand more information before proceeding to rank x and y. Consider two alternative interpretations of x and y. Interpretation A is that person 1 is rich while 2 is poor, and x is a situation without an income tax while y is one where rich 1 is taxed for some welfare programme benefiting poor 2. Interpretation B is that 2 is a miserable torturer always unhappy but less so when he can torture, while 1 is a resilient visionary who suffers of course when tortured, but who is kept buoyant by the vision of the future to come. In this case, x stands for both being free and y represents 1 being tortured by 2. While 1 is worse off under y than under x, he is better off than that miserable wreck 2 both in x as well as in y.

Suppose we agree that given those welfare numbers, the alternative of taxation is superior to non-taxation. Are we then under an obligation to

---

[22] Bernard Williams (1973) describes utilitarianism as a case of 'eudaimonistic consequentialism', eudaimonism being the principle of regarding 'the desirable feature of actions is that they should increase or maximize people's happiness' (p. 79). Note also that 'eudaimonism', on this interpretation, is not the same as welfarism since it too is concerned with judging actions rather than social states.

[23] Assumptions regarding measurability and interpersonal comparability should also be specified (see Sen (1970)). If we choose cardinality with full interpersonal comparability, these numbers are unique except that we can take a positive affine transformation of the entire set of numbers. None of the arguments that follow is affected by such a transformation.

[24] Cf. Hammond's (1976) 'Equity axiom' which is a strengthened generalisation of the 'Weak Equity Axiom' used in Sen (1973).

accept that the alternative of torture is also superior to non-torture? This is indeed so under welfarism.[25] In the welfaristic vision the two comparisons are identical, since they involve the same personal welfare magnitudes. But clearly other things might be relevant that do not operate in the same way in the two cases. Values that accept the right to freedom from torture may not assert any immunity from taxation.

If now a 'discriminating' judgement is made (taxation yes, torture no), and welfarism is violated, would this lead to any violation of end-statism? None at all. The different judgements under the two cases still relate to information about the end-states, e.g. whether y stands for taxation or torture. So there is no need here to go outside the end-state framework.

This also raises the more general question as to whether libertarian values require the rejection of an end-state approach. They clearly must if libertarian values are to embrace property rights that can be decided only on the basis of historical facts (e.g. legitimate inheritance in Nozick's (1974) entitlement theory). Or the right to receive the 'value' of one's labour (including 'dated' labour), as under some interpretations of the Marxian system. But what about the more traditional values of personal liberty, e.g. freedom from interference of movement, reading, speech, etc.? Acceptance of the special status of such freedoms in matters that are 'personal' would certainly violate welfarism,[26] but there is no obvious conflict with end-statism as such. Interferences with movements, reading, speech, etc., are just as much a part of the end-state as are the personal welfares and illfares caused by such interferences.

Turning now to consequentialism, how the states x and y are ranked vis-à-vis each other under the two interpretations has no *necessary* bearing on whether consequentialism is accepted. For anyone concerned with his action in this case, there are two quite distinct questions: (i) 'How should I, as an observer, rank the states as outcomes (including descriptions of my actions if any that form a part of that state)?' (ii) 'How should I act?' For welfarism, the answer to question (i) will be: by taking account just of the personal welfare values, without discriminating, say, between whether these welfares or illfares are due to taxation or torture. No answer to question (ii) has yet been given in this. For consequentialism, the answer to question (ii) is: by taking account just of the answer to question (i) and by acting accordingly. No answer to question (i) is implied by this.

---

[25] Strictly speaking, this will be the case only if the two pairs of social states occur in the same list X. There is no difficulty in enriching the descriptions so that this happens, retaining the same personal welfare numbers. Two types of contrasts can be easily embedded in two pairwise comparisons from the same set of social states X.

[26] Indeed, it even leads to contradiction with allegedly the least controversial social welfare principle which happens to be welfaristic in a limited way, viz., the Pareto principle, for any social decision function with unrestricted domain; see Sen (1970, 1976).

Welfarism and consequentialism are, thus, quite independent of each other on this interpretation. I have not asserted that this is the only meaning of consequentialism that could be found in the literature: it is certainly one meaning that *is* found.

There *is*, clearly, the possibility of distinguishing between the information that is relevant to judging actions (and similarly institutions, practices, etc.), and the information that is relevant to judging states that result from such actions (and institutions, etc.). Consequentialism, as interpreted here, asserts that the two informational demands must be identical.

Distinctions between different approaches to moral issues can be re-examined in the light of investigating the information sought and the context in which such information is to be used. This relates closely to the informational analysis of moral principles with which the rest of the paper has been concerned.

REFERENCES

Arrow, K. J. (1951): *Social Choice and Individual Values*, New York: Wiley, 1951; 2nd ed., 1963: Arrow (1963).

Baier, K. (1977): 'Rationality and Morality', *Erkenntnis* **11** (1977), 197–223.

d'Aspremont, C. and L. Gevers (1977): 'Equity and the Informational Basis of Collective Choice', *Review of Economic Studies*, **46** (1977), 199–210.

Deschamps, R. and L. Gevers (1978): 'Leximin and Utilitarian Rules: A Joint Characterization', *Journal of Economic Theory*, **17** (1978), 143–63.

Hammond, P. J. (1976): 'Equity, Arrow's Conditions and Rawls' Difference Principle', *Econometrica*, **44** (1976), 793–804.

Hammond, P. J. (1977): 'Dual Interpersonal Comparisons of Utility and the Welfare Economics of Income Distribution', *Journal of Public Economics*, **7** (1977), 51–71.

Hansson, B. (1968): 'Choice Structures and Preference Relations', *Synthese*, **18** (1968), 443–58.

Hart, H. L. A. (1973): 'Rawls on Liberty and Its Priority', *University of Chicago Law Review*, **40** (1973), 534–55; reprinted in N. Daniels, ed., *Reading Rawls*, Oxford: Basil Blackwell, 1974.

Herzberger, H. G. (1973): 'Ordinal Preference and Rational Choice', *Econometrica*, **41** (1973), 187–237.

Kanger, S. (1976): 'Choice Based on Preference', mimeographed, Uppsala University; presented at the Reisenburg Symposium on Decision Theory and Social Ethics.

Marx, K. (1875): *Critique of the Gotha Programme*. English tr. in K. Marx and F. Engels, *Selected Works*, vol. 2, Moscow: Foreign Language Publishing House, 1958.

Maskin, E. (1978): 'A Theorem on Utilitarianism', *Review of Economic Studies*, **45** (1978), 93–6.

Nozick, R. (1974): *Anarchy, State and Utopia*, Oxford: Basil Blackwell, 1974.

Rawls, J. (1971): *A Theory of Justice*, Cambridge, Mass.: Harvard University Press, and Oxford: Clarendon Press, 1971.

AMARTYA SEN

Roberts, K. W. S. (1976): 'Interpersonal Comparability and Social Choice Theory', *Review of Economic Studies*, forthcoming.

Schwartz, T. (1976): 'Choice Functions, "Rationality" Conditions and Variations on the Weak Axiom of Revealed Preference', *Journal of Economic Theory*, **13** (1976), 414–27.

Sen, A. K. (1970): *Collective Choice and Social Welfare*, San Francisco: Holden-Day, and Edinburgh: Oliver & Boyd, 1970.

(1973): *On Economic Inequality*, Oxford: Clarendon Press, and New York: Norton, 1973.

(1974a): 'Choice, Ordering and Morality', in S. Körner, ed., *Practical Reason*, Oxford: Basil Blackwell, 1974.

(1974b): 'Informational Bases of Alternative Welfare Approaches', *Journal of Public Economics*, **3** (1974), 387–403.

(1976): 'Liberty, Unanimity and Rights', *Economica*, **43** (1976), 217–35.

(1977): 'On Weights and Measures: Informational Constraints in Social Welfare Analysis', *Econometrica*, **45** (1977).

Suppes, P. (1966): 'Some Formal Models of Grading Principles', *Synthese*, **6** (1966), 284–306; reprinted in P. Suppes, *Studies in the Methodology and Foundations of Science*, Dordrecht: Reidel, 1969.

Watkins, J. (1974): 'Choice, Orderings and Morality: Comment', in S. Körner, ed., *Practical Reason*, Oxford: Basil Blackwell, 1976.

Williams, B. (1973): 'A Critique of Utilitarianism', in J. J. C. Smart and B. Williams, *Utilitarianism: For and Against*, Cambridge: Cambridge University Press, 1973.

Reflections on the state of nature

J. E. J. ALTHAM

So many philosophers have made use of a fictional state of nature that one may wonder whether it is not an inevitable device in moral and political thought. Yet the fiction of a state of nature has been used unconvincingly, or at best inconclusively, as often as it has been used at all, so that one may wonder whether it is not necessary to avoid recourse to it. It is easy to become at the same time fascinated by the apparent power of the concept of a state of nature, and exasperated by the possibly insurmountable difficulties of using it in a way that can carry general conviction. If a theory of the state of nature could be devised that marked off the area of its proper use from the area where it overreaches itself, the predicament just described would be escaped. But there is little prospect of such a theory, since the notion of a state of nature has a Protean character that makes it improbable that it can be held fast within a general theory. The essay seeks only a more limited kind of enlightenment than would be afforded by a general theory. It concerns itself with just one kind of state of nature, and tries to assess the prospects for its use. Only at the end shall I make some tentative remarks with rather broader scope.

One possible way of beginning to classify states of nature is by how much morality is built into them. In particular, the state of nature may be used to explain morality itself, or it may assume a morality, or elements from one, to explain or justify something else, usually government or some particular form of government. It is the latter kind of state of nature that I shall be discussing. As will be seen, I incline towards an unfavourable view of the prospects for a state-of-nature philosophy of this kind.

The most famous recent example of a state-of-nature philosophy of this kind is Robert Nozick's *Anarchy, State and Utopia*,[1] and especially the first part of that book. Nozick there defends a minimal state, and argues that only a minimal state is justified. A minimal state is one whose functions are never exactly defined, but include protection against force, theft and fraud, and enforcement of contracts, and exclude coercing citizens into positively helping others, and prohibiting activities to citizens for their own good.

[1] New York, Basic Books, 1974.

Because modern governments extensively and increasingly perform functions excluded by Nozick, and most political writers think that this type of action is permissible for a government, and because on the other hand there are few anarchists, Nozick's arguments that *only* a minimal state is justified have so far received more attention than his arguments that a minimal state *is* justified. This emphasis, however, can easily lead to an unbalanced view of the book as a whole. For Nozick's conclusion that *only* a state with minimal functions is justified is not an optional extra; it is intimately bound up with the strategy for refuting the anarchist. I shall be probing some weaknesses in the execution of that strategy, and in the strategy itself. In so far as I succeed, the discussion will have indirect repercussions on the problems of going beyond the minimal state, but I do not have space to go into these.

Lawrence Becker has recently written 'Robert Nozick's arguments against anarchism in *Anarchy, State and Utopia* seem to me to be as conclusive as philosophical arguments can get on this issue'.[2] That is a remarkably strong endorsement, but one from which I shall give reasons for dissenting.

Nozick supposes people living in a state of nature, that is to say without any sort of government. This state of nature is specified by two components, namely how the inhabitants may morally behave, and how they do behave. In both respects John Locke is followed closely. Each person is as it were surrounded by a moral territory whose boundary no other may cross without his permission. Actions that cross nobody's boundaries are permissible. Harming a person, or interfering with what he may permissibly do, are the kinds of things that cross his moral boundaries. The morality is a morality of rights that imposes side-constraints on what may be done. In form as well as in practical import it is contrary to consequentialism. All rights moreover, at least at this stage in the story, are rights of individuals, and none is a right to receive anything.

The factual component is that most people respect each others' moral rights, but some violations do take place. That supposition in turn brings into play further moral considerations, namely that the injured party and his agents may exact compensation from the boundary crosser, and *anyone* may *punish* transgressors. Again the qualification 'at least at this stage in the story' must be added to the last clause.

Two necessary conditions for the existence of a state are declared to be crucial. One is that an agency, to count as a government, must have the requisite sort of monopoly over the use of force, and the other is that it must protect everyone within its territory.

A government satisfying these conditions is argued to emerge as follows (in baldest outline; the details are often subtle and complicated). It is inefficient for each person to enforce his own rights. Entrepreneurs go into

[2]   Note 3 to Ch. 6 of *Property Rights*, London, 1977, p. 126.

business, selling protection and enforcement policies. Individuals transfer their rights to enforce their rights to these firms. One of these firms naturally becomes dominant, or they federate so that there is a single system that dominates. The dominant agency has a *de facto* monopoly over the use of force; only it has the power to oversee the use of force, and to rule on its permissibility. There *may* be independents who do not become clients of the dominant agency, but the latter has the right, on behalf of its clients, to prohibit the independents from enforcing their rights privately if it regards their procedures as risky, providing that it makes compensation for so doing. The eventual upshot of this rule is something at least very close to universal protection.

Among the most important claims made for this process, and for the state that is the result of it, are the following. First, that the state emerges in a morally permissible way. Secondly, that it emerges without anyone intending that it should. Thirdly, that it has no rights not possessed by individuals in the state of nature. And fourthly, that so long as it confines its activities to the exercise of these rights, the condition of man under the state is superior to his condition without government, in that his rights are more securely and efficiently protected.

The aims of carrying out the strategy are mainly two. One is to answer the question 'why not anarchy?', i.e. to *justify* the state, or rather a particular kind of state. The other is to *understand* the political realm. The Lockean state of nature is the best anarchic situation one could reasonably hope for. If even out of this favourable state of affairs a state would emerge of which the four claims of the last paragraph can be made, the state is both justified, and explained completely in terms of the nonpolitical.

It would be wonderful if it all worked, but it does not. First, Lawrence Becker, in the quotation I gave, seems to be claiming more for the argument than its own author. For Nozick acknowledges an obvious gap, namely that the moral theory assumed is not by any means fully defended. Indeed, it is not even fully stated. And he makes a general acknowledgement at the beginning of the book that his work is an exploration, not a finished and complete whole. I do not wish to dwell for long on the fact that the moral theory is insufficiently defended, but one need is so desperately urgent that it must be mentioned. If in the state of nature a person does have any right to any of the resources of others to meet any of his needs, Nozick's limitation of the state's functions to the minimal ones will be in peril. For such a right would provide a way of justifying the state's intervention to make sure it was satisfied, that others *did* provide from their resources to meet others' needs. So it is an urgent matter to prove that there is no such right as, for example, the right to be cared for when sick.

That point is rather obvious. I mention it because of a further reflection it prompts, which is that in the light of it it can be seen that Nozick's justification of the state should not be seen in terms of the category of need. Unlike many uses of the state of nature, Nozick's is not of the general form that the state exists because it is needed. For if it were of this form, one could take issue by pointing to other needs that will not be met, or not met well, without the state's activity, and the state would then cease to be a minimal one. But such an argument would misconstrue Nozick, for whom need does not really come into the picture. At best, for him, we can say that the state is needed because it legitimately emerges, but not that its emergence is legitimate because it is needed. I shall argue later that this is a source of weakness in his general approach.

I next wish to bring out a few minor weaknesses, to get them out of the way before the main assault. The first of these is a weakness in so far as the argument is directed against anarchists, and it is suggested by Section VIII, Part II, of Book III of Hume's *Treatise of Human Nature*. Hume is maintaining a difference between the need for justice and the need for government. The former he thinks is universal, the latter not so. In particular, where the possessions and pleasures of life are few and of little value, society may subsist without government. For predominantly, the occasions on which a person's rights are violated are ones where he possesses an object of which he can be deprived, and which is of use to one who deprives him of it. If there are few such objects, or few opportunities for depriving their possessors of them, there will be few occasions for violations of rights. If people are poor, and there is little trade or other contact between isolated families, there may be so few invasions of others' rights that government never gets established.

Hume's explanation of government is in terms of human need, but the need is there only in a particular conjunction of circumstances. It requires human avidity, and short-sightedness, so that people fail to keep clearly in view their common interest in the observance of justice, for government to become necessary. But it also requires adequate opportunity, which is not there in all conditions of men, for avidity to be exercised.

Now although Nozick's explanation of government is not in terms of need, Hume's ideas in this section can be adapted to fit his framework. Nozick's is essentially an economic explanation of the state. The process that starts from the state of nature gets going because of voluntary exchange between individuals and entrepreneurs offering protective services. Such exchanges do not take place unless both sides find it worth while. There has to be a set of protective services and a price such that the individuals find it worth while to pay that price for those services, and entrepreneurs find it worth while to provide those services, at that price. Unless that is true, the process does not get started. Now the private protective agencies are supposed to be continuously operating firms, and mention is made on p. 117 of their 'enduring administrative structures, with full-time specialized personnel'. Moreover, to satisfy the requirement of moral permissibility they must administer justice using fair procedures, and we may suppose that to get clients they must be moderately effective. So they have to carry out detective work, and pursue and apprehend suspects. There must be some guarded place where suspects may be detained. There must be the whole apparatus needed for a fair trial. And there must be provision for carrying out sentences. As we all know, such procedures and facilities are expensive. If people are poor, there is little trade, travel is difficult and crime is rare, there may be no price at which an entrepreneur offering protective policies that observe moral constraints would get enough customers, unless the price was so low that the entrepreneur went bankrupt.

Hume may not be right about the conditions for the emergence of government, but it is immensely plausible, if one goes in for a state-of-nature strategy at all, to think that there are conditions of human life which do not start the Nozickian process. The Humean conditions are sketched only for purposes of plausible illustration. Other possibilities result from changing the assumptions about human rationality and motivation, for example. Now if there are conditions in which the state would emerge, and others in which it would not, it is important, both from the point of view of explanatory theory and from the point of view of refuting anarchism, to characterise these conditions. So long as we do not know from *what* anarchic circumstances the state would come into being, there is an obvious gap in our explanation, in that we shall not have specified the initial conditions satisfactorily. And the anarchist may take heart, for *perhaps* there is an anarchic condition of men both more attractive than the poor one described by Hume *and* such that in it there would be no need of the state. Indeed, one could almost say that it is precisely the hope of such a condition that sustains anarchism.

Hume seems to me superior to Nozick in that he does try to bring out that to get to the state you need to make assumptions about motives, rationality, and material circumstances, and in that he tells a plausible story about all three. It is far from clear from his book what Nozick's own account would be. However, for all that has been said so far, this is merely a gap that could be filled without too much difficulty. One may on the other hand not be very confident that the gap can be filled. In philosophy gaps in the argument tend to be the places where serious difficulties lie concealed. Here is just one speculative possibility: for the process of administering justice to satisfy moral constraints, the procedures used must be fair and reliable, and therefore, as we have seen, elaborate and expensive. Moreover, the full panoply has to be used from the start. An entrepreneur cannot, in this field, enter business in a primitive, cottage-industry kind of way. That is not morally permissible. He therefore needs a certain amount of capital to get going. This suggests the possibility that because of the inefficiency of the state of nature, nobody in it could acquire enough capital *by morally permissible means* to be able to go into business in this way. If so, the explanation of the state is undercut. For either the process to the state would not get going, or it would, but would involve morally impermissible acts on the part of the agency that becomes the state. Thus perhaps it would turn out, if the economic conditions for the emergence of the state were specified, that it took the state to bring them into being; in which case the explanation would be null because circular.

The next problem is that it is not at all clear what the condition *is* that the state should emerge by morally permissible means. The fullest statement Nozick gives is on p. 115 'the *de facto* monopoly grows by an invisible hand process and *by morally permissible means*, without anyone's rights being violated and without any claims being made to a right others do not possess'. It is far from clear what Nozick is getting at here, and one reason for the unclarity is that if this quotation is taken absolutely literally, then it is quite simply *untrue* that nobody's rights are violated in the series of transitions to the state. On the contrary, the protective associations, one of which attains a monopoly, come into being only because some men transgress the bounds of the Lockean law of nature and violate people's rights. Let us then try a second interpretation. Perhaps the point is that nobody's rights get violated *by the agency that eventually becomes the state*. But Nozick's own description of how one agency becomes dominant suggests that this also is untrue. For according to that description, there are initially several protective associations, and there will be disputes between clients of one and clients of another in which each association will decide (in good faith) in favour of its own client. In such a case the agencies *do battle*; that is to say, the disagreement is portrayed as being settled by force. The association, or federation, that in the end attains supremacy, will have fought and won frequently. For this association not to have violated anyone's rights requires first that it is morally permissible to settle the disagreements that arise by force, and secondly that the agency that attains supremacy is always in the right in the battles it engages in. The first requirement is nowhere shown to be met, and it is a gross implausibility that the second should actually be the case. There is nothing here to set at rest the anarchist's doubts as to the legitimacy of the state.

A third interpretation would be that the association that eventually comes to dominate does not *intentionally* violate anybody's rights, but this too seems not to be what is required. For first, it is not very close to what Nozick actually says. Secondly, it strains credulity, and therefore undermines the explanatory purpose, to suppose that an association which judged disputes involving its own clients with complete impartiality would ever become dominant. Is honesty *invariably* the best policy for such a business? Thirdly, it is not clear how important it is that violations of rights by an agency acting in good faith should be unintentional. Is the anarchist going to be satisfied to be told that the state can emerge and in the process violate others' rights only unintentionally?

I thing it is necessary to get clear that from the point of view of refuting anarchism, the mere fact that rights are sometimes violated is neither here nor there. Rights may be violated because of men's defects of character and general fallibility, and if they are violated only for these reasons no anarchist other than the most absurdly utopian need take exception. What is needed to refute the anarchist is something more like a set of transitions from anarchy to government which is in relevant ways no worse from the point of view of violations of rights than anarchy itself. There are two ways in which a transition could be worse off than anarchy from this point of view. One is that a violation of rights is a causally necessary condition of a transition taking place, that is a violation by the agency that survives the transition. The other is if some agency is set up in the course of these transitions which has, as part of its function, to perform activities which essentially involve violations of rights. Nozick's story seems not to involve any steps that, on his and anarchists' premises, are impermissible in the second way. But it is not clear that it does not involve steps that are impermissible in the first way.

So far I have drawn attention to what seems to be a gap in Nozick's story, namely that he has not specified the contingent circumstances in which his process would get started, and I have tried to bring out some difficulties with the use made of the notion of the state's emerging by morally permissible means. I mentioned that I regarded these as minor weaknesses, and I look at them in that light because there seems no need to despair of making repairs to the narrative to eliminate the weaknesses. I now turn to something fundamental. It is fundamental to Nozick's enterprise that no new rights should emerge with the state. If that part of it fails, then he cannot succeed in his objective of explaining the political realm in terms of the non-political, nor in his desire to refute anarchism. For one great anarchistic objection to the state is that in it some people appear to have special rights to do things to others against their will, rights that not everybody has and which have not been conferred on them voluntarily by the citizens. Such rights he regards as illegitimate. Nozick's reply is of the form that they are not special after all; they do *not* come into being only with the state, but arise naturally by transfer from rights everybody does have. But I do not believe that this strategy is successfully carried out in Nozick's book, nor that it can be made successful.

The crucial consideration is the government's right to punish. Nozick has

J. E. J. ALTHAM

to find the source of that right in rights of individuals in the state of nature. One possibility would be to find it in the right of individuals to assign rights by means of a contract. That is of course the classical solution, and not one that Nozick pursues. He wants the state to emerge by an invisible-hand process, and the hands involved in contracts are thoroughly visible. Contract theory is precisely one that *acknowledges* that new rights emerge with the state, and seeks to explain how. It is equally impossible for him to find the source of the government's right to punish in any notion of there being a need for a body with such a right. That line also is incompatible with the no-new-rights thesis. And obviously, in a state-of-nature framework the government's right cannot be merely a customary one. That seems to leave only one resource; somebody must have a right to punish in the state of nature, and this is of course the view adopted. Since in the state of nature if anyone has a right to punish all do, all do have this right.

Now the project of justification is here, as it usually is, one of justifying something *to* somebody, and as against something else. And if one wishes to justify government to a libertarian anarchist, a powerful way of doing so will be to do so on anarchistic premises. Since libertarian anarchists do believe in the primitive right of all to punish, assuming this right is legitimate in argument with them. But the idea that in the state of nature all have a right to punish is one that Locke himself realised would not naturally commend itself to many of his readers, and the same remains true to-day. The explanation of a government's right to punish in terms of an individual's right will be no explanation at all unless the individual's right is rendered less in need of explanation than the government's. For most of us who are not anarchists, that requires that some work be done on the right of all to punish.

Consider first Locke's two main reasons for asserting the right of all to punish. One is that the law of nature would be in vain if no one in the state of nature had the right to execute it, and the other that an offender becomes dangerous to mankind in general. Nozick mentions these without dissenting from them (p. 137), but without explicitly endorsing them either. I shall comment on them as they might occur in Nozick's framework, leaving the features peculiar to Locke out of account. It seems clear that these two reasons ground the right of all to punish on need: without someone to punish offenders, something will not happen that needs to happen. This is dangerous ground for the Nozickian framework, for once one begins to ground rights on need, questions will spring up about other needs, and awkward questions asked about why they too do not give rise to rights. Secondly, even if the Lockean reasons are usable, they are double-edged. They give reasons why *someone* should have the right to punish. To reach the conclusion that all have, the further premise is needed that in the state

140

of nature all have the same rights. Now rights, and the state of nature generally, are here being regarded as very close to facts. The argument is of the form 'Because of this and that, people *have* these rights'. But the question is not what the state of nature is really like, or would be like if it existed. It is about what description of it, as a pure fiction, will serve certain explanatory purposes. The question is then whether it serves explanatory purposes to ascribe the right of all to punish to individuals in a state of nature, for Lockean reasons. An objection which now looms up concerns the possibility of *rival* explanations. Thus if it is true, as indeed I concede, that there is reason for *some* agency's having the right to punish, an obvious rival to the idea that all have it is that the reason is a *direct* reason for the state. Thus an argument might run, in very bare outline: Someone is needed to execute the law of nature. Nobody has that right in the state of nature. So there is reason for getting out of the state of nature by having a government. This form of explanation promises to be much more economical than one that goes *via* the right of all to punish. Indeed one might ask what role the intermediate stage, where all have a right to punish in the state of nature, is really playing, since it turns out in the end that this arrangement, of open punishment with no government, does not work well enough to survive.

It could, however, be argued that we deprive ourselves of possible insight if we adopt the shortcut to the state just suggested. For to gain maximum understanding of the political realm, we should cast about for any means to avoid entering it. If it is found that we enter it from the state of nature despite adopting even fairly extreme measures to avoid doing so, the justification of the state will be all the stronger. One might compare one form of argument running like this: in the state of nature everyone has rights, including the right to punish, and from that government emerges by an invisible-hand process, with another form running like this: *even* if, *however absurdly*, we ascribe the right to punish to all in the state of nature, the state will still emerge by an invisible-hand process. The trouble is that Nozick's strategy requires an argument of the former kind. The reason is that the latter does not satisfy the condition that no new rights emerge with the state. For that, it *is* necessary to treat the ascription of the right of all to punish as having some independent merit. So the counter-argument that adopting the line of the previous paragraph sacrifices insight is not after all available within Nozick's general strategy.

The section in *Anarchy, State and Utopia* entitled 'The Right of All to Punish' (pp. 137–42), is really rather astonishing. For in it Nozick presents a formidable battery of difficulties in the way of seeing how the right of all to punish would actually operate in the state of nature, and eventually even tentatively amends his description of this state, so that no longer does he say that *each* person has a right to punish, but rather that all should *jointly* act to punish or to empower someone to punish. So the right of each actually to punish gives way to the right of each to a say in the ultimate determination of punishment. And as he himself points out, this requires some institutional apparatus within the state of nature itself. And as he also points out, this emendation goes against the previous conception that all rights are rights of individuals. (This explains why I put the qualification 'at least at this stage in the story', in my initial outline of Nozick's argument). One thing that astonishes about this section is that its author does not see how radically it affects his entire account that he has made this modification to the right of all to punish. On the contrary, he seems to think he can use this modification to reinforce his conception of the dominant protective agency's entitlement.

All this is rather amazing. For consider, under the revised conception, what an entrepreneur must do to set up a protective association. He can no longer offer to punish, taking over the rights of his clients to do so. He has instead to offer to *represent* them, taking over their right to *a say* in the ultimate determination of punishment. Then where is the reason for rival agencies to fight, and for one to become dominant? For the representation is not of their *interests*, which are liable to clash, but rather of their opinions on public matters, most of which may touch their interests hardly at all. It is clear that the whole story needs to be retold.

It is not easy to say what considerations carried the heaviest weight in inducing Nozick to modify the doctrine of the right of all to punish in this way. His shift in position is made *via* an avalanche of questions he puts to himself, most of them remaining unanswered. But one important set of considerations concerns the problems of *coordination*. If anyone may punish an offender, co-ordination is needed to ensure, for example, that he is not punished again and again by different people for the same offence. A possible solution to such problems might seem to lie in allowing that the victim has some special authority over punishment of the offender. This idea is, however, quite rightly rejected. Apart from obvious problems such as multiplicity of victims, or the victim's being dead, there is the point that the offender does not owe his own punishment *to* the victim. Punishment is in this unlike compensation. So one who punishes is not acting especially on behalf of the victim. He is rather acting on behalf of everybody.

A specific problem Nozick raises concerns mercy. In a state of nature, would it be permissible for an individual to be merciful, and either refrain from punishing an offender altogether, or decide to punish him lightly? If he does this out of mercy, it is hard to see why others should accept the decision. Another may decide that since the first punisher let the offender off, it is all right for him to take his place and punish instead. Then an act of mercy would be of no effect, and it would be difficult to see why it should be *called* an act of mercy at all.

What these considerations seem to me to bring out is that if one is punishing, one is doing so on behalf of everybody, and for that to be so there must be a degree of recognition on the part of others that one's decision carries authority. Subject to possible procedures for appeal – and how on earth are these to be organised in the state of nature? – the execution of one's sentence on an offender must be recognised to end the matter. This in turn means than an individual acting alone to punish on behalf of everybody has just that feature that the anarchist finds objectionable in the state. By whatever route it comes about that *he* is to punish, rightly, *this* offender, in that particular case he then has an authority that is his alone, for he alone decides for everybody, and his decision ought to be respected. In a crucial respect the punisher is in the position of the state vis-à-vis, not only the offender, but also the public at large.

This reflection can be turned back onto Nozick. If, instead of each having the right to punish, we say only that all have it, acting jointly, then this does not merely require institutional apparatus within the state of nature. Rather, we have something that already has a crucial feature of the state, the peculiarity being that everyone participates in the judicial function, or at least may so participate.

Thus the anarchist is suffering from a misunderstanding if he thinks he can have punishment in the state of nature, while avoiding the features he finds objectionable about government. Punishment involves authority, and authority is inherently monopolistic in its own sphere. The choice is between a lot of little, individual, uncoordinated, inefficient, monopolistic authorities, and the kind of system that is more readily described as the state.

It therefore seems that overall the ascription of the right to punish to all in the state of nature neither does nor can serve explanatory purposes. If this is so, the consequences for this kind of state of nature theory are far-reaching. For it would seem then that there can after all be no explanation of the political realm wholly in terms of the non-political, if this is understood, as it naturally is, as including the requirement that political rights be all explained in terms of prepolitical rights. The quest for such an explanation founders on the state's authority in the matter of punishment. If one finds the source of this in something that is not itself a right, then the state's right is a 'new' one. If one finds its source in something that *is* a right, the only candidate has itself a political dimension.

There seem to be three main kinds of state-of-nature theory. The kind that was for a long time dominant is the theory of the social contract. But, to stick my neck out with a large and undefended generalisation, social contract theory has turned out to be unstable. The terms of the contract are determined by men's needs and interests, if the theory does not presuppose a morality, and then, as we may learn from Hume, it is the interests and needs themselves that are doing the real work in explaining and justifying government. The contract, even if a useful expository device, can be eliminated. On the other hand moral requirements may be built into the contract, and in that case – as in the philosophy of John Rawls – it is the ethical requirements that are doing the real work, and again the contract becomes just a device of presentation. The second type of state-of-nature theory is the type to which the theory of *Anarchy, State and Utopia* belongs. In this type the explanation is neither in terms of needs nor interests. We are to come to understand and justify the state by seeing how it might legitimately come about without anyone intending it to. The prospects for this style of theorising now look bleak, because it looks as though one has to put so much *into* the state of nature that the state of nature itself is as much in need of explanation as the state itself. And it leaves the real source of the state's authority in the matter of punishment unsolved. The latter point may also give this kind of theory some instability. For if one must locate the source of the state's right to punish in the *need* for such a right, then we may be able to adapt the Humean objection to contract theory and say that in the end it is this need that explains the state. The rest is unnecessary complication.

In general I think this conclusion is right. If state-of-nature theory has a role to play it will be because (and this is the *third* kind) it helps us to understand and justify the state in terms of interests and needs that it serves, or might serve. Unfortunately to say that is to say very little. The big problems only start here, with questions as to what to count as a need, and *what* needs and interests one may appeal to in explaining and especially in justifying the state.

APPENDIX

The discussion of the first draft of this paper, and in particular remarks made by Richard Tuck, make me think that it is desirable to defend in an appendix one argument in the paper. This is the claim that the problem of coordinating punishments in the state of nature requires that punishment, even in a *prima facie* apolitical condition of man, already has a feature that anarchists find objectionable in government.

It could look as though the problem of co-ordination were merely a technical one. If this were so, it could be put to Nozick that his retreat from the right of all to punish is premature, as he has not exhausted the possibilities of technical solutions. For example, who is to punish in a given case might be settled by making appropriate use of a randomising device.

If some such solution were to work, it might look as though it would also prevent the transition mentioned above. As an objection to Nozick, it is unclear whether the point has weight, but it does not hold against my argument. For my point here does not concern the difficulty of attaining co-ordination *per se*, but rather what the need for co-ordination reveals about the position of the punisher, irrespective of how the co-ordination is achieved.

This can be brought out by imagining the problem of co-ordination to be solved. Suppose that once a crime has been committed the various agents involved in administering justice – the detectives, judges, and so on – are all decided by lot. The details of this are of no moment in the present connexion. What is important is that once the decisions have been made, nobody not appointed has any right to punish. For if any did, the decisions would be of no effect, and the problems of possibly being punished again and again for the same offence would be back with us. Also, just because these problems exist and the need for a mechanism is there, there is reason to assert that *before* the decisions are made by lot nobody has a right to exercise any function in the administration of justice (although each may be eligible for appointment). Consequently, at no time is it true that *each* has the right to punish. Hence the mechanism of appointment by lot assigns rights not otherwise possessed. It thus violates the 'no new rights' thesis. Further, in some sense of that much argued-over word, the individuals must *consent*, or agree to the mechanism. Thus we are by now well away from the invisible hand, and close to contract theory.

Again, if the problems of co-ordination are really to be solved, it must be the case – subject to appeals – that the decision of those appointed be recognised to end the business so far as the crime in question is concerned. That gives the agents an added aspect of authority. So far as I can see, this amounts to those administering justice being in effect just like state officials. They are appointed by a public, recognised procedure to fulfil defined functions, in carrying out which they exercise authority which is both generally recognised and theirs alone. They are indeed only temporary officials; but within the present context that is irrelevant. For the anarchist's objections to the state are ones of principle, and a principle that is contravened for a brief period is still contravened.

The idea of solving the co-ordination problem by lot is merely for the sake of illustration. Other technical solutions will have the same consequences, that those who have the right to punish in a particular case are alone in having that right, and are, relative to the concerns of anarchism, just like state officials. The point then of adducing the problem of co-ordination is to uncover the fact that punishment inescapably involves something which, from an anarchist's point of view, is tantamount to government.

Is there a free-rider problem, and if so, what is it?[1]

RICHARD TUCK

In the writings of those modern political theorists whose techniques and assumptions are derived from the traditions of welfare economics, one particular problem has often been taken to be of paramount importance from the point of view of state activity. It is the so-called free-rider problem. A good example of what this problem is, and what it is taken to imply, is provided by John Rawls's remarks on the subject in *A Theory Of Justice*:

> Where the public is large and includes many individuals, there is a temptation for each person to try to avoid doing his share. This is because whatever one man does his action will not significantly affect the amount produced. He regards the collective action of others as already given one way or the other. If the public good [by which Rawls means, as I shall mean in this paper, an indivisible and non-excludable good, available to any member of the population whether he has contributed or not, like a defence force] is produced his enjoyment of it is not decreased by his not making a contribution. If it is not produced his action would not have changed the situation anyway. A citizen receives the same protection from foreign invasion regardless of whether he has paid his taxes. Therefore in the polar case trade and voluntary agreements cannot be expected to develop.[2]

The *locus classicus* for this view is the famous work by Mancur Olson, *The Logic of Collective Action*, and it has since been given more precise handling by such people as James Buchanan and (in the most formal terms) Russell Hardin and Michael Taylor.[3] (Rawls's exposition is in fact a relatively imprecise one, though as we shall see it is close to our basic intuitions about the problem.)

It has been customary for political theorists to accept that this argument is a good one, and to direct their energies towards devising strategies to cope

[1] In addition to my fellow participants in the Thyssen Group meeting, I should like to thank Margaret Sommerville for her help in discussing this problem.

[2] J. Rawls, *A Theory of Justice* Oxford 1972 p. 267.

[3] M. Olson, *The Logic of Collective Action* Cambridge Mass. 1965; J. Buchanan, *The Demand and Supply of Public Goods* Chicago 1968, *The Limits of Liberty* Chicago 1975, and with G. Tullock, *The Calculus of Consent* Ann Arbor 1962; R. Hardin, 'Collective Action as an Agreeable n-Prisoners' Dilemma', *Behavioural Science* XVI 1971 pp. 472–81; M. Taylor, Anarchy and Cooperation London 1976. See also A. Downs, *An Economic Theory of Democracy* New York 1957, for the same argument applied to voting.

with it. The most popular has undoubtedly been some mechanism of social coercion, despite the fact that such mechanisms characteristically depend on co-operative action by the people concerned, and that the argument is therefore likely to turn into a *regressus ad infinitum*. Among less hard-headed political theorists, the damaging consequences of free-riding have seemed to be a good argument for necessity of some principle of justice: what is wrong about free-riding is not that it is harmful, but that it is unfair to other people. The problem here has always been that it is not clear how to move from the proposition that an action is unjust or unfair to the further and vital proposition that we should not act unjustly. A sceptic is unlikely to be persuaded of the necessity of acting justly by the use of a free-rider argument. Among other theorists (particularly Buchanan and Tullock) the preferred mechanism has been a variant of the curious doctrine associated originally with Knut Wicksell, that any collective decision should require *unanimity*. Clearly, this solves the free-rider problem, but at such social cost that the cure seems worse than the disease.

The main purpose of this paper is not to propose yet another solution to the free-rider problem, but instead to question whether it is a problem of this kind at all. I take it first that what is important and interesting about free-rider problems is not that they are examples of a clash between individual interest and collective social principle, but rather that they arise in cases where the application by individuals to their own conduct of a particular social principle leads to results considerably at variance with a co-operative and communal application of the same principle. This is a distinction which has not been made sufficiently clearly in the modern literature on the problem, for many discussions (including large parts of Olson's) turn on the question of whether individuals seeking to maximise their *own* welfare will succeed in thereby maximising the *collective* welfare. In such cases, the individuals are applying to their own actions a different principle (one of rational egotism) from the principle that is to be applied to their collective action (one of collective optimisation), and the peculiarly worrying features of a free-rider problem do not arise. Other problems, to do for example with liberty, may arise, but they lack the paradoxical character of the true free-rider problem.

But Olson and most other writers have also claimed that a free-rider problem arises for *altruists*. Olson has said that his argument

does *not* necessarily assume the selfish, profit-maximising behaviour that economists usually find in the market place. The [argument about free-riding] offered here holds true whether behaviour is selfish or unselfish, so long as it is strictly speaking 'rational'. Even if the member of a large group were to neglect his own interests entirely, he still would not rationally contribute towards the provision of any collective or public good, since his own contribution would not be perceptible...

The only requirement is that the behaviour of individuals in large groups or organisations of the kind considered should generally be rational, in the sense that their objectives, whether selfish or unselfish, should be pursued by means that are efficient and effective for achieving these objectives.[4]

This more general point about the rationality of free-riding *whatever* one's principles is the most interesting and important feature of the discussion.

Two principles have been canvassed either explicitly or implicitly in the modern literature as suitable for the generation of free-rider problems – the utility principle and the principle of Pareto optimality. Most of what I shall have to say in this paper will be concerned with the utility principle, but I should like to deal briefly with the Pareto principle first – that is, the principle that if at least one member of a society prefers x to y, and no member prefers y to x, then the society should prefer x to y. A substantial part of the modern literature takes the prisoners' dilemma of classical games theory to be a paradigm of the free-rider problem,[5] and argues as follows. We can imagine a situation in which the alternatives available to the 'players' are to contribute to or not to contribute to (defect from) a common enterprise. This matrix can then be constructed

	C	D
C	x, x	z, w
D	w, z	y, y

where C represents 'contribute', D 'defect', and $w > x > y > z$. In this situation, D dominates as a strategy for each player, since he will be better off with D whatever the other player does. And yet CC is Pareto-optimal to DD, the state of affairs that will actually result.

But this is a problem or a dilemma only if the players are primarily rational egotists. If their primary purpose is to achieve not the outcome which benefits themselves most, but the Pareto optimum for their society, and they rank the possible outcomes according to the Pareto principle, then the one thing they will *never* do is to prefer DD to CC. The priority of CC to DD is in fact the only ranking which the Pareto principle specifies in this situation – none of the other possible pairs are capable of being ordered by it. To make any further choice between outcomes, the players would have to employ a subsidiary principle (which cannot be egotism, since the application by each of them of that principle leads to either no result or one at variance with the primary principle). Further discussion of the problem is thus dependent on the nature of that subsidiary principle, whatever it might be. What this shows is that Pareto optimality is an unsatisfactory principle to consider as a context for free-rider problems – the looseness and

[4] Olson op. cit. p. 64.
[5] This is particularly true of Russell Hardin and Michael Taylor – above n. 3.

RICHARD TUCK

indeterminacy with which it specifies social rankings make the problems of its application far wider than simply the possibility of free riding.

The strength of the utility principle, on the other hand, has always seemed to be that it avoids these problems of indeterminacy – it is capable on most occasions of specifying one or a limited number of equally desirable outcomes. But that makes the free-rider problem a particularly serious one for the utilitarian. In the case of the utility principle, the characteristics of the problem as I have outlined them have always been clear; it is related to the question which dates back at least to Hume about whether a utilitarian should keep to general rules – the question which was exhaustively debated in the 1950s and 1960s between the exponents of 'rule' and 'act' utilitarianism. It can often seem that if in every circumstance we choose as individuals that course of action which apparently maximises utility, we prevent the creation of general social practices which would increase utility still further. A familiar example is that of the man who argues that if he waters his garden in a drought, he will increase his own utility and not significantly diminish the utility of his fellow citizens. Viewed in isolation, his watering of the garden maximises utility; but if everyone makes the same calculation, utility is not maximised.

At first sight, it is not obvious that a free-rider problem *will* arise in a community of utilitarians. Brian Barry has commented on Olson's application of his theory to altruists (a comment which refers mainly to the utilitarian argument),

This is surely absurd. If each contribution is literally 'imperceptible' how can all the contributions together add up to anything? Conversely, if a hundred thousand members count for something, then each one contributes on the average a hundred-thousandth. It it is rational for workers in an industry to wish for a closed shop, thus coercing everyone to join the union, this must mean that the total benefits brought by the union are greater than its total costs. (Otherwise it would be better not to have the union.) But if this is so, it must mean that anyone who wished purely to maximise the gains of workers in the industry would join the union voluntarily... Suppose, for example, that (up to some point) for every pound spent on a public good a thousand people will derive ten pounds' worth of benefit each [I think Barry must mean *in toto*]. An altruist (who might or might not be one of the potential beneficiaries) would clearly find a good use for his funds here. But it would not *pay* one of the potential beneficiaries to contribute, because the benefit *to him* from giving a pound would be only one new penny (ten pounds divided by a thousand).[6]

It is certainly the case that if each contributor is able to say with assurance that his contribution represents a greater increase in either the average or total utility of the group than would his own consumption of it, then he seems

[6] B. Barry, *Sociologists, Economists and Democracy* London 1970 p. 32. A similar argument against Downs's theory of voting is to be found in his *Political Argument* London 1965, pp. 328–330.

150

to have a utilitarian motive for contributing. (The distinction between average and total utility, often important, does not seem relevant here.) The same point has been made at greater length by David Lyons, who argued in *Forms and Limits of Utilitarianism* that 'rule' utilitarianism collapses into 'act' utilitarianism because in principle it is possible to describe actions and their consequences in sufficient detail to distinguish between those which are harmless though they break an apparently desirable rule, and those which are in fact disutile. (One needs to be careful here that one is not led into the mistaken idea that Lyons's theory justifies the keeping of normal rules by utilitarians – it would if applied lead to some pretty unorthodox practices.) The most important category of actions which he has dealt with are those involving so-called 'threshold effects', such as (his example) walking on the grass. It is clearly the case that whether or not our walking on the grass conduces to overall disutility depends on circumstances – in particular, how many other people have walked on it. Thus up to a certain 'threshold' it will be legitimate for us as utilitarians to walk on it, while at the threshold it will not be. Circumstances change beyond the threshold: once the grass is wrecked, it is wrecked, and there is no reason why we should not march all over it. But in a society of utilitarians, that stage should never be reached: they will all abstain at or near the threshold.[7]

This argument is plausible for diachronic activities, in which each participant knows what his predecessors' actions have been. Synchronic activities are more difficult: how can a community of utilitarians arrive (without open agreement or institutional sanctions) at the utilitarianly optimal allocation of resources? The work of Thomas Schelling on co-ordination games, applied in this area by David Lewis and J. J. C. Smart, has shown the way in which they can do so.[8] Assuming that each member of the community is a utilitarian and knows that his fellows are the same, and that each person can work out independently what the utilitarianly optimal allocation is, then it should be possible for them so to co-ordinate their activities that the allocation is achieved. Suppose they calculate that the optimum number to walk on the grass is 10 (any more, and there will be a decrease in utility), and there is a population of 100, then each member of the population can independently give himself a probability of walking on the grass such that if they all give themselves the same probability, the number walking on it will ordinarily be 10. In this case, the most plausible probability for each person to give himself is 0.05 (i.e. a 1 in 20 chance), which gives a probability that not more than 10 will walk across the grass

[7] D. Lyons, *Forms and Limits of Utilitarianism* Oxford 1965.

[8] T. C. Schelling, *The Strategy of Conflict* Cambridge Mass. 1960; D. K. Lewis, *Convention* Cambridge Mass. 1969 and 'Utilitarianism and Truthfulness', *Australasian Journal of Philosophy* L 1972 pp. 17–19; J. J. C. Smart and B. A. O. Williams, *Utilitarianism For and Against* Cambridge 1973 pp. 57–61.

of 0.99 (an individual probability of 0.06 gives 0.96, while the superficially obvious probability of 0.10 (1 in 10) gives a collective probability of only 0.58). Such a strategy is salient, since it is the most obvious way for the population to arrive at the commonly-desired result.

This line of argument has seemed to many people to dispose of any free-rider problem for the utilitarian. The utilitarian will not keep any rules in a simple-minded way, but he will be capable of so moderating his activity that no overall disutility results. However, this argument rests on an assumption which is crucially *not* made as part of the free-rider thesis put forward by Olson or Rawls. The assumption is that each contribution does make a real though small difference – as Barry said, 'if each contribution is literally 'imperceptible', how can all the contributions together add up to anything?' But that assumption can be weakened without falling into absurdity – indeed, arguably it *must* be weakened.

The essence of the problem is related to the ancient paradox of the Sorites – one of the great paradoxes, such as the Liar, whose importance is still recognised. It has recently attracted the attention of a philosopher of language, for it seems to raise a number of interesting questions in that field;[9] and logicians too are becoming interested in it again. In one version, it goes as follows. There can never be a heap of stones. This is because one stone does not make a heap; but the addition of one stone to something that is not a heap can never transform it into a heap. Therefore there can never be a heap of stones. Alternatively, there can never be anything but a heap of stones. A similar argument was used to the effect that all men are (or are not) bald.

The paradox takes its force, as Crispin Wright has perceived, from the vagueness of our criteria as to what is to count as a heap – there simply is *no* straightforward criterion such that after and not before *n* stones we have something which is to be described as a heap, and which is to play the role assigned in our activities to things which fall under such a description. But given the absence of such a criterion, it is indeed correct that no *particular* stone is sufficient to make the necessary transformation.

This has profound consequences for the utilitarian, which are obvious if we simply imagine a society of utilitarians who wish to have a cairn built by co-operative labour to guide them in their wanderings in the mountains. Each person has to put on one stone – but because of the vague nature of the criterion for achieving a *cairn*, each member of the society can rightly argue that *his* stone is not necessary.

To understand how this argument works, we can assume (as I have been

[9] See the papers collected in *Synthese* 30 (1975) and C. Wright, 'Language-Mastery and the Sorites Paradox', G. E. Evans and J. McDowell eds, *Truth and Meaning* Oxford 1976 pp. 223–247.

assuming throughout this paper) that the utilitarian is correct in his belief that a reasonably precise value can be assigned to every social practice, including public goods. But what is to be evaluated is of course not the thing itself, but the function it performs – a defence force is of value only in so far as it performs a particular service on which we can (in theory) set a precise value. Being protected from foreign attack, we can say (forgetting about free riding for the moment), is worth £n to the society; the defence force does so, and costs us £p; $n > p$; therefore it is worth paying for. The problem is that just as in the case of a heap of stones, our criteria as to what is to count as protecting us from foreign attack are essentially vague.

The question is, let us say, how far one tank is a necessary component of the defence force in its job of protecting us. We can imagine a possible future history in which one tank *does* make all the difference, but we can also imagine an indefinite number of equally plausible future histories in which it does not. There is simply no clear-cut means by which we can say that *this* agglomeration of military hardware is a defence force, and anything less would not be, any more than such means are available to pick out what counts as a cairn. This is not to deny (as is often done) that the utilitarian can attach a precise value to the service performed by the institution; it is to break the chain of argument at a different link, and to deny that he or anyone else can show precisely how *that* institution performs the service, and other institutions on which less money has been spent would not.

This is even the case with something like a national health service, though less obviously. In general, any reduction in the current level of public expenditure on health care seem obviously unjustified – unlike a smaller defence force, a smaller health service surely represents a direct and immediate disutility (somebody dying for lack of a kidney machine, let us say). But that looks like a plausible argument only if we imagine our money purchasing direct medical assistance such as a kidney machine. If we take it that our money is going to the administration, then we can quite reasonably ask the same question about its necessity as we can about our contribution to a defence force – for while an administrative machinery is undoubtedly necessary, we have no means of saying precisely how large it should be. The difference between the two segments of the health service is given simply by the different ease of determining how effectively each performs its function: if we became unclear about how far such things as kidney machines are necessary for health care, then we would become uncertain about our contributions in that area also.

If this is right, then all the old problems of the free-rider seem to return for the utilitarian. Each participant in a co-operative enterprise can argue that since there is no evidence that his contribution is necessary for achieving the desired outcome, it would make more sense for him to bestow his resources on some project where it is clearly beneficial. And of course, at some stage so many people will have acted on that principle that there is quite definitely no point in anyone making a contribution. It is instructive to compare this state of affairs with that which arises when there is a definite commodity to be bought. Suppose a group of ten people want to buy a billiard-table they see advertised for £50. They know that if each of them puts in £5, there is a definite incentive for the others to do likewise, since the good can only be bought for £50 and not for £45 or even £49. The free-rider problem arises precisely because public goods are characteristically not like that – the amount that they can be bought for is indefinite, because what is being bought is essentially indefinite.

However, it would be a mistake to leave the matter there. While there *is* a free-rider problem for the utilitarian, it is not one that should be taken seriously; we have seen that it is connected with a *paradox*, and the essence of paradoxes is that their conclusions should not be believed (for if they were, they would cease to be paradoxes, and become merely good arguments). To see that this is so, we need only consider what the position would be not of a group but of an individual were he to use the Sorites argument as a basis for his actions. He could be a shepherd who wishes to build a cairn of stones by himself to guide him in the hills. On setting out in the morning, he can reason as follows. If I work all day, I will have a suitable pile of stones by nightfall. But one stone added to a collection of other stones makes a negligible difference – it can never be enough to tip it over the edge and into a heap. It takes a certain amount of time and effort to find a spare stone. If I do not start immediately, I will still have a heap of stones at nightfall, since the stone I could have picked up in the next few minutes would have made no difference to the outcome. But the same applies to the next stone, and the next: there is no point in ever beginning. Moreover, at some time in the day it will be clear that I have passed the stage where I will have enough time to build a cairn, and after that point there is certainly no benefit to be gained by piling up stones.

This line of reasoning is *prima facie* just like the utilitarian's. Both men wish to see the eventual outcome; both believe that an individual contribution to that outcome is negligible, and therefore that there is no point in making it. Clearly, there are various possible disanalogies that must be considered before we can accept this. The most obvious one is that the shepherd is in control of the whole sequence of his action, while the isolated utilitarian (we have supposed) is only one among many similar people. Surely that will make a difference? Would we not have to accept (say) some extreme theory of discontinuous personal identity to make the analogy hold?

The problem with this response is that it is not clear what difference the shepherd's control over all his actions makes. If the point is parity of reasoning – that is, if the shepherd thinks like that about the first stone, he will think like that about subsequent stones – then while that might be true, it does not seem to invalidate the reasoning. What it invalidates is the stone-piling. It is no use saying, 'If you think like that each time, you will never get the cairn built, and therefore you ought not to think like that': that amounts simply to an assertion that the reasoning is false, and not to the required explanation of *how* it is false.

Instead of parity of reasoning, one might appeal to the fact that the shepherd is capable of determining a rule to govern his actions, in a way that the isolated utilitarian can not. Thus he might say, rightly, that he will have a cairn if he works from daybreak to nightfall (but not *only* if he does so), and that the application of that rule to each individual action will lead him to pick up a stone. The difficulty here is twofold: first, on what grounds will the shepherd arrive at such a rule? And second and more importantly, what is it in the situation that makes him apply the rule to the particular instance? If it is said that he will not get a cairn unless he applies the rule in each instance, then that is plainly false: by the Sorites argument, the particular stone in question makes no difference to whether or not he gets a cairn. (The parallel with some of the arguments used in free-rider problems is obvious). And without some argument of that kind, there seems to be no good reason why he should guide all his actions by his self-imposed rule. None of this requires the acceptance of a weak theory of personal identity; it is not the case that the shepherd is free-riding his alien future selves, it is simply that he cannot be shifted from his belief that there is no point in going to a lot of trouble about negligible increments.

What the parallel between the fee-rider problem in social action and this kind of dilemma in individual action shows, I believe, is first that the free-rider problem is not in fact a problem of *political* theory alone – it is merely a particular application of a general logical problem. And second that because it is a general logical problem, the political theorist should not be particularly worried by it. We would think it extraordinary if individuals started to go to elaborate lengths to ensure that they were forced to perform these kinds of iterative tasks: surely it should seem just as extraordinary that societies go to such lengths. We cannot live in this world without disregarding the Sorites argument, or more accurately treating it as what it is – a *paradox*. We have to treat minute increments as non-negligible, even though the Sorites argument seems to establish that they ought not to be treated as such. At the moment we lack the necessary formal equipment for dealing adequately with the Sorites, but that is a problem for the logician and not for the political theorist.

I should like finally to make some general remarks about the significance of the argument which I have been presenting. Among its most important consequences is that the old question of the relationship between justice and utility should perhaps be re-opened. It has become almost axiomatic that a normal principle of justice cannot be derived from the utility principle, but if the problem of justice is reformulated as a free-rider problem, it is not clear that it *is* impossible. A utilitarian might take the Humean line that universal confidence in (say) stable property ownership or continued personal freedom is desirable; the problem has traditionally been that a particular defection from such a universal practice in the interests of local utility would not sap that confidence, though iterated defections would. In form this is identical to the arguments we have been considering about (for example) defence forces: the way in which a particular social institution actually fulfils its function (in this case, generating universal confidence) is essentially indeterminate and a particular 'unjust' action makes no difference. But if it is right to ignore such considerations, it becomes much easier for a utilitarian to generate a principle of justice from within his theory. There might be other problems (for example, why should such universal confidence be desirable?) but a traditionally major one seems to be removed by this line of argument.

A further consequence is that a common defence of social coercion is weakened. It has seemed to many people that even a society of utilitarians would require coercion in order to get them to co-operate, and that coercion is therefore in some way fundamentally necessary to social life, whatever the psychological facts about the members of the society. If my argument is correct, that is not so: the old vision of a society which is both utilitarian and liberal may still be worth pursuing and the flight from utilitarianism characteristic of the last fifteen years may be unwarranted.

Contract, coercion, and consciousness

JOHN MAGUIRE

My aim in this paper is to present some leading elements of Marx's theory of society and politics. In presenting them, I shall be concerned with the role of ideas such as 'exchange' and 'power' in his thinking, and shall therefore be relating his thought to some contemporary discussions in exchange theory. I shall also follow the main lines of what Marx has to say about the kind of knowledge which social actors have of their society. Finally, I shall raise some considerations about what differentiates the mode of activity of people in communist society, and their mode of relating to one another, from those of capitalist society.

'DIVIDED HISTORY' AND SOCIAL COHERENCE

The best place to begin a discussion like this is Marx's basic conception, called variously his 'materialist conception of history' or his 'economic determinism'. Central to this conception is a notion which I shall call 'divided history'. Although Marx does not use this term, it aptly characterises what he sometimes designates as 'human pre-history' or 'the reign of necessity'. It denotes all those historical epochs lying – in Marx's schema, at least – between communal and communist society. Towards the end of his life, Marx took a deep interest in the then-emerging science of ethnology, recording with delight the indications in the work of Lewis Henry Morgan and others that the earliest forms of human society had been communal. This was in fact a confirmation in Marx's eyes of a conviction which he and Engels had shared since writing the *German Ideology* in 1845–46. Although apparently discredited nowadays, the idea of 'primitive communalism' is of interest to us chiefly for its role in Marx's ideas.

It is difficult to characterise 'communal' society, either in general terms or from Marx's own writings. He seems to have had in mind a situation where there was little or no distinction between the life-activities of different individuals; where people 'possessed' but did not 'own' goods (i.e., they had personal regular use of them, but could not dispose of them, and if a person left the community to live in another his/her goods reverted to the

157

community); and, as a result of such states of affairs, there was no conflict between the interest of the individual and the rules of the community. Marx does not deny that there were 'criminals' in communal society, and that they had to be constrained; his conception is that for the 'representative' (and majority) citizen, there was no need for law-enforcement, because what they spontaneously wanted to do was what the society regularly required.

Whatever we think about the coherence and plausibility of this conception, its chief interest for our purposes is to mark a contrast between it and the 'divided history' which succeeds it. Marx follows Hegel in seeing a certain early form of community as in some respects superior to what followed it, particularly in the spontaneous unity within it between the desires of the citizen and the requirements of the social order. He also follows Hegel, however, both in seeing this as no more than a rudimentary version of the truly ideal society, and in hailing its downfall as historically irreversible and necessary for human progress. This downfall is attributed to different factors by the two thinkers: for Hegel, it is 'individualism'; for Marx, the 'division of labour'.[1] Marx's notion of 'division of labour' is both socially broader and historically much older than the notion as found, say, in Adam Smith. It refers to the process, beginning with the break-up of early communal society, whereby there emerged significant differences between the life-activities of kinds of individuals, so that some were farmers, other crafts-persons, others judges and so on.

Marx believes that there was a quality of 'transparency' about communal society: from whatever the vantage-point, each citizen could make sense of what happened and why it happened. No part of the social process was either puzzling to, or in any important sense hidden from, the gaze of the citizen. In this sense, the important fact about the division of labour for Marx is a negative one: once division of labour emerges, then it is no longer possible for anyone to have such a view of the resultant social totality. This is not due to some bias or blind-spot on the part of anybody; it is due to the fact that there is no longer any vantage-point from which the whole social process can be grasped as a whole. Individuals can make sense of their own sphere of activity, but not of those of other kinds of individuals, nor of the interrelations of different spheres. Thus it is possible for their actions to issue in results which they had not intended and do not necessarily understand correctly.

If this 'divided history' has lost the coherence of communal society, it does not follow that divided history is 'one damn' thing after another'. The whole point of Marx's historical materialism is to argue that the long period between communal society and the communist society which he believes will end the whole process is marked by a 'series of forms of human intercourse'.

[1] The relevant discussion in Hegel appears in the *Phenomenology of Mind*, especially Section V.B.

These forms of intercourse are social formations based on specific modes of production. A mode of production is a specific set of forces of production (human labour, materials and machinery) patterned into a specific set of relations of production (relationships of property, and work-relationships); Marx believes that the mode of production sets constraints on the rest of the social formation: its political system and its consciousness or 'ideology'.

I have argued elsewhere that this theory does not require what I have called a 'temporal priority thesis'.[2] In other words, Marx need not (and frequently does not) postulate that periods of social transformation are always initiated by a transformation in the mode of production, with consequent changes at the other levels of the social formation. The 'priority' of the economy can be put forward in another manner. No matter whether the period of transformation is started at the political level (as in the case of conquest, which Marx twice specifically discusses), the level of ideas (which is admissible but unlikely from Marx's point of view) or the level of the mode of production, it will come to an end only when there have emerged political structures and types of consciousness which meet the requirements of the mode of production made possible by the forces of production available to the society.

On this formulation, the theory is not a vacuous 'equilibrium' theory to the effect that when things are not harmonious there is conflict. It has more explanatory bite than that, because it carries the claim that other levels of society will fall into line with the economy *rather than vice versa*. Michael Evans has attacked the interpretation of Marx in terms of 'correspondence', arguing that any statement to the effect that 'A corresponds with B' is equivalent to 'B corresponds with A'.[3] This is not so. If you 'fall into line' with my wishes, I can change your plans by changing mine, but you have not the same freedom. In the same way, Marx's theory is a 'correspondence theory' with an independent variable in the economy. In other words, during a period of social transformation, any number of wild ideas and political blueprints can be floated: people may set themselves to recreating a distant past or realising a visionary future; by chance, indeed, they *might* hit on the form of consciousness or the pattern of political relationships which just suits what is economically feasible; but whether or not this is so, only those ideas and patterns of relationships will survive and become established, which enable the establishment and development of the mode of production. At the end of the day, then, the society will have the consciousness and the politics needed by its economy, rather than having the economy dictated by the most popular idea or blueprint.

Marx believes that when a coherent social formation of this kind has

[2] In 'Marx's Historical Materialism: Hegelian Roots and some Problems' (unpublished paper, 1975).
[3] Evans, M., *Marx* (London 1975), p. 65.

JOHN MAGUIRE

emerged, there will have emerged a class-structure, a division between those who own and control the means of production (materials and machinery) and those who have to work for them. Here we encounter a quite important unclarity in his thinking. Sometimes he seems to conflate the division between owners and workers with what we might call 'occupational' divisions (e.g. between doctors and teachers, or between engineers and carpenters) under the broad title of 'division of labour', which is at best unhelpful. At other times, he argues that the two are distinct, but necessarily related: 'i.e., the existing stage in the division of labour determines also the relations of individuals to one another with reference to the material, instrument and product of labour'.[4] This unclarity raises problems particularly for the analysis of modern capitalism, where there are grounds for arguing that differences between the kinds of work people do are often as important as differences between workers and non-workers as factors in stratification.

For our purposes, it is sufficient to note that the notion of 'divided history' is being amplified to include a succession of forms of 'division' of workers and non-workers, and that for Marx this is the division (being central to the relations of production) which sets its stamp on the rest of the social formation. As we shall see, this division is essentially one of power, setting limits to the bargaining freedom of the respective parties. A point to note at this stage is that Marx seems to attach weight to a distinction between two species of power. I have argued elsewhere[5] that it is possible to detect in his usage a difference of terminology which neatly catches this distinction. When Marx speaks of '*Gewalt*' he tends to be talking about unstructured situations where people are in conflict over what will be the shape of the social structure. When he speaks of '*Macht*' he tends to have in mind structured situations, and the extent of social actors' ability to get their way within them. I shall base a distinction between 'force' and 'power' on this usage, and say that 'power' is what enables me to get my way within a structure (in ways which will be elucidated later), whereas 'force' is what enables me to acquire a position of 'power' in an unstructured situation.

Given this terminology, we may say that a class structure emerges when certain social actors possess the resources which give them power over others. Once they have this power, it becomes more and more likely that the non-owners will yield to it and even gradually cease to resent it. Nothing more than the sheer necessity of materially surviving, and the impossibility of indefinite resistance, is needed to explain this stage in the process. But before it is reached, the power involved has had to be achieved, very often as Marx puts it by 'very bloody means', not only in the colonies in the

---

4 Marx, K. and Engels, F., *The German Ideology* (Moscow 1968) p. 33.
5 See 'Marx on Ideology, Power and Force' in *Theory and Decision*, VII, (1976) No. 4, pp. 315–29.

nineteenth, but also in the homeland of capitalism in the sixteenth, seventeenth and eighteenth centuries.

THE STRUCTURE OF CAPITALIST SOCIETY

In the remainder of this paper, I shall be concerned almost entirely with the characteristics of one social formation within divided history, namely the capitalist one. The mode of production of this society most clearly exemplifies the distinction of owning and non-owning classes, having one group, the capitalists, who own all the means of production (i.e. the factory and everything in it) and a group who own nothing except their own productive energy or 'labour-power'. The kernel of the social process is the exchange between these two classes, and its consequences.

It is here that Marx claimed, with justification, to have made a major advance beyond classical economics. Nowadays, the labour theory of value may be disputed or totally rejected by economists. It should be remembered that in Marx's day it was the accepted basic theory even of his opponents, the 'bourgeois political economists'. Given its premises, which he shared, Marx was quite justified in emphasising the scandal represented by the phenomenon of profits. Profit was a scandal not only in the moral sense, but, more relevantly here, in the scientific sense. Given a theory of market economy, whose basic 'rule' was the exchange of equivalents, how did one explain the fact that one group in society – the capitalists – put in $£X$ at the start of the market period, and extracted $£X + x$ at the end of it?

Marx's answer hinges on the peculiar nature of one particular exchange, that between the capitalist and the worker. Marx always insisted that this was a fair exchange of equivalents: the worker was not getting in wages less than the value of his productive energy, or 'labour-power'. However, what made Marx qualify this exchange at times as 'a sort of exchange' was the very fact that it was only his labour-*power* that the worker was exchanging. The worker was not exchanging his *labour*, which at the time of the contract was by definition yet to be performed; he could exchange his labour only if he already possessed the commodity in which, according to the theory, it was embodied. This could never be true under the institutional assumptions of capitalism, because it would involve abolishing the capitalist's ownership of the means of production.

So far, then, we could re-interpret the exchange as the worker's undertaking to work for the capitalist in return for a two-sided coin: his wages, plus the permission to work. But of course these *are* only two sides of the same coin, and the worker's permission to work is at the same time his obligation to reproduce the value given him in his wages. But there is still more to it. It is a basic premise of the theory – still in important respects accepted even today – that the vendor of a commodity alienates control over the buyer's use of it. This means that there is no stipulation in the contract as to how long or how intensely the worker will have to work in the factory. It may immediately be objected that, at least in the modern economy, this is no longer so: trade union negotiations have set firm limits to the 'normal working-day'. I could reply that trade unions have not yet been allowed into the model but, apart from the speciousness of such a response, there is no need to do so. The limitations on hours do not determine the *intensity* of work during the hours worked, which probably explains the importance of productivity deals in the modern economy. More crucially, even if hours and intensity of labour were regulated, there would still be no automatic equality between the value represented by the wage and the value created by the worker during the production period. In other words, while the worker is getting a fair market exchange for the commodity – labour-power – which he exchanges, the use of that commodity gives to the capitalist, in all but the most extraordinary circumstances, more value than he has had to pay out in wages to buy it. The difference is *surplus*-value, otherwise called profit (the difference between the two names not being relevant to our present concerns).

EXCHANGE AND POWER IN CAPITALISM

As we shall see later, the worker does not in fact perceive his situation in terms of the theory of surplus-value. For the moment, however, I am interested in the objective nature of the exchange between worker and capitalist, granted that both perceive it simply as a market exchange between 'labour' and 'wages'. It is significant that in the very first sentence of the very first work he ever wrote on economics, Marx declared that 'Wages are determined by the bitter struggle [*feindlichen Kampf*] between capitalist and worker.'[6] It is often and correctly observed that Marx here is in a sentence overthrowing the notion that the laws of the economy are 'natural' or 'iron' laws, and insisting that they are the forms and results of human activity. This is not only true but important; however we should not overlook a different but related implication of Marx's dramatic assertion.

In an article from which as will emerge I have received much stimulation, Jack Lively begins his discussion of exchange theory by a characterisation of three broad kinds of social theory. The first kind (including contractualist, utilitarian and classical economic theories) emphasises individual intentions; the second emphasises shared values, and the third emphasises the emergence of patterned social development, as explanations of social order and

6   Marx, K., *Early Writings* (ed. and tr. Bottomore, T.B.) (London 1963), p. 69.

coherence. Lively tells us that all three types of theory have stressed 'the limited efficacy or even the positive disutility of political intervention in social arrangements, the marginal use of politics'.[7] Lively locates Marxism as one of the theories of the third kind; however, his general comment applies only in a restricted way to what Marx has to say. If, as we shall shortly see, Lively endorses the attempt made by Peter Blau in his *Exchange and Power in Social Life*[8] to include at least certain power relations within the ambit of exchange theory, he would appear to applaud the general aim of overcoming the compartmentalisation between 'economic' and 'political' modes of theorising. If so, he ought perhaps to recognise Marx as an ally in this endeavour, since this would appear to be one of the implications of Marx's treatment of the worker/capitalist exchange. We shall arrive at a fuller statement of this point by a closer examination of Marx's analysis.

Consider the bargaining-positions of the two parties. The worker is dependent on striking a bargain in order to live: he has no resources to fall back on, and therefore must get a weekly wage. The capitalist on the other hand has accumulated savings which cushion him against even a fairly prolonged stoppage or lockout, and therefore – particularly in the absence of trade unions – will almost certainly have the upper hand. Note that this does not remove the freedom of the exchange: the worker is free to sell his labour-power to whichever capitalist will take it on the best terms, and is in that sense in the same position as any seller of a commodity. This Marx emphasises is a real advance over preceding economic systems. While the slave or serf simply worked as assigned and forced to work, the worker in capitalist society has a real measure of choice as between buyers of his labour-power, and to that extent can bargain over the wage he receives. But he is not free, of course, not to choose *some* capitalist. This is why Marx is being more than just capriciously paradoxical when he tells us that the worker selling his labour-power is 'compelled to sell it voluntarily'.[9] Here we come onto the vexed topic of exchange and power, freedom and compulsion.

In his attempt to incorporate power-relations within exchange terms, Blau draws the line at straight coercion. He says that 'there is an element of voluntarism in power – the punishment could be chosen in preference to compliance, and it sometimes is – which distinguishes it from the limiting case of direct physical coercion'.[10] Lively objects that this narrows coercion down to direct physical manhandling, whereas the notion is necessarily wider in significant ways. He argues that Blau's root error is the insistence on voluntariness as a necessary condition of exchange. Lively deals with the

[7] Lively, J., 'The Limits of Exchange Theory', in Barry, B. M. (ed.) *Power and Political Theory* (London and New York 1976), pp. 1–13. The quotation is from p. 1.
[8] Blau, P. M., *Exchange and Power in Social Life* (New York 1964).
[9] Marx, K., *Capital*, Vol. 1 (London 1886; reproduced 1938), p. 761.
[10] Blau, *op. cit.*, p. 117 (quoted by Lively, p. 9).

well-known example of Hobbes's 'sovereignty by acquisition', and concludes: 'I may agree on an exchange as the best I can get in the circumstances, but to talk of my decision as thereby "voluntary" is to drain the notion of free choice of all that normally we think characterizes it.'[11] This move seems to me to be both unfortunate and unnecessary. We might as well respond to Lively that to characterise a choice as 'non-voluntary' is to drain the notion of choice of all that normally we think characterises *it*. Not only is it not true that there can be non-voluntary choices; it is unnecessary to propose such a notion, and it lands us in problems which we need not have.

It is not necessary, if we distinguish clearly our choosing between alternatives, from the determination of the alternatives between which we choose. If I am compelled in making a choice, I am compelled not *as to* the choice but *into* the choice. For example, if someone asks me to wash his car, I can and probably will refuse. But if he threatens to bash my head in, he thereby transforms my choice from 'washing *versus* non-washing' to 'washing *versus* non-washing-plus-bashing' with (in the case of the present writer, at least) a predictably different outcome. Whatever my 'freedom of choice' or 'voluntariness' is, he has in no way interfered with it as such; what he *has* done is significantly alter the context or scope within which it operates. I believe that this presentation will handle all the valid points which Lively makes, and goes on to make about zero-sum conflicts and so on; in that sense, I see his breaking of the entailment between 'exchange' and 'freedom' as unnecessary.

I also see it as undesirable, since it raises the phantom of what a 'really free exchange' would be, and I believe that that is a misleading and false question. We shall see below that even the notion of a 'freely-*entered* exchange' is a highly problematical one, but the notion of 'free exchange' can be simply rendered straightforward by saying that all exchanges are free, but always only in respect of certain ranges of alternatives. In other words, the interesting question about any exchange is not whether it is free, but what it is free in respect of. In this perspective, a social actor's (or group's) power becomes the ability to determine the range of choice available to another social actor (or group); this, incidentally, is a perspective on *power* with which Lively would agree.

On these terms, the worker makes a voluntary exchange within a range determined by the capitalist. The worker can refuse to make a wage-contract only if he is prepared to starve, or if he wins the pools, or if he can successfully challenge the whole institutional structure of capitalist private property. If the worker attempts this last, the capitalist has a range of powers, in the sense that he can add disincentives to the choice of rebellion, which will herd the dissident back into the fold.

[11] Lively, p. 9.

KNOWLEDGE AND POWER IN CAPITALISM

The problem of knowledge in capitalist society can best be posed by bringing together what we have had to say about the structure of capitalism and what we have had to say about exchange and power. Let us begin by reconsidering the structure.

We have said that the crucial feature of this structure is the worker/ capitalist exchange, and its consequences. We have seen that the chief consequence of this exchange is the production of surplus-value, or profits. It is now necessary to explicate what is meant by calling this state of affairs 'exploitative'. There is a common-sense notion which confuses exploitation with someone's having more social goods than someone else, but that will not do. In fact, I could exploit someone and gain less than they did (as is the case with the predicament, frequently invoked by well-heeled conservatives, of the pensioner living on a few low-yielding shares in a company.) The notion of exploitation involves (a) taking something from somebody which is rightfully theirs, while preventing them from gaining access to it; or (b) using them to gain something for ourselves in a way which they would not, other things being equal, choose, or (c) a combination of (a) with (b), which means that we are abusing them to get at something which also is rightfully theirs. Marx's notion of exploitation is of the (c)-type: not only is the worker being compelled to work for the capitalist in the sense of being forced to 'bring him' something; the 'something' is itself a *product* of the worker's activity, and thus in itself rightfully his.

Indeed, things are worse than that, because the fact that the worker hands over (as it were) the *product* of his activity increases the capitalist's ability to force him to work for him. Marx traces this irony in an electrifying passage in the *Grundrisse*, from which I hope that I may be allowed one fairly long quotation:

He has produced not only the alien wealth and his own poverty, but also the relation of this wealth as independent, self-sufficient wealth, relative to himself as the poverty which this wealth consumes, and from which wealth thereby draws new vital spirits into itself, and realizes itself anew. All this arose from the act of exchange, in which he exchanged his living labour capacity for an amount of objectified labour, except that this objectified labour...now appear as posited by himself, as *his own product*, as his own self-objectification as well as the objectification of himself as a power independent of himself, which moreover rules over him, rules over him through his own actions.[12]

The problem, however, is that all this 'appears' only to the scientist equipped with the theory of surplus-value, and not at all to the social actors involved. The explanation of this fact is already contained in what we have said. People live and act in markets, and work in factories. Their experience

[12] Mark, K., *Grundrisse* (tr. Nicolaus, M.) (London 1973), p. 453.

is that of receiving a wage, which entitles them to work so as to 'earn' the wage. They do not bring together the two aspects of their experience – market and factory – as does Marx's theory. This is not due to any stupidity on their part, any more than early civilisations were stupid to 'see' the sun revolving around the earth: that is the way things appear (i.e. manifest themselves) to the observer.

Capitalist society, if I may wax poetic for a moment, thus does not 'disclose' itself to its agents. There is a peculiar depth to the hiddennesss of the capitalist process. In a slave or serf society, it was possible literally to see the surplus produced by the workers over what they received: the slave built pyramids or what have you, and received scant food and skimpy clothing; the serf physically transported his 'tribute' to the lord of the manor. This is why Marx emphasises the necessary dependence of such social formations on non-economic ideologies and relationships (politics in the ancient and religion in the medieval world) to preserve their economic systems from questioning and/or attack. In capitalism, however, the one process – the economy – both exploits the worker and secretes the ideology which cloaks the exploitation. As we shall see, this does not mean that capitalism has no need of *political* ideology – the trappings of representative democracy, the 'contract' between the citizen and the state, and so on. But these are only a backdrop to the central process, which is the worker's acquiescence in the wage-relationship because he perceives it as a market exchange, and does not see what a 'kind of an exchange' it is.

I have elsewhere examined the status of Marx's conception of ideology, and argued that it is vital not to interpret ideology as a set of lies told to the poor by the rich.[13] Not only do the rich not spend all their time telling lies to the poor; in any case the 'lies' would not go down nearly as well as they do, were it not for the fact that they are accurate accounts of part of the worker's experience. Market-exchange is an illusion (a misleading reality), not a hallucination. If we reflect on the quotation which I have given from the *Grundrisse*, we will see that the ideology works: a worker is a worker is a worker. By acting as a worker he 'reproduces' himself as worker and the capitalist as capitalist. It thus makes sense for him to go on acting as he previously did, for the reasons which he previously had for so acting.

As I have presented it here, we see an ideology (whether religious, political or economic) as a functional necessity, not just an incidental curiosity, of Marx's notion of social formation. In other words, when Marx deals with ideology, he is not, as he is often thought to be, simply dismissing 'bourgeois nonsense'. He is at least as much supplying the 'account of the situation' required to give the actors involved the reasons and motivations to act in the ways posited by the theory. This means that it is significantly

[13] See note 5.

false to say, as tends to be said by followers of the 'Verstehen' school and of the approach represented by Peter Winch in Anglo-Saxon philosophy,[14] that Marx somehow downgrades or trivialises the role of the agent's consciousness and reasons for acting in social science. Not only does his treatment of ideology disprove this claim; it proves the very opposite. Marx bothers to develop a theory of ideology precisely because he is aware that the social process would break down, were it not that the agents of the process have a view of their situation which gives them reasons for acting in ways which, as they see it, prove 'self-validating' and are therefore reinforced. This is why Marx is so keen to show us how they 'feel as much at hom as a fish in water among manifestations which are separated from their internal connections and absurd when isolated by themselves'.[15] The quarrel between the Marxist and the 'Winchean', then, is not one between the denial and the affirmation of the importance of the agent's view of his situation.

The 'Winchean' would be entitled to complain if, in adding further aspects to the picture, the Marxist posited these aspects as themselves issuing in social behaviours, without any connection between situation and behaviour in the agent's motivation. But this is not what Marx does. He insists that the aspects of the social process not understood by the agents are aspects *resulting from*, and *underlying*, conscious behaviour, in the sense that because they are produced as unintended and unperceived consequences of what people do, and because as a matter of fact they bring about a repetition of the original situation in which people first acted, they continue to 'serve up' to people the same reasons for acting as they originally had; he never asserts that they 'bring about human action' in the mechanistic kind of way which the Winchean finds implausible. In other words, Marx's argument about 'surplus-value' and the actions of capitalists and workers, is exactly the same as Winch's argument about 'liquidity preference' and the actions of businessmen.[16] It is not necessary that either of these concepts be grasped as such by the agents (and in Marx's theory it would be disastrous for capitalism if the workers *did* grasp it as such). It *is* necessary that, in terms of the basic concept, we should be able to explicate how the world looks – in terms different that but theoretically derived from the basic theoretical concept – to the agents required to act as the theory postulates. The value-process appears to the worker in terms of wages for work, to the capitalist in terms of profit for enterprise; while that goes on being so, they in fact fulfil the value-process without grasping it as such.[17]

[14] Winch, P., *The Idea of a Social Science* (London 1958).
[15] Marx, K., *Capital*, Vol. III (Moscow 1959), p. 760.
[16] See Winch, p. 89.
[17] *Grundrisse*, pp. 196–7.

As much, then, as the whole of this movement appears as a social process, and as much as the individual moments of this movement arise from the conscious will and particular purposes of individuals, so much does the totality of the process appear as an objective interrelation, which arises spontaneously from nature; arising, it is true, from the mutual influence of conscious individuals on one another, but neither located in their consciousness, nor subsumed under them as a whole. Their own collisions with one another produce an *alien* social power standing above them, produce their mutual interaction as a process and power independent of them.

Lest the reader think that I have conflated Marx and Winch, I should emphasise that the quarrel between the two views, albeit not on the territory where it is sometimes mislocated, is nevertheless a real one. This is because the kinds of factors which, Marx believes, 'contextualise' the agent's view of the situation are so profound and crucial as to alter the whole focus of the 'Verstehen' approach. Just after the passage quoted above, Marx tells us that the reason why social structures crystallise into tyrannous powers (whether due to the tyranny of 'nature' or to that of 'chance') 'is a necessary result of the fact that the point of departure is not the free social individual'.[18] This brings us right back to our notion of 'divided history', particularly as it appears in the *German Ideology*. In that work, Marx concedes the point that 'individuals have always built on themselves'. He adds however that they have had to build 'on themselves within their given historical conditions and relationships, not on the "pure" individual in the sense of the ideologists'.[19] Marx's claim is that, in divided history, there cannot be 'pure' individuals, in the sense that there will always be a discontinuity between the individual's consciousness and activity, on the one hand, and the social interrelationships which flow from and in turn underlie that consciousness and activity, on the other.

What we have said about knowledge in this section amplifies what we have said about power in the preceding one. We have seen that the capitalist's power lies in his ability to determine the alternatives between which the worker may choose. Not only that, but if the worker tries not to have to make this 'economic choice', the capitalist is able to determine the alternatives which he faces in his 'political choice' between conformity and 'rebellion-plus-penalties'. We now have to incorporate ideology into this schema.

As we have seen it so far, ideology is a 'natural secretion' of the economic process. As the capitalist also is a social agent, he just as much as the worker will regard his situation as natural and self-justifying. In other words, the capitalist also is a 'victim' of the ideology (i.e. the one who will cry all the way to the bank). In this situation, the roles of capitalists and worker, and the ideological images which they have of them, will recurrently validate

---

[18] *Grundrisse*, p. 197.   [19] *German Ideology*, pp. 94–5.

and reinforce one another, and there will be no tendency towards conflict or disruption. As I have argued elsewhere, the fact of 'system-maintenance' here – i.e. the absence of questions and *a fortiori* of challenges from the workers – should not be put down to an exercise of power on the capitalist's part. Of course he is exercising power *in being* a capitalist, but he is not exercising power *to remain* a capitalist. We can attribute the system's maintenance to its own recurrent operation.[20]

I make this point in order to distinguish this situation from a similar but subtly different one, where the worker has begun to realise the injustice of his situation, or at least where the capitalist has realised the possibility of his doing so. If I know that somebody knows or can know X, I must myself know what X is; in other words, this situation arises where the capitalist himself 'sees through' the ideology, at least to the extent of realising that there are alternative possible states of affairs, which would attract the worker if he conceived of them. Thus in the case in question the capitalist is no longer a mere 'victim' of the ideology. At this juncture, he can begin to use the ideology as a manipulative weapon. He can use it either to *distort* the worker's perception – by leading him to misinterpret items of his experience – or to *limit* it by causing him not to perceive, or to overlook, certain other items, or both.

This ideological or manipulative activity is a further species of power, in that it determines the alternatives between which the worker may choose, by simply closing some of them from his consciousness. It can be used at economic or other levels of society. The capitalist can in various ways try to persuade the worker of the fairness of the market exchange, or he can sell him the image of himself as free, equal and sovereign citizen, thus either distracting him from his economic woes or misleading him into thinking that political expression will cure them. Finally, the capitalist can offer the worker the vision of a celestial equality (or even a celestial revenge) which again either distorts or excludes certain perceptions of his economic condition. In this context I should restate what I have already said about ideology and lying; it is not true that ideology is *never* a set of lies told by the rich to the poor, but it is true that ideology is neither essentially nor most interestingly such. Moreover, the sense in which ideology is not a set of lies is the secret of its success when it *is* a set of lies.

SOME THOUGHTS ON IDEAL EXCHANGE

It will be now be clear that the mode of human relationships in capitalist society is that of exchange, involving (in the senses presented already) reciprocity and voluntariness. In this concluding section, I want to turn to

[20] See note 5.

some considerations about the alternative form of society to capitalism: communist society. I am not going to discuss the question of the possibility of such a society. We shall define it as the kind of society which Marx envisaged as being really possible where a people had undergone advanced capitalist development (in which sense the relevance of the Soviet model is slight). I am interested, in this section, in how human relationships in communist society will differ from exchange in capitalist society.

As a starting-point, we may say that Marx's objection to the worker/capitalist exchange is not an 'absolutist' one to the effect that man's productive energy should not be subjected to exchange at all, but rather an objection to the exploitative context and consequences of the exchange. After a transition period (which sometimes he calls by contrast 'socialism') Marx says, full communism will be instituted. It will not be true that there will be *no* economic process even here. However, the productivity of human labour, and the possibilities of automation, will make it possible for society to produce its material requirements with a relatively small amount of its time. Only then, when 'all the springs of cooperative wealth flow more abundantly – only then can society wholly cross the narrow horizon of bourgeois right and inscribe on its banner: From each according to his abilities, to each according to his needs!'[21]

It seems to me that this kind of system is nearest to what Heath classifies as 'generalized reciprocity', where everyone contributes (in this case) productive effort according to their ability, without any specific type or rate of return, but is thereby assured of having their own needs met.[22] In a sense we might call this an exchange between the individual and society, 'society' being represented by whatever individual happens to fulfil my need at the particular time.

It is curious thing about Marx's vision of the alternative society that, as the exchange nexus is thus loosened in matters economic, it seems in some ways to become more direct in other areas. I said as a starting point that Marx objects to the precise form rather than the mere fact of the worker–capitalist exchange, and I still hold to that. On the other hand, however, he does also attack for example the 'sense of having', and the way in which money leads us to suppress our appreciation of the specific characteristics of goods, seeing them only as homogeneous 'commodities'. Ultimately, I believe, this represents an objection not to the idea of exchange or reciprocity, but rather to the dominance of a single narrow calculus in all our perceptions.

I must admit that Marx does seem to envisage certain satisfactions in

[21] Marx, K., 'Critique of the Gotha Programme' in Marx, K., *The First International and After* (ed. and tr. Fernbach, D.) (London 1974), p. 347.
[22] See Heath, A., *Rational Choice and Social Exchange* (Cambridge 1976), pp. 57 and 119–20.

communist society which must be termed 'gratuitous', in that they require no return whatsoever: 'in your enjoyment or use of my product I would have *immediately* the satisfaction, and the consciousness, of having in my work satisfied a human need, of having objectified *human* nature and thus having created the object corresponding to another human being'.[23] Perhaps I should say that Marx envisages certain satisfactory *aspects* of communist activity as gratuitously satisfying, since in this passage he goes on to say that I would have the satisfaction of 'having proved myself in your thoughts and in your love'. It is difficult not to regard love as having a 'feedback' element – we are never content to know that we are loved in people's interiority, but want either to encounter or be able to count on manifestations of it. Indeed, Marx elsewhere spells out the 'direct reciprocal' side of the picture:

Let us assume *man* to be *man*, and his relation to the world to be a human one. Then love can only be exchanged for love, trust for trust, etc... If you love without evoking love in return, i.e. if you are not able, by the *manifestation* of yourself as a loving person, to make yourself a *beloved person*, then your love is impotent and a misfortune.[24]

It might be objected that the analogy between this and economic exchange is limited. I am sure that there are many respects in which it is so, but there *are* respects in which they are alike. The fact that, as Marx sees it, by being a lover I have to evoke a response from *some* lover but not necessarily any particular one is in fact directly akin to what happens on a market. I do not exchange with this particular person as such; rather, the person I end up exchanging with is the one from whom I get the appropriate response. In Marx's conception of loving relationships here, as in a market, there are both a 'searching' and a 'negotiating' phase.

One thing about human relationships in Marx's alternative society is that they will be 'free' in a way in which present ones are not. It is not very easy to isolate this freedom. When discussing exchange and power in an earlier section, I argued that all exchange is by definition 'free' or 'voluntary', and that therefore the search for 'free' or 'really free' exchange was a non-starter. I went on to say that what was in question was whether exchanges were freely *entered*, in the sense that people were free not to choose any of the alternatives offered. Various criteria have been offered for such a freely-entered exchange (although by authors who, as has already emerged, do not use or might even reject my argument on 'free exchange'). I think that there is a very valuable clue in Lively's argument that the defect in Hobbes's account of 'sovereignty by acquisition' is that of seeing the contract as one 'made of free choice which consequently entails a moral obligation to obey'.[25] Surely it is true that the kinds of bargains we regard

---

[23] Translated from 'James Mill' in Marx, K., *Texte zu Methode und Praxis* II (Munich 1968), p. 180.
[24] Marx, K., *Early Writings*, p. 194.   [25] Lively, p. 9.

as 'free' in the relevant sense are the kinds we would be prepared to hold to. I do not intend to follow this clue here, firstly because I have nothing useful to say about it at present, and secondly because I suspect that it can adequately be handled only in the context of a theory of the ideological element in customary morality.

I shall briefly follow up another clue, offered by Anthony Heath. He suggests that a good criterion is whether both parties are better off at the end of the exchange than in the pre-bargaining position.[26] If so, then it represents a positive gain to both, and it is plausible to claim that both entered it voluntarily. This is helpful, but needs to be worked out a bit more. It is not strictly true that, if I am better off after than before an exchange, then I was not coerced into it. This is because we have to separate the ability of power-holders to make compliance attractive from their ability to make non-compliance unattractive: they give with one hand, and take with the other. It is not strictly impossible that an insane millionaire landlord should threaten to knock down my house if I do not leave it, while thrusting a ten-bedroom mansion on me as an alternative. I will naturally leap at the offer, but if, for the sake of it, I pretend not to want to move it will quickly emerge that I must. Thus I can end up better off than before through an exchange into which I was coerced.

Thus we should reformulate Heath's criterion to read that an exchange is freely entered if I am not prevented from remaining in the pre-bargaining position and being as well off as before (a version which Heath himself employs shortly after the above argument).[27] Once armed with this criterion, we are ready to move, but we are faced with quite a long journey. As I have already argued, exchanges are always 'free in respect of...'; presumably, the kind of exchange which we are seeking is one which is free (i.e. freely entered) in respect of the whole range of relevant factors. In the situation of 'ideal exchange', presumably, nobody must be determining the range of alternatives between which I have to choose. But even then if, as we have seen to be the case, my agreement in such exchanges fulfils my *needs*, it is not clear that I can always choose to remain in the original position and be as well off as before: choosing whether or not to fulfil our needs for food, or indeed for affection, is not clearly a more capricious affair than choosing whether or not to give our sandwiches to a bully.

To a certain extent this all depends on whether we programme 'needs' into or out of our concept of the 'self'. If the former, we still have to recognise that certain needs can be 'inserted' into the self by manipulation of the kind discussed earlier. Perhaps we could arrive at an outline definition of 'ideal exchange' as exchange which we enter and make at the prompting of needs which have not been manipulated, but which are in some sense 'natural'.

<hr/>

[26] Heath, p. 19.　　　　[27] Heath, p. 20.

At this point, I believe, the concept of ideal exchange has an irreducibly evaluative component. One way of getting over some of the problems involved is the distinction between 'deficiency needs' (without fulfilling which we will decline in some respect) and 'growth needs' (without fulfilling which we remain just where we are). Armed with such a distinction (if it can actually be applied unproblematically) we could then have two stages of ideal exchange: the first, where we were impelled into the exchange only by our own natural deficiency needs, and the other where we chose whether or not to fulfil whatever growth needs we were aware of.

Index

Index